HEADHUNTER

5-73 CAV and Their Fight for Iraq's Diyala River Valley

PETER C. SVOBODA

CASEMATE
Philadelphia & Oxford

AN AUSA BOOK
Association of the United States Army
2425 Wilson Boulevard, Arlington, Virginia, 22201, USA

Published in the United States of America and Great Britain in 2020 by
CASEMATE PUBLISHERS
1950 Lawrence Road, Havertown, PA 19083, USA
and
The Old Music Hall, 106–108 Cowley Road, Oxford OX4 1JE, UK

Hardback Edition: ISBN 978-1-61200-927-8
Digital Edition: ISBN 978-1-61200-928-5

A CIP record for this book is available from the British Library

Printed and bound in the United States of America by Integrated Books International

Typeset by Versatile PreMedia Service (P) Ltd

For a complete list of Casemate titles, please contact:

CASEMATE PUBLISHERS (US)
Telephone (610) 853-9131
Fax (610) 853-9146
Email: casemate@casematepublishers.com
www.casematepublishers.com

CASEMATE PUBLISHERS (UK)
Telephone (01865) 241249
Email: casemate-uk@casematepublishers.co.uk
www.casematepublishers.co.uk

Front cover: U.S. Army soldiers of Bravo Troop, 5th Squadron, 73rd Cavalry Regiment, 3rd Brigade Combat Team, 82nd Airborne Division react to contact from anti-Iraqi forces during a mission in Al Haymer, Iraq, July 12, 2007 (Defense Imagery Management Operations Center)

To Dad AATW!

Contents

Foreword

One of the most lasting images in military history is that of Leonidas and 300 Spartans fighting to their deaths against a massive Persian army in order to guard the retreat of the Greek army from the "Hot Gates" of Thermopylae. It is remembered for the Spartans' stunning display of bravery and patriotism in the face of overwhelming odds.

Lieutenant Colonel Drew Poppas couldn't have chosen a better comparison for the 5th Squadron, 73rd Cavalry Regiment. The story was aspirational. It was Poppas' vision of what the newly formed unit would become and an embodiment of the values which would prepare them for the dark and dangerous road ahead.

Poppas defined for them who they were and, by invoking the Spartans, he gave them a picture and a model of what that looked like. This cultivated in his men the belief that anything was possible, and that they could stand toe-to-toe with any adversity. They would be spread thin, they would be outnumbered, and they would face disheartening odds. But like their warrior brethen, they would never accept defeat, and they would never quit.

He told the men of the 5th Squadron, 73rd Cavalry (5-73 CAV) who they would be, and he led them to becoming who they could be. Together, this team of 400 paratroopers excelled.

In Iraq they were the smallest unit in their parent organization and they were spread the thinnest. They were intended to be an economy of force operation—no one ever would have imagined that this small squadron would win major battles, hold the most ground, and accomplish so much during their deployment.

Over 30 percent of the men in this unit received valorous awards for their heroic actions. A team of Hollywood scriptwriters couldn't conjure up a unit of paratroopers who achieved more: a young paratrooper firing the .50-caliber machine gun from the cupola of the Humvee while his buddy in the vehicle applies a pressure dressing to his shattered wrist; a medic—with total disregard for his own safety and without orders—moving under an intense whizz of bullets to save another paratrooper's life.

5-73 CAV also sustained the highest casualty rate of any unit in proportion to its size. One out of every four men was killed or wounded. These are men who understood that whether they were a cook or a mechanic or a support team member, every single one was a war fighter first and foremost.

The paratroopers of 5-73 Cavalry Squadron made history during their time in Iraq, but the battles they fought weren't won in the moment. They were won every day, piece by piece, in that place where real success is born—through the sort of leadership and preparation which creates a culture of excellence.

Pete Svoboda has done a superb job of capturing what made 5-73 CAV a truly outstanding unit. Svoboda provides a detailed history of the unit from their formation to their challenges throughout Iraq. He captures not only their most striking adversities and their most stunning victories but the comradeship with which they served each other while they served their country. *Headhunter* will leave you feeling certain that these men truly deserved to be called American Spartans.

Lieutenant General William B. Caldwell
U.S. Army, retired

Preface

Immediately after he completed jump school in August 1944, my father volunteered to serve as an instructor at the Airborne Demolitions School. After graduating from Officer Candidate School as an infantry Second Lieutenant he was assigned to the 508th Parachute Infantry Regiment following the surrender of Germany. He was subsequently assigned to the 504th Parachute Infantry Regiment of the 82nd Airborne Division which had returned to Fort Bragg, North Carolina. He would go on to serve as counterintelligence officer during the Korean War and remained in the Army Reserve, retiring as a Lieutenant Colonel. I have vivid memories of his paratrooper jump boots and the silver jump and glider wings on his uniform that signified his being part of the paratrooper community.

My idea of trying to chronicle the role the 82nd would play in the war on terrorism seemed to be a natural extension of his story and those of paratroopers who deserved to have their stories told.

In 2003, I began to pursue telling the story of the 82nd's deployments to Afghanistan and Iraq. At the time, no one could have known that this two-theater war would become such a long-term commitment of troops and treasure.

As someone who had never pursued or researched such an endeavor, I had no idea that the writing process would take such an enormous amount of time. Interviewing paratroopers from each deployment meant spending hours contacting them, lining up, conducting and recording interviews. The vast majority of those interviews were conducted by phone. Often, follow-up interviews were conducted and I always requested photos to provide me with a visual of what the interviewees had experienced. Transcribing the interviews was a key part of beginning the writing process. I found it easier to read hard copy in order to find common threads. In turn, this approach allowed me the ability to mirror the timeline I followed based on the narrative from the unit citation that had been submitted for award consideration.

Crafting a readable work for a potentially diverse reading audience and the framing of a cohesive, page-turning account that would inform readers of the sacrifices and bravery exhibited by these paratroopers was always my goal.

I continued to interview members of the 82nd through November 2007, when I spoke with Colonel Bryan Owens, then commander of the 3rd Brigade which had recently returned from Iraq. At the end of the interview I asked if he would recommend another person to interview. "Have you spoken to Drew Poppas?" Owens indicated that Poppas had quite a story to share. When I got off the phone with Drew I knew that this was the story that I would focus on. The 15-month deployment of the 5th Squadron, 73rd Cavalry Regiment, 3rd Brigade Combat Team, 505th Airborne Infantry Regiment, 82nd Airborne Division to Iraq would become my writing commitment to these paratroopers and their families.

Military members who serve in combat are in constant danger of being injured, wounded or killed. Losing a team member is traumatic but continuing the mission is essential. Add to that the stresses of family separation, being exposed to a foreign culture that most find unfamiliar, and the sectarian violence that was such a large part of the fight. They would live and work in austere conditions, conducting patrols and missions out of combat outposts that were established to help protect the local populations from the violence perpetuated by Al Qaeda and other terrorist cells.

This story is a microcosm of what many of our military members have experienced in both the past and the present. Although the nature of warfare has changed to some extent, what service members experience in combat has not. The comradery, danger and stress that is part of warfighting appears to be the essence of what service members relate to, in whichever era they serve. During the 15 months that 5-73 CAV was deployed, 22 members of the squadron were killed. In this same period of time, service members from other units were wounded or killed by enemy fire, including paratroopers from the 3rd Brigade of the 82nd who were also fighting insurgents. They faced similar dangers and also made every effort to accomplish their mission.

I interviewed every person who agreed to tell their story and have made every effort to corroborate each detail. That said, I'm certain that I have missed more than one firefight or improvised explosive device detonation. The squadron had only one day that the entire unit stood down. That was Christmas Day, 2006.

There are many more stories to tell. Elements of the 82nd have deployed to Afghanistan and Iraq throughout the war on terrorism. The granite memorial at Fort Bragg has hundreds of names displayed to honor those who've been killed in action during these deployments. My hope is that through this work I have begun to share the experiences of these paratroopers and their loved ones so that their service and sacrifice are never forgotten.

Introduction

They appeared as small specks that covered just a piece of the early morning dawn. The uninformed would be uncertain as to their origin or purpose. As they increased in size and the powerful sounds of jet engines filled the air, however, the casual observer was provided with an awe-inspiring sight. As the formation of massive air force cargo planes carrying hundreds of paratroopers approached the drop zone, the sky seemed to come alive with anticipation, energized with what was about to happen.

Inside each aircraft, airborne warriors from the U.S. Army's 82nd Airborne Division prepared to execute a mass tactical airborne operation. Their primary mission: to deploy within 18 hours of notification, conduct a forcible entry parachute assault and secure key objectives for follow-on military operations. The 82nd's legacy was forged on the World War II battlefields of Sicily, Italy, France, Holland, Belgium and Germany. Elements of this storied unit have been part of military campaigns in the Dominican Republic, Vietnam, Grenada, Panama, Afghanistan and Iraq. Nicknamed the "All American Division," the 82nd is the U.S. Army's only airborne division. Its members are all entitled to wear the coveted maroon beret signifying that they are on jump status, ready to deploy into combat by parachute.

This is the story of 300 of these paratroopers, airborne reconnaissance scouts and infantry brethren along with a 103-member company of support paratroopers deployed to Iraq's enemy-infested Diyala River Valley in July, 2006. The 5th Squadron, 73rd Cavalry Regiment—better known as 5-73 CAV as well as Headhunter (a nod to the squadron commander's call sign) and Task Force 300—was composed of three troops (Alpha, Bravo and Charlie), a headquarters troop, mortars, medics and the forward support company (known in 5-73 as Delta Troop). The squadron spent 15 violent months confronting the Al Qaeda terrorists who had a stranglehold on this vast region located in eastern Iraq.

According to the squadron's senior sergeant, Command Sergeant Major Ray Edgar, the history of 5-73 is long and varied. The squadron's origins go back to the relatively small "airborne cavalry mafia community" of the Charlie 73 scouts, the ground

A paratrooper stepping forward to the door (Senior Airman Jodi Martinez, 1st Combat Camera Squadron)

A paratrooper exiting the aircraft (Senior Airman Jodi Martinez, 1st Combat Camera Squadron)

A paratrooper in the air (Senior Airman Jodi Martinez, 1st Combat Camera Squadron)

reconnaissance element of the 82nd Aviation's 1-17 Cavalry. This proud cavalry tradition even had an airborne armor element: 3-73 Armor had provided Sheridan armored reconnaissance-fighting vehicles, air-transportable/parachute-capable light tanks whose lineage and honors included Panama, Haiti, and the liberation of Kuwait. Edgar recalled that "we weren't an integral part of the infantry brigade because we weren't a slice element, we were a division asset as a reconnaissance organization." In support of the infantry force, these recon paratroopers were jumping with them, going on training exercises with them and delivering the protective firepower on the drop zone. According to Edgar, in spite of the fact that the equipment was old and had seen some rough service, the paratroopers of Airborne Thunder "managed to make it work and we had a real strong work ethic."[1]

The 82nd would see the expansion of the cavalry, using the 1-17th CAV/ Charlie 73 CAV scouts who, along with casing the colors[2] of the 3rd Battalion, 505th Airborne Infantry Regiment, provided the personnel for the creation of the 1-73, 3-73, 4-73 and 5-73 Airborne Reconnaissance Squadrons or RSTA, short for reconnaissance, surveillance, targeting, and acquisition. When it was decided by the army's senior leaders that there was a need to bring RSTA functions down to the brigade level it became imperative to fill these units with cavalry scouts.[3]

Filling the squadron with cavalry scouts was a problem because there weren't enough to go around. In order to fill out the ranks, infantry riflemen would be used. These front-line combat troops are trained to "close with and kill the enemy with overwhelming force." The two groups of warfighters considered themselves different and, in some ways, better than the other. Chalk it up to rivalry between the branches. Combining the two occupational specialties into a cavalry squadron had its own unique set of challenges. The common thread was that they must all be jump qualified, ready to parachute into harm's way, but blending the cavalry scout and infantry rifleman skill sets wasn't going to be nearly as difficult as blending two distinctly different and equally proud mindsets into a cohesive fighting force. The running joke was that the scouts had to be taught to get out of their trucks and the infantrymen had to learn to get *in* the trucks tactically. There was the "close with the enemy" mentality of the infantryman versus the "gun truck and heavy weapons" mindset developed by the scouts' affiliation with the armor/cavalry branch. Ultimately, when the two were combined a unique and potent fighting force was to emerge.

Since the days of the U.S. Army's Parachute Test Platoon, when 50 volunteers stepped forward on June 26, 1940 to become this experimental airborne nucleus, not much has changed about how paratroopers jump from an aircraft in flight.

The paratroopers jump from a height of 1,000 feet while the aircraft is flying at a speed of 125 knots (just under 150 miles per hour). Dressed for combat in their tan, medium and dark gray digital pattern Army Combat Uniforms and Kevlar helmets, each paratrooper is loaded with their main parachute packed in a deployment bag strapped to their back along with a reserve located at waist level. All the tools of combat go with them: weapons at their sides, rucksacks attached at their front underneath the reserve chute, which serves as a backup in case the main parachute malfunctions. As the drop zone nears, a sense of uneasiness and fear that never completely goes away is palpable. One veteran 82nd paratrooper and jumpmaster, Sergeant Major Pete Johnson, recalled that, "What the hell am I doing up here?" seems to be a common paratrooper refrain. The paratroopers receive "20 minutes" and "10 minutes" time warnings from the jumpmaster. The air is thick with anticipation.

The jumpmaster, along with a safety, runs the jump, making sure all the procedures are followed correctly. Each jumpmaster begins to signal their "stick" of paratroopers who will be shortly filling the sky. Verbal commands and hand signals are delivered in unison due to the engine noise and to ensure that everything is done according to the book. "Get ready." "Outboard personnel stand up." "Inboard personnel stand up." Commands from the jumpmasters are met with the echo of the paratroopers repeating each command and moving in unison. The tension is high, the concentration absolute. The slightest deviation in this procedure could mean injury or death to one or more of the paratroopers. "Hook up." The sound of metal snap hooks can be heard attaching to the anchor line cable, the cables that run down each side of the aircraft.

The command to "check static line" makes certain that each paratrooper is clipped and secured to the anchor line cable. "Check equipment" is next. This ensures that nothing is broken, out of place or attached improperly. It's the second time that this check has occurred. The first time, a jumpmaster has given each paratrooper a detailed inspection before they were even loaded on the aircraft. "Sound off for equipment check." From the very back of the aircraft each paratrooper signifies "OK," and gives the next paratrooper in front a sharp tap. The signal is continued until it gets to the number one paratrooper, who notifies the jumpmaster, "All OK, Jumpmaster."

The air force loadmaster opens the jump doors, conducts a safety check and hands it over to the jumpmaster saying, "Your door army." The jumpmaster begins a series of safety checks to ensure the jump door and surroundings are good to go. Leaning slightly out of the door, the jumpmaster makes sure that no hazardous conditions exist outside the aircraft. The jumpmaster and safety continually observe the paratroopers along with conditions inside and outside of the aircraft. The jumpmaster conducts a 30-second reference point check, one last "clear to the rear," checking for safe conditions and issues the one-minute warning. The paratrooper in the number one position steps toward the door and hands the safety the static line. The jumper turns and orients to the center of the open jump door and awaits the final command.

"Go." The indicator light turns green and the jumpmaster simultaneously gives the command to the paratroopers to begin exiting the aircraft. Training kicks in and the process is executed from muscle memory. Upon clearing the aircraft, the jumper rotates his or her elbows firmly into their sides, both hands over the end of the reserve parachute with fingers naturally spread. The jumper then bends their body forward at the waist to look over the reserve to see the toes of their boots while continuing to count, two thousand, three thousand, four thousand, five thousand, six thousand, at normal cadence. Pushed by the wind, pulled by gravity, each paratrooper falls to earth executing a one-thousand count in anticipation of the opening shock that comes when the parachute deploys and the canopy fills with air. During this critical time the main parachute canopy and suspension lines that attach the parachute to the tight harness that the paratrooper is wearing are pulled from the deployment bag on the paratrooper's back.

If the main parachute malfunctions then the paratrooper must quickly deploy the reserve chute. There are only precious seconds to react before the paratrooper hits the ground at a speed that will most probably critically injure or kill. Falling towards the ground, the once deafening sound of jet engines and wind is replaced by the slow descent that the parachute provides once the canopy fully deploys. Each paratrooper uses the risers that are part of the parachute harness to steer the parachute in order to avoid other paratroopers and objects such as trees.

After the transition from the cacophony inside the aircraft, then into the aircraft's jet stream for those six seconds, the almost deafening silence of the descent is one of the most peaceful yet tense episodes that a paratrooper experiences. Constantly on the lookout for other jumpers, the paratrooper is also checking the rate of descent, and trying to steer towards assembly areas—or more than likely the softest piece of drop zone to reduce the jarring impact of landing.

The absolute worst part of the jump is the landing. You know it is coming; the ground rushes up at you and the wind always seems to increase, which means that both jumper and parachute are at the mercy of the wind. You always feel that you are falling faster than you are, and you know that it is going to hurt on impact. Some hyperventilate while others are super relaxed. There doesn't seem to be any way to soften the impact or mentally prepare for it.

As each paratrooper prepares to land, their knees are slightly bent and feet are together so the legs act as springs to help cushion the landing and avoid injury. The parachute landing fall or PLF is the procedure that is executed in order to avoid being injured upon landing. There are five portions of the body that must contact the ground in sequence: balls of the feet, calf, thigh, buttock, and pull-up muscles, in order to minimize the potential of an injury occurring. If all goes well, each paratrooper will collapse their parachute, remove their harness and prepare to execute the mission. Remember that in combat, as the paratrooper descends, the ground at the other end is foreign soil that is being defended by an enemy soldier who has the tactical advantage to wound or kill the paratroopers.[4]

These airborne warfighters are trained to take the fight to the enemy no matter where they wind up on the battlefield, no matter how many or how few of their fellow paratroopers are present to execute the mission. Everything from Humvee gun trucks to artillery howitzers can also be dropped by parachute to support the airborne assault. They live by the Rule of LGOPs or Little Groups of Paratroopers:

> After the demise of the best airborne plan, a most terrifying effect occurs on the battlefield. This fighting spirit dates to the early hours of June 6, 1944 when thousands of paratroopers who were supposed to be dropped in the fields behind the beaches of Normandy, France were widely scattered. Many wound up forming into small groups and proceeded to engage the enemy. In turn, the actions of these paratroopers helped to both confuse and slow the enemy thus contributing to a successful landing by allied troops on the Normandy beaches. Well trained, armed-to-the-teeth and lacking serious adult supervision, they collectively remember their commander's intent as "March to the sound of the guns and kill anyone who is not dressed like you." Happily, they go about the day's work.[5]

Many of the 5-73 CAV paratroopers had grown up in the post 9/11 world of terrorism. Regardless of the reason why they had joined the army and volunteered to earn their jump wings, each of these paratroopers was about to be tested in combat, many for the first time.

On July 21, 2006, the issuing of the Mobilization Order had set in motion the furious pace of deployment along with the inevitable and tearful good-byes.

August 7, 2006 would find the squadron boarding planes at Pope Army Airfield, adjacent to Fort Bragg, heading to Kuwait. A stop here would acclimatize the paratroopers to the desert heat while they continued to fine tune their warfighting skills. Headhunter was the squadron commander's radio call sign and it would become synonymous with 5-73's ability to bring the fight to the enemy.

CHAPTER I

Push Forward

The 82nd's senior leaders had to find the right person to lead 5-73. It would need to be someone who was innovative, extremely flexible, able to adapt quickly and a creative thinker—a leader willing to explore new ways to make this cavalry force more lethal and able to adapt to new missions.

In the summer of 2005, a three-day creative leadership workshop was held. All of the 82nd's battalion commanders, lieutenant colonels and their command sergeant majors attended. The goals were to get the participants to appreciate their individual strengths and weaknesses, share these observations with their peers and finally identify how these traits affect the organization. One of the exercises attempted to determine whether each individual would be able to quickly adapt to a situation or was so rigid that it would be difficult to adapt. Everyone took the test, then the facilitator identified each participant beginning with the most rigid and working his way down the list to the most flexible. When it was all said and done, Lieutenant Colonel (LTC) Andrew "Drew" Poppas was identified as the most flexible, the most adaptable, innovative and creative person of all the potential candidates.

As a result, Poppas would command the 82nd's first cavalry squadron. He'd graduated from the United States Military Academy at West Point in 1988, being commissioned as a Second Lieutenant. After completing the Infantry Basic Officer Course, he received basic jump wings for graduating from airborne school. Poppas earned his ranger tab after successfully completing the grueling nine-week course designed to train soldiers to develop small unit leadership and patrolling skills that are applied in a variety of combat simulations, often operating during the hours of darkness in all types of weather and terrain while being placed under extreme mental and physical duress including lack of sleep. Poppas was first assigned to command a rifle platoon. He moved through the ranks and had various assignments leading up to commanding a battalion of airborne infantry when he got the nod to command 5-73 CAV.

Even though Poppas had not commanded troops in combat, he possessed all the right traits: personable, adaptive, flexible and willing to take the risks necessary to

Poppas, Sylvia and Hercik (Andrew Poppas)

accomplish the mission. A favorite expression exemplified his caring nature: "You have to give a hug to get a hug." Squadron Chaplain Craig Honbarger, a former enlisted soldier who had rediscovered his faith and decided to pursue a military ministry, was 5-73's spiritual leader. Honbarger observed that Poppas made everyone "feel like they're his quarterback" leading the way to "get it done."[1]

Poppas would have as much latitude as possible to facilitate the formation of this new piece of the brigade combat team. There would be a large number of paratroopers to choose from since they would be used to staff both 5-73 CAV and other cavalry squadrons that were being formed. Poppas gave this analogy to one of his troop commanders: "It's like managing the Yankees and getting ready to win the World Series. You've got your pick of super stars to choose from to make it happen."[2] It was indeed a unique opportunity.

Command Sergeant Major Ray Edgar was the senior enlisted paratrooper. Edgar knew many of the senior non-commissioned officers who would be filling the ranks due to his previous assignments with the 82nd. He'd returned to Fort Bragg to find that there were privates he had served with who were now platoon sergeants.

As the command sergeant major, Edgar would make certain that the enlisted members were performing to standard. He'd act as the eyes and ears for Lieutenant

Colonel Poppas in all matters related to the enlisted soldiers, provide advice and make recommendations to the commander and staff regarding issues that pertained to enlisted personnel. Poppas emphasized to Edgar the need to develop and maintain "a disciplined organization that I [Poppas] could employ in combat because if they're ill-disciplined or ill-trained then the greatest commander in the world can't do anything with them." Poppas urged that "there can't be any daylight between us."[3]

Captain Mike Few would command Alpha Troop, Captain Stephen Dobbins would have Bravo Troop and Charlie Troop would be led by Captain John Carson.

Mike Few was a West Point grad, had been a tank platoon leader then a tank company executive officer and had seen combat during Operation Iraqi Freedom I. He'd also spent some time back in Iraq on a staff supporting special operations missions. Described as being analytical, he wanted to win the war on terror and was focused as well as forceful regarding how to do so.

Dobbins had graduated from The Citadel, a four-year military college located in Charleston, South Carolina, where he was commissioned through the Army Reserve Officers Training Corps (ROTC) program. He had a previous combat tour in Afghanistan serving with a heavy weapons company. Dobbins was known for his quick wit and sarcastic sense of humor.

After graduating from Texas Tech Carson had earned his commission through Officer Candidate School and was branched infantry. He'd been in command of a rifle company prior to joining 5-73 CAV. A passionate and selfless leader, Carson worked diligently to balance the welfare of his organization with accomplishing the mission.

Each troop would have a senior non-commissioned officer or NCO at the rank of First Sergeant. They provided the troop commanders with the support, guidance and years of experience in the enlisted ranks that were essential to mission success. Alpha Troop had Tim Metheny, Bravo's was Michael Clemens and John Coomer Charlie Troop's.

Metheny had extensive combat experience prior to the deployment. According to Command Sergeant Major Edgar, Metheny would demonstrate "the deepest sense of loyalty to the organization, working tirelessly to achieve exceptional results on the battlefield."

Michael Clemens was described by Edgar as a "highly intelligent, critical thinker with deep tactical knowledge. He could be counted on to approach complex combat situations calmly with logic rather than emotion." Edgar observed that, as Charlie Troop's First Sergeant, John Coomer was a "skilled at planning and executing training events." Due in part to his time as an instructor at the Ranger Training Brigade, Coomer proved to be a "tremendous asset during close-quarter battle live-fire training" prior to the deployment. All the first sergeants were found at the "tip of the spear" on many occasions fighting alongside of the younger, less experienced enlisted paratroopers.[4]

Captain Andy Hercik was the squadron's Fire Support Officer which meant that he planned and executed fires in order to set conditions for the maneuver using artillery, mortars, attack aviation and close air support from the air force to support the mission. Commissioned out of Ohio University's ROTC program, Hercik had been an enlisted soldier in the Ohio National Guard prior to being commissioned and had a previous Iraq deployment. According to First Sergeant Donnie Workman, Hercik was a "mammoth of a man," nicknamed "Mongo"; a massive country boy who always seemed to have a dip in his mouth.[5] All serious one minute, laid back the next, he demanded excellence from his troops.

Major Brett Sylvia filled the S-3/operations slot. Sylvia was an interesting addition to the group. Commissioned in the engineer branch after graduating from the U.S. Military Academy, Major Sylvia brought a broad background to the table. The army chief of staff believed leaders should be pentathletes, establishing a comprehensive set of skills due to the "dynamics of the contemporary operating environment."[6] LTC Poppas was not thrilled when he learned that an engineer officer had been selected to fill this important position on the squadron's staff. He was of the mindset that an officer without infantry experience couldn't do the job. However, when he learned that it was Sylvia, Poppas welcomed him with open arms, remarking that he felt as if he'd "just grabbed the brass ring," signaling his high marks for Brett and how fortunate 5-73 CAV was to be getting him.

Poppas had met Sylvia while they were both working at the Pentagon and knew that he was getting an extremely sharp individual. Captain Dobbins described Sylvia as having an "eight-pound brain."[7] Sylvia had taken advantage of his time while attending the School of Advanced Military Studies at Fort Leavenworth to fine tune what he referred to as his "combined arms maneuver skills knowledge base." Sylvia had his doubts about if or when others would welcome him. He noted that the infantry community was known to be "somewhat parochial," having the "if you ain't infantry you ain't shit" attitude regarding non-infantry types. Sylvia observed that the airborne infantry community in the 82nd was extremely tight knit so being welcomed and accepted was going to take some work.

Some of the junior officers attempted to test Major Sylvia. Seeing the writing on the wall, Sylvia quickly refreshed his memory regarding maneuver doctrine and then began "sharpshooting" his junior adversaries. "Do you know the three ways to withdraw?" inquired Sylvia. The captain in question gave him a puzzled, confused look. Sylvia continued the attack, noting that "you're an infantry officer and you're supposed to know this stuff." Sylvia had the upper hand as the captain offender withdrew from the verbal assault.[8]

Physician Assistant or PA Major Brad Rather would lead the combat medics. Rather was a prior service enlisted paratrooper rifleman who often greeted his medics with phrases like, "Morning bitches." Rather had gone back to school to become a nurse then had the opportunity through a pilot program to go to PA school on the army's ticket. According to Rather, he had "the institutional knowledge due to being prior service." Doctors on the other hand learned how to be a provider and then tried to catch up on army knowledge. So, when a new physician arrived, they were taught how to zero and fire their weapon, wear their basic combat load and how to assemble an aid bag.

Rather had the opportunity to move to another unit prior to 5-73 deploying. He noted that "I didn't see a rationale of me going to a new unit with medics that I haven't trained and deploying to combat with people that I didn't know when I had a vested interest in the medics that I'd trained in wanting to be there and take care of them, and I knew everybody in the squadron."[9] Lieutenant Colonel Poppas agreed, stating that Rather was a "known entity." Poppas fought hard to keep Rather in the squadron. The paratroopers knew that Rather was going to do everything in his power to take care of them, "and that helps a soldier with the mindset that, hey I know that if I get hurt, Doc Rather is going to be there to take care of me, so I don't have to worry about it, I'm going to get after it and take care of the mission."[10]

Rather emphasized that the medics needed to be trained "to a higher standard than what a regular medic got in the army." Advanced skills like inserting a surgical airway, placing a chest tube or performing needle decompression required more training along with reinforcing these skills to ensure that the medics were proficient.[11] Rather asserted that the medics needed to have "a chance to save someone's life at the point of injury on the battlefield." Advanced trauma life support teams were established and spread out amongst the three troops—as Rather put it, "to stop the red stuff from leaking out of the body."[12]

Each platoon in each troop had a medic assigned. The squadron broke new ground to figure out the best way to deploy the various levels of what's referred to as the "echelon of care" from self-aid, to buddy aid, to combat lifesaver, to combat line medic, casualty collection point and arrival at the battalion aid station. In addition to combat patient care, medics also looked after a variety of other medical needs from ensuring that the paratroopers remained hydrated to foot care.

There were three teams: one led by Rather, one by Dr. Larry Robinson, better known as Doc Rob or L-Rob and the third by Sergeant First Class Jonas Woodruff, the medical platoon sergeant whose skill set had been fine-tuned so he could fill the position. Robinson was the battalion surgeon whose background was in family medicine. He didn't have a good handle on operational medicine and tactical combat casualty care when he arrived at 5-73 CAV but he was a likable guy with a friendly smile who was a quick study, was eager to learn and quickly picked up the necessary skills.

As the squadron deployed to Iraq 5-73 CAV became a maneuver element with the same mission as the infantry battalions that they would have traditionally supported. Even artillery soldiers were patrolling and securing patrol bases. The squadron used their recon skills to find the enemy, close with and destroy them. Digging a hole in the ground, overwatching a target using observation posts and small kill teams after moving by ground or air assaulting in were the tactics that proved to be extremely successful. 5-73 CAV came into the battlespace with, as Captain Few described it, having "a force advantage, superior weapons systems, troops and other assets."[13] The enemy would have the information advantage. They knew the terrain, could terrorize the population and often could disappear at will. A critical piece was reaching out to the locals in order to gather the intelligence needed to track down and destroy the enemy. Operating covertly by inserting in hours of darkness provided the element of surprise.

Due to the need to mix cavalry scouts and infantry riflemen the decision was made before Headhunter deployed to cross-level the infantry and cavalry platoons so that the scouts and riflemen were evenly distributed to ensure the most effective mix. Platoons had corresponding colors for the purpose of differentiating them. 1st Platoon was Red, 2nd Platoon was White, 3rd Platoon was Blue, headquarters was Black, and mortars were Green.

Alpha Troop stayed cavalry pure with all three platoons filled with cavalry scouts. Bravo Troop had one platoon of infantry (Bravo Red) while Bravo White and Bravo Blue were cavalry. Charlie Troop had Charlie Red cavalry, while Charlie White and Blue were infantry. So, Bravo and Charlie Troops each had 25 to 30 riflemen in an infantry reconnaissance platoon and each cavalry reconnaissance platoon had 16 scouts, a medic and a Fire Support Team forward observer better known as a "FISTer." The FISTer directed fire support from artillery, mortars and/or army attack helicopters. Calling for a fire mission, or Apache gunships, the FISTer provided map coordinates, the requested type of munitions and any other details that ensured that the mission was on time and on target.

From cooks to mechanics, the Delta Troop paratroopers provided a host of functions that were essential to the squadron's success in Iraq. They handled a variety of roles beyond their normal jobs including prisoner of war detention, setting up snap checkpoints and serving as reinforcements. Combat logistics patrols placed them in constant danger of attack. The Delta Troop paratroopers gave the commander flexibility and the economy of force.

Alpha and Bravo Troops were assigned 81mm and 120mm mortars. With two guns each, the squad had one 81mm and one 120mm. There were 11 soldiers assigned to the entire section: a sergeant first class, two staff sergeants and then eight corporals or specialists and below. Charlie Troop had a 60mm mortar section, two three-man gun teams and a section sergeant. The mortar is a smooth-bore tube with a baseplate, bipod for the tube to rest on and a sight that allows the mortar to provide the proper distance to target. The mortar rounds are fin-stabilized ammunition that explodes when the round strikes a target. It's a crew-served weapon, with a crew of three to fire the weapon system.[14]

5-73 along with the rest of the 3rd Brigade began to arrive in Kuwait on August 9, 2006. The paratroopers started to acclimate themselves to the weather. The summer was at its peak in August with temperatures soaring into the 120-degree range. "Hot as balls" was a favorite refrain used to describe the extreme summer heat.

Equipped for combat, each paratrooper was wearing their digital patterned Army Combat Uniform with sand-colored boots, full kit including helmet, and body armor with several ballistic plates. A tactical vest was issued to attach various pouches for carrying ammunition along with other basics such as self-aid/buddy aid supplies for wound care. Individual weapons had a standard ammunition load of 210 rounds in 30-round magazines for the M4 carbine (rifle) and if assigned as a grenadier, between 15 and 20 explosive rounds for the M203 grenade launcher, which attached to the underside of the rifle barrel on the rail system. Depending on the mission a three-day assault pack or rucksack was carried by each member, which when combined with the heat of the day placed quite the initial strain on the paratroopers.

The Humvee gun trucks the squadron was issued carried 1,200 rounds for the .50-caliber machine gun with 400 additional rounds in the rear cargo space; same for the M240 machine gun and the M249 squad assault weapon better known as the SAW. The machine gun could be changed out with the Mark 19 grenade launcher, a belt-fed weapon system that fires 40mm grenades. With their ability to move around the battlespace with the gun trucks, a cavalry platoon had more firepower than an entire infantry company, which was three times its size.

Extra water and rations were the other two essentials. Staying hydrated was essential. It was not usual to consume two liters of water in 30 to 60 minutes, especially when doing building clearances. Even with hydration packs carried as part of the soldier's kit, with a water bladder holding up to three liters, everyone ended up carrying IVs so that whenever possible they could be used for rapid rehydration. Three MREs or Meals Ready to Eat along with six 32-ounce bottles of water per day were the minimum carried in the gun trucks. So, with five soldiers per truck and figuring on average a five-day supply each gun truck was carrying six cases of MREs and eight cases of water. If told to prepare for three days, pack for five!

From Kuwait, 5-73 flew to Balad then to Forward Operating Base (FOB) Warhorse to have equipment issued. Along with the weapons systems, radios and equipment needed for the Iraq battlespace, 5-73 received the assigned Humvee gun trucks. Gun trucks were going to be an integral part of this deployment. Alpha and Bravo Troops were 100 percent mounted using the Humvee. A top turret had either a Mark 19 grenade launcher or a .50-caliber machine gun mounted in the cupola along with an a SAW for added protection. According to Captain Few, the organizational table allowed for "only three scouts to be assigned to each truck and there are five seats in each gun truck."[15] The crews were rounded out with medics and forward observers.

Typically, a scout platoon had six trucks; 5-73 CAV went down to four. With the loss of two trucks per platoon, there was a net loss of six trucks per troop. Charlie Troop only had three trucks in the troop: a command vehicle, a cargo truck for the mortars and a Light Medium Tactical Vehicle, a light utility truck used for moving supplies. While in Iraq, Charlie Troop received 20 up-armored Humvees for theater-provided equipment. The squadron even received John Deere Gators, all-wheel drive all-terrain vehicles or ATVs that were used to transport supplies, move troops and evacuate casualties. The Gators were easily loaded onto a Chinook helicopter.

The transition to up-armored gun trucks had just begun and it was going to take some time to get through the process, so frag kits were installed as a stopgap measure to protect the paratroopers. First, a set of doors were installed. Next, a steel plate covered the bottom of the truck. Another plate covered the fuel tank and another covered the wheel wells.

Along with the latest and greatest, Lieutenant Mike Anderson, one of Alpha Troop's junior officers, noted that "some old Bosnia shit," stock from the army's mission to keep the peace in Bosnia, was in the mix with "shitty weld-shop ghetto armor." Plenty of work orders were generated to "unscrew all the crappy vehicles."[16] Upgrades were completed as time permitted and trucks went to FOB Warhorse to have the work done.

The scouts and the riflemen continued to grow on each other, sort of. The infantry Joes needed work on how to operate the heavy weapons. The scouts provided the maintenance and operations training for the .50-caliber machine gun and the Mark 19 grenade launcher. According to Anderson, the "high-school drama" all but disappeared with the squadron's departure from Kuwait.

As the squadron prepared for the coming fight, Lieutenant Colonel Poppas believed that the army's "warrior ethos" had to reach down deeper in order to inspire his paratroopers. To do that, Poppas chose the epic tale of the 300 Greek Spartan warriors who sacrificed their lives in the Battle of Thermopylae. These 300 stood against a Persian force of roughly 250,000 and fought to the death, taking what some historians estimate was the death of 20 Persian soldiers for each Spartan warrior who was lost.

The modern-day warriors of 5-73 CAV stood as one just as their ancient warrior predecessors had done. According to Poppas the Spartans were "committed to the formation," maintaining the integrity of the phalanx, warriors marching forward in line, their *doru* swords at the ready and their *hoplon* shields interlocked to protect not only the warrior but his comrade to the left and right.[17] They became "the living embodiment of the Spartans." These "consummate professionals" looked down on individualism and were continuously strengthened in their resolve that "in this formation, everyone has to fight." Their leaders faced the same hardships thus helping to ensure that the "vision of the formation" remained strong and steadfast.[18]

This ethos found its way into all the squadron's preparations for combat through the study of fear along with its effects, using the Spartan tenets to effectively lead troops, recognizing the loyalty that warfighters had for one another by virtue of their dependence on one another for survival and mission completion along with the realistic and tough training that helped prepare them for the life and death "battle-focused" realities of combat.

The legend of the Spartan warrior was destined to give the warfighters of 5-73 CAV a unique sense of inner strength that saw them through an unknown future filled with many challenges and dangers. It unknowingly tested the resolve that the legacy of these ancient warriors was instilling in these paratroopers. Before it was all over, they would refer to themselves as Task Force 300, a proud reference to their Spartan warrior brethren.

CHAPTER 2

Alpha Troop and Patrol Base Otis

The squadron leadership had been under the assumption that when Headhunter arrived in Iraq, they were headed to Salah al-Din Province with the rest of 3rd Brigade of the 82nd since 5-73 CAV was organic to or permanently assigned as the cavalry squadron for the brigade. That assumption abruptly changed.

The day before flying into Iraq, Poppas was informed that one troop was to be detached to another unit for a separate mission. Mike Few and Alpha Troop would go to the area surrounding Baqubah, the provisional capital of Diyala Province. Alpha would supposedly be there for 30 days to get a handle on the conditions in the area surrounding the city and the outskirts.

The Diyala River flows directly through this area and many of the villages are located on its banks. The area from Muqdadiyah to Baqubah is referred to as the "breadbasket of Iraq" and historically is part of the Fertile Crescent.

Towns and villages like Zaganiyah had all the signs of a community living in peaceful co-existence with a mix of Sunnis and Shias, functional government institutions and religious leaders known as imams who seemed moderate. However, a storm of epic proportions brewed below the surface as tribal and sectarian differences that had been gaining strength for many years began to clash. The area was about to erupt into the perfect space for insurgents to attack civilians, creating both panic and suspicion. Captain Few recalled that extremists were fighting to "undermine the religious and ethnic tolerance of the Iraqi people in order to gain control of territory and resources."[1]

The paratroopers of 5-73 had to become familiar with the factions battling for control in Iraq. One of the main Shia groups was the Badr Corps, an Iranian-backed group whose members had prolifically infiltrated the Iraqi army and the police. Even though Badr worked with the Iraqi government, its members attacked Sunnis and competed with another major faction, Jaysh al-Mahdi, for power and influence among the Shia.[2]

At the time, the New Ba'ath Party, the 1920 Revolutionary Brigade, and Jaysh Muhammad were the most prominent Sunni Rejectionist groups. The Sunni

Patrol Base Otis (Josh Kinser)

Rejectionists chose to attack coalition forces in an effort to press them to leave Iraq and restore Sunnis to power. They demanded security improvements in Sunni and mixed areas, disarmament and demobilization of Shia militias, a coalition exit timetable, the elimination of de-Ba'athification (a plan implemented by the Coalition Provisional Authority to purge all Ba'ath Party members from the Iraqi government) and amnesty for Sunnis who had rebelled against the Iraqi government.

Ongoing attacks by Jaysh al-Mahdi, along with the presence of Badr and Jaysh al-Mahdi members in the Iraqi police service, perpetuated Sunni persecution.[3] Executions were conducted by death squads whose members came from various terrorist, militia, and illegal armed groups, and in some instances the Iraqi security forces. Shia as well as Sunni executioners were responsible for a tremendous uptick in sectarian violence during this time and were principally targeting civilians.

Another adversary to confront was the Sunni extremist group Al Qaeda in Iraq which had in its ranks both foreigners and Iraqis who desired to establish an Islamic caliphate in Iraq.[4] Their goal was to drive the foreign occupiers from Iraq along with subjugating the Shia. Initially, this Al Qaeda affiliate was a partisan force attempting to muscle its way into the ancient tribal political-social networks. The insurgents determined that a firm stronghold in Zaganiyah would give them the strength needed to pursue their caliphate goal.

During the spring of 2004, Al Qaeda's infiltration of Zaganiyah began. Its leader in Iraq was Abu Musab al-Zarqawi, a jihadist from Jordan. He attacked coalition forces but also mercilessly attacked Shia groups. Beheadings and gruesome torture of Shias were often displayed and filmed. DVDs were distributed to Shia villages.

In 2005, Zarqawi declared an "all-out war" on Shias and the Iraqi government. Zarqawi envisioned a Sunni caliphate, an Islamic state. However, Bin Laden and Zarqawi did not see eye to eye on the killing of fellow Muslims, be they Shia or Sunni. Bin Laden also did not care for Zarqawi and his cohorts' plans to attack Shia places of worship.[5]

It was decided that in order for Alpha Troop to gain the upper hand, they would set up shop in no man's land between the Sunni and Shia portions of Big and Little Abu Saydah out of what became known as Patrol Base Otis. The patrol base would serve as the demarcation line between the two factions. "Fuck it, we're going to live here so we know what's going on," Captain Few declared.[6] By road, it was about 45 minutes northeast of Zaganiyah considering that gun trucks always had to drive defensively in order to protect against improvised explosive devices, commonly known as IEDs. On the other hand, on foot moving through the palm groves it was only a 10-minute trip between the two towns.

The house that was chosen afforded solid force protection. There was a school next to it and an abandoned lumberyard down the street. Otherwise, there were no other buildings nearby. HESCO barriers, dirt- and rock-filled liners wrapped in heavy gauge wire mesh, were stacked and surrounded the patrol base. They served as a protective blast wall as well as a means of blocking the street from potential vehicle attacks. The main house was two stories tall. The building height provided a clear line of sight so that any approaching target could be observed, stopped and if necessary destroyed before it did any damage to the paratroopers. In addition to the barriers that formed the outside of the wall concertina wire was strung. Guard towers secured all four corners.

The three platoons were rotated out of the base every three or four days depending on the mission. One platoon was always committed to the quick reaction force mission. This force provided reinforcements in the event more firepower was needed if a platoon or patrol made contact with the enemy. There were two platoons at the patrol base. Platoons got most of a day off every four days. That time was used for maintenance and a chance to grab a cup of coffee. All the latest communications technology was at their disposal. The base ended up having a freezer and some generators. The resupply routinely included burgers, hot dogs and occasionally even lamb which was a local favorite.

Alpha Troop was operating out of Patrol Base Otis while most of the remaining coalition forces were moving back into the forward operating bases better known as FOBs. The top commanders in Iraq at the time had decided to shift to a plan that focused on coalition forces working out of four super FOBs. Operations or patrols ran out of these bases and troops returned, never having had the opportunity to understand and address local problems or threats. Counterinsurgency doctrine seemed to be in a state of flux at this time. The approach of "clear, hold, build" was still in its infancy.

Along with the decision to establish a patrol base, the challenge of mission planning was a constant, complicated problem. Just to enter someone's house, a mission packet containing the operations order along with the evidence justifying a mission had to be submitted and approval had to come from the brigade commander unless troops were taking direct enemy fire. The process was similar to building a case by law enforcement to submit a request for a search warrant and presenting it to a judge for approval. It was a pain in the ass and placed severe restrictions on how effectively troops could accomplish the mission.

Then there were the Rules of Engagement. The rules were based on a method of distinguishing a life-threatening scenario from a non-life-threatening one. The "Escalation of Force" or "Show, Shout, Shove, and Shoot" was straightforward "in a perfect world."[7] In many instances, the enemy couldn't be distinguished from the rest of the population. Uniforms were seldom if ever worn by the enemy. Enemy fighters blended into and were protected by the population many times out of fear of reprisal.

One veteran 5-73 paratrooper, Sean Ventura, remembered:

> Escalation of Force stages were more commonly referred to as *Shout, Show, Shove, Shit!!* The fear of being wrong and making a bad shoot hung just as heavily on the shoulders of young men barely out of high school. Was I right? Was I overreacting? The flat rural terrain and cramped, twisting city streets added another dimension as suicide car bombers could drive up on you in an instant, reducing the Escalation of Force to a more realistic *See, Shoot* dynamic as the bongo truck bore down on you. Fear was so omnipresent that it was almost forgotten, becoming just another aspect of daily life with the sweet tickle of little spikes every time you interacted with a local. They existed in a similar dynamic of permanent fear pervading daily life to the point of driving sensible people crazy. Crazy enough to ignore the foreign man carrying a rifle and shouting at them in a strange tongue.[8]

Alpha Troop began to unravel who the bad guys were and how to stop them. Captain Few and Staff Sergeant Josh Kinser searched the digital intelligence files trying to figure out the details of this complex environment. Kinser was a combat veteran with a previous deployment to Iraq. He was a section leader and later a squad leader who also served as Alpha Troop's intelligence coordinator. Information networks were developed. The three years of assessments were at their disposal to data mine and were used to paint a common operating picture. After finishing up an 18-hour day running his section, Kinser spent hours with Captain Few working the intel. "Who's this guy, who is he talking to? How does he know this guy?" Each linkage brought more clarity to who the enemy was and the complex web that each group had built.

A special operations team showed up one day as they were preparing for a capture/ kill mission, looking for intelligence on a suspect. Kinser gave them his pitch. "This is this guy, and he's talking to this guy and this is his brother who just came back from Iran. And this guy's been doing this," and here are the pictures to prove it. The long hours spent searching files paid off. Alpha Troop developed a clear picture of their enemy while insurgent groups used different tactics to learn about Alpha Troop.

A dinner invitation brought Captain Few and Kinser face to face with Al Qaeda and Jaysh al-Mahdi leaders. Unbeknownst to the Iraqis who thought that they were just "dumb Americans" Kinser understood Arabic and even took pictures of the suspected terrorist leaders. Unfortunately, this approach was short-lived. It wasn't long before Kinser's secret got out and he became known by the locals for his ability to understand the language. On one occasion, Kinser had been approached by a police officer in a town full of dirty death-squad cops. Pointing at his nametape, the cop said in English, "Ahh Kinser, I heard of you. You are the one who speaks Arabic." Kinser didn't recognize him. When he checked his name in the registry, the cop was dirty, a member of the Mahdi Army. The place was full of all sorts of bad guys including Iranian intelligence agents. Kinser declared that "if people recognize my face as they do because of me speaking Arabic and what I do, then they sure as shit are going to recognize my name on my chest."[9]

The 80 paratroopers of Alpha Troop engaged the roughly 100,000 Iraqis who were part of a hundred different tribes. An area recon was initiated. Who were the key leaders and what was their sphere of influence? It was learned that Sheik Septar was a very influential and powerful leader in Zaganiyah. Septar was a shrewd character. Playing both sides, he was also in communication with Al Qaeda, which was sending secret messages to the sheik proposing business contracts and military treaties through couriers consisting of farmers, taxi-drivers, and women. Captain Few recalled that the purpose of these contracts and negotiations was to devise a cooperative agreement under the ever-popular "the enemy of my enemy is my friend" principle.

By accepting the offer, Sheik Septar agreed to partner with Al Qaeda to destroy their opposition whether it was the government, Western support or the Shia militias. Septar supported Al Qaeda with fighters, arms, and information. Al Qaeda promised to enter into agreements to smuggle weapons and foreign fighters from Syria, along with allowing Septar to send his most able fighters to Al Qaeda training camps. The sheik had a tough time wrapping his brain around "the extremist ideology of Al Qaeda that was rooted in Salafism, the ultra-conservative reform branch or movement within Sunni Islam. Septar enjoyed smoking cigarettes and drinking alcohol." According to an operational summary generated by Alpha Troop, Septar initially "perceived Al Qaeda in Iraq as an extreme band of thugs with little capacity to expand."[10]

In the wake of the uncertainty surrounding Septar, Al Qaeda began to explore other options. Ali Latif Al-Zuharie, a 28-year-old criminal, filled the void. Ali Latif had started his religious Wahabbi studies years earlier, then after being recruited by Al Qaeda he traveled to Mukisa and began his military training. He was trained in standard military skills and ended with the skill unique to Islamic extremists: martyrdom operations. After the completion of his warfighter training, he spent time reinforcing his previous religious indoctrination. Al Qaeda recognized his dedication to the cause and brought him into the terrorist fold.

Ali Latif returned to Zaganiyah and began to recruit possible candidates along with establishing a stronghold in the village. From the spring of 2004 to the spring of 2006, Abu Musab al-Zarqawi, the leader of Al Qaeda in Iraq, reportedly visited Ali Latif to encourage, mentor and provide guidance for future operational planning. Although relatively minuscule at the time, Al Qaeda in Iraq successfully established a presence in Zaganiyah. In the coming days, this foothold would prove decisive.

Another layer of complexity was the wealthy and influential Sheik Rohkan. He was a former member of the Special Republican Guard. Word was that he'd been injured numerous times in combat during the Iran–Iraq War leading commando teams into Iran using the cover of darkness to sneak up on and kill sleeping Iranian soldiers. A land mine ended his military career by destroying his knee. Rohkan was not your average enemy fighter. Josh Kinser reflected that he may have been "playing a game with us, maybe he was Al Qaeda the whole time, but Rohkan wasn't your average dumbass with an AK47."[11]

While using Syria as a safe haven, Rohkan received word that the Shias were getting out of hand and his help was needed. That's when he brought a force from Syria. Rohkan's fighters started murdering large numbers of Shias in the streets. The police chief was murdered: Rohkan's goal was to take over the entire police force. Operatives in Syria as well as Al Qaeda thought that they were going to team up with Rohkan. "No, this is my town," Rohkan declared. Josh Kinser noted that Rohkan didn't have any interest in being a "religious zealot." His focus was on making a power grab for himself.[12]

After weeks of work mapping through this complex environment, and without warning, Alpha Troop got pulled out of the patrol base in Abu Saydah in the middle of October. Speculation was that somebody in a much higher pay grade with a big-base mentality trumped the patrol-base approach. Captain Few went to the village leader, known as a mukhtar, and encouraged him to leave, offering to provide him with safe transit. The mukhtar declared that he wouldn't be driven away and a short time later, he met a violent death at the hands of his enemies.

The violence continued to escalate causing the tribal and governmental ties of the Sunni residents to be destroyed.

Alpha shifted its fight to Zaganiyah. Small kill teams were dispatched each night for a week to the opposite shore side of the Diyala River to recon potential enemy activity. A quick-reaction force and fire support were at their disposal in the event that a firefight developed. The Alpha Troop's tactical operations center spent tense nights waiting for them to make contact. The enemy was elusive and the continuing complicated, time consuming process of not being able to go into a house without getting a mission packet approved made it feel, according to Captain Few, like "a cluster fuck."[13] Coupled with the fact that the locals refused to talk out of fear of violent retribution or loyalty to the insurgent cause, this made for an intel-gathering nightmare.

Patrols began "finding shit left and right," recalled one of the Alpha Troop platoon leaders.[14] The second night they were observing what appeared to be some sort of safe house that was being guarded by suspected insurgents who were actively patrolling the immediate area.

The armed suspects were checking the riverbank using spotlights to see if someone had been watching them. The enemy fighters worked four-hour shifts. One night, the observation post, which was less than 100 meters away from the suspected safe house on the other side of the river, picked up Arabic-speaking men talking in a dialect other than Iraqi, possibly Egyptian. Their conversations were recorded and an interpreter confirmed that it was an Egyptian dialect. Indicators continued popping up. On another night, a group of old men who turned out to be enemy cell leaders were observed having a meeting. Permission was requested to hit the target but the request was denied due to restrictions placed on coalition forces by the Rules of Engagement.

This insurgent activity coincided with continued attacks on the police. A call was received that the Iraqi police station was going to be attacked. Aggressive patrolling conducted by elements of Alpha Troop over the previous two weeks allowed Captain Few and his paratroopers to respond in force to assist the police. An air weapons team, composed of two Apache attack helicopters, was requested to reinforce the position.

The Apaches took full advantage of their ability to stand off from their target, flying at an altitude of 2,000 feet and at a distance of four or more kilometers using advanced sights to detect enemy movement. With the pilot seated behind and slightly above the front seat gunner position, the two pilots generally work in tandem lining up their targets.[15] A variety of missiles gives the gunner a choice of which would be the most lethal based on the target. A 30mm chain gun mounted under the nose of the aircraft rounds out their ability to inflict maximum damage on the enemy.

The Apache pilots couldn't find the target so Captain Few got on the radio and offered to help locate the position for the pilots. The gunships were sent down the path leading from the police station to the house Alpha Troop had been watching. Captain Few instructed the gunships to "look for enemy fighters running from the palm groves into the house carrying weapons."[16] Within three minutes the Apaches had engaged and killed eight enemy fighters.

Al Qaeda responded with leaflets dropped at the police officers' homes warning them not to return to work. On October 20, friendly forces reinforced the police station. Captain Few attempted to conduct a hasty governance meeting with the local sheiks. No one showed up, and the police force unraveled. It was decided by Iraqi authorities to reinforce the police station with the Baqubah Emergency Response Force, a paramilitary unit molded after the Iraqi Special Operations Forces brigade.

The following day, the situation rapidly deteriorated and Alpha Troop helped the local police patrol the streets. On October 24 the enemy attacked once more. A platoon was sent up to reinforce. The enemy had blocked the entrance points with buried explosives—a series of six improvised explosive devices or IEDs were found. Bomb disposal techs eliminated that threat. Mike Few sent another platoon in from the north through Abu Saydah; Al Qaeda sent a wave of attacks to disperse the Iraqi reinforcements. Friendly air support pounded the insurgents; Al Qaeda counterattacked by placing a defensive belt around Zaganiyah. This firefight resulted in the deaths of 10 enemy fighters and four paratroopers being wounded. The police reinforcements stood their ground and drove the attackers back.

Using the situational intelligence along with the ever-increasing level of attacks on the police and civilians, a mission packet was formulated to destroy the Al Qaeda safe house in Zaganiyah. It was located on the Diyala River in a corner alley of the town. Operation Shaku Maku (Arabic for "What's up?") required, according to Captain Few, "a 70-page mission packet" along with a video recording of the enemy patrolling the area.[17]

To underline the need for the mission, there was a rumor floating around that a contract had been put out by Al Qaeda to assassinate Captain Few and Alpha Troop's platoon leaders. So, there was a sense of urgency to the operation and it was getting increasingly personal. The insurgents had a roving patrol, which was observed from an Alpha Troop hide site using a camera with night-vision capabilities. During the early morning hours, several high-level leaders speaking a Syrian or Saudi dialect moved into the palm groves to meet. Afterwards, they returned to the target house. Rohkan had strategically picked this house, since it was backed up in a corner and the streets were too narrow for coalition gun trucks to maneuver.

Approval was received to initiate the mission and it was set for the night of October 31. 3rd Platoon and Captain Few were across the river in sniper/ambush positions. The hide site included a medic, machine gun and a sniper team. They took up their positions around 10:00 p.m. 1st Platoon was given the job of conducting the raid on the house. Aerial photography and imagery were utilized to provide additional intel on how to approach it. 1st Platoon's gun trucks moved up in total darkness along Route Canal. Along the Berm Road was a culvert that went into the southwestern portion of Zaganiyah, and it skirted south along some palm groves. The palm groves were directly west of the safe house and north of Berm Road. It was suspected that the Al Qaeda cell was hiding weapons and bomb-making materials in the groves. The enemy fighters used the canals to escape capture during searches of Zaganiyah.

The original time on target was between 2:00 and 3:00 a.m. An artillery barrage had been planned to strike the palm grove in order to prevent enemy fighters from escaping that way. Air weapons teams composed of two Apache gunships armed with missiles and 30mm guns were also on station to support the mission. The reality of suppressing the enemy using the gunships was that the palm groves were so thick with vegetation it would be extremely difficult to spot any enemy movement using the Apache's optics.

For some unknown reason, the artillery mission failed to deliver. As a result of this lapse, 1st Platoon began to receive enemy small-arms fire as they entered Zaganiyah. By now it was daybreak and the paratroopers moved straight into the target. Al Qaeda fighters had placed logs across the road, which blocked the approach to the safe house. In support of the raid, First Sergeant Tim Metheny had linked up with two platoons of the Iraqi army and right at daylight they began to provide suppressive fire to keep the insurgents pinned down. One of the assault gun trucks created a breach by ramming the Humvee through a brick wall so the platoon could get to the target house, quickly bypassing the enemy obstacles. As the various coalition forces began their approach to the target, car horns began to sound. The enemy early warning system had been activated. Enemy fighters began to scramble from the safe house using women as human shields. A flare fired from the hide site hit the building, sent the women scattering and exposed the enemy fighters who in turn were killed.

An enemy sniper was also trying to escape, attempting to use suppressive fire to cover his movement. The paratroopers were struggling to place accurate fire on the insurgent. Firing one round to make sure the next shot would be dead on from a borrowed rifle after his own malfunctioned, one of the paratroopers fired a second shot that killed the sniper, striking him in the head. An amazing feat of marksmanship using someone else's rifle!

Once the enemy safe house was cleared the palm groves had to be searched. Before they entered the palm groves, however, attack helicopters were ordered to initiate suppressive fire on enemy positions in the palm grove in an effort to limit any enemy attempts to ambush the paratroopers. Several of the enemy were tracked down and captured in the palm grove.

Despite having a $10,000 bounty placed on their heads by the enemy insurgents, the Alpha Troop leaders arranged a meeting with Sheik Septar and what Captain

Few referred to as "100 of his closest friends" immediately following Shaku Maku. The captain had his interpreter, who was from Zaganiyah, call Septar to guarantee the safety of the Americans attending the meeting. The sheik repeated the guarantee three times which meant that if something were to happen, according to local custom, their neighborhood could be burned to the ground. Septar gave his word, but Captain Few wasn't satisfied. Apache gunships were performing dry runs over the building during the meeting as a reminder. As Few, Kinser and a single paratrooper security detail entered the building they removed their body armor to illustrate to the Iraqis that they were not afraid of the insurgent threats.

Septar accused the paratroopers of massacring women and children. He demanded $100 for each dead Iraqi. Captain Few shot back and proceeded to talk Septar through the events of the previous morning, telling them how the insurgents used the women as human shields. As the captain recounted the gruesome details the faces of the assembled elders according to Captain Few "visibly shuddered." The captain told the assembled leaders that even though the national government was unstable and appeared to be extremely biased the alternative of Al Qaeda and Sharia law was fraught with evil.

Shaku Maku was successful in stopping the violence in Zaganiyah for several weeks. There weren't any attacks on the police stations and the police stopped beating up civilians. Sheik Septar, who was Sunni, began talking to the police who were Shia. Captain Few recalled that "everybody started getting along." Within days of Shaku Maku Alpha Troop got the word that once again they were being pulled out, this time to rejoin the rest of the squadron. Supposedly, it was because conditions had improved. The Joes were pretty pissed off about it. "If we leave it's going to get fucking ugly," Few told his superiors.[18]

By the middle of November, the police station had been suicide bombed and the police were in complete disarray. Al Qaeda and The Islamic State of Iraq seemed to have gained a foothold.

Just in the month of October Alpha Troop had conducted over 190 missions. Upon returning to the squadron, 2nd Platoon would be detached to a Provisional Reconstruction Team mission in Baqubah thus reducing Alpha Troop's combat power by another platoon. It wouldn't be long before Alpha Troop, along with the rest of the squadron, would be engaged in an unexpected and deadly new operation. In a twist of irony, 5-73 CAV would return to the Diyala River Valley five months later to the fight of their lives.

CHAPTER 3

AO Headhunter

While Alpha Troop wrestled with its mission in Zaganiyah, the remainder of the squadron was assigned to a different unit. The area of operations for 5-73 CAV, known as Area of Operations or AO Headhunter, was the remainder of Diyala Province, located in eastern Iraq between the outskirts of Baghdad and the Iranian border. The total area of approximately 4,550 square miles is roughly the size of Connecticut.

With Alpha Troop gone, Headhunter was left with Bravo and Charlie Troops, the Delta Troop forward support paratroopers, the headquarters troop, two mortar sections, a sniper section and one platoon serving as squadron reserve to conduct combat operations. The goal was to start running a series of four-day operations to get a feel for the battlespace followed by a two-day rest and refit. The intelligence reports indicated that supplies and enemy fighters were entering Iraq at the Iranian border and that this pipeline led right through Diyala. Lieutenant Colonel Poppas encouraged his subordinate leaders to aggressively develop the situation, engage the population and let it be known that Headhunter was on the prowl for the enemy.

As the S-3, or squadron operations boss, Brett Sylvia got his marching orders from Lieutenant Colonel Poppas. Sylvia emphasized the squadron's goal: "at the end of it... you don't need to send another unit out here because we did it!" It wasn't about patrolling and making some improvements. The goal was to aggressively execute a campaign plan that resulted in defeating the insurgents. An audacious plan executed by a squadron that wanted to win. The challenge was that there hadn't been any significant friendly force presence for over a year in this part of Iraq. Headhunter planning efforts focused on what Major Sylvia referred to as the "quest for intelligence" that would ultimately provide the necessary ingredients to develop a campaign plan.[1]

The first squadron-level mission began on August 26, 2006 and lasted two weeks. 5-73 CAV less Alpha Troop moved into AO Headhunter and began pursuing enemy fighters. It was important to develop a working relationship with the Iraqi Security Forces including the Department of Border Enforcement, the Iraqi army and numerous Iraqi police elements organized in the more densely populated areas. Various intelligence, surveillance and reconnaissance platforms including ground

Jeff Loehr's truck after the detonation on October 16, 2006. Loehr was the first to be WIA by an IED (Brad Rather)

A close-up of Loehr's truck (Brad Rather)

sensors were used to identify routes along the Iraq–Iran border that were being used to smuggle bomb-making materials into Iraq. The paratroopers were exposed to how the Iraqi army operated, what, if any, government institutions were in place, the local economy and ability to sustain support in these towns along with the composition of enemy forces. One common thread quickly became readily apparent: there weren't any military-age males around when the soldiers were. This was a sure sign that Al Qaeda had radicalized these men.

As the intelligence picture was refined the problem set became clear. First, there was the porous border between Iraq and Iran that allowed for the movement of explosives, which comprised the eastern edge of AO Headhunter. Shepherds and local villagers with tribal heritage focused primarily on moving accelerants from Iran or harvesting the munitions left over from the Iran–Iraq war, which were sold to the highest bidder.

Next was a group of radical Sunnis south of Balad Ruz, known as "the Council." The Council was a Wahabbist-minded group that had chosen violence to wrest control of the region following the fall of Saddam Hussein. These insurgents had set up a network of training camps for Al Qaeda foreign fighters, safe houses and an early warning system across southern Diyala. Since there hadn't been a government presence in the area for several years, at this point in 2006 Diyala was fertile ground for Al Qaeda. One of the terrorist group's tactics was to infiltrate an area with a mixed population, destabilize it and in turn establish a base of operations. Foreign fighters also found it easy to transit the province, moving from the Syrian border through northern and central Iraq. Ba'athists and ex-army officers took control of Diyala following the end of Saddam Hussein's regime, creating "a hotbed of activity."[2]

The Al Nida tribe was another challenge. When Saddam Hussein was in power this tribe had been given both land and financial support in return for helping secure the border between Iran and Iraq along with strengthening Saddam's Ba'athist agenda in Diyala Province. Following the collapse of Saddam Hussein's regime, the Al Nida tribe lost all its power and influence. The tribe turned to peddling accelerants and intelligence to the highest bidder, primarily Sunni insurgents, which led to the tribe's preaching the violence of Al Qaeda. Criminal activities like carjacking, smuggling and money laundering helped to fund their efforts to strengthen control of the province. The disruption of elections in the province was also part of the Al Nida's efforts to retain their tribal dominance.

Finally, there were concerns about Kurdish expansion into the sector, which had the potential of leading to what one operational summary referred to as "regional instability."[3] At the time, the Kurds permitted the smuggling of accelerants or munitions over their border if the price was right, with the understanding that these explosives wouldn't be used to target Kurds.

For almost two weeks, 5-73 had been maneuvering through the sun-crested Zagros Mountains, the key terrain feature in the Diyala River Valley. With the help of the intelligence staff, Major Sylvia laid out the problem in Diyala to Lieutenant Colonel Poppas. Headhunter didn't have the combat strength to deal with all of these objectives at the same time but the campaign plan needed to ensure achievable end-state conditions that included Iraqi forces being able to provide the security necessary to keep insurgent groups at bay, eliminate the smuggling of explosives over the Iran–Iraq border and establish a peaceful forum to address sectarian issues. The plan needed to be accomplished using the limited squadron assets and to correspond with plans that were formulated by higher headquarters.

Charlie Troop under the command of Captain John Carson was given the Iraq–Iran border. They focused on interdicting smugglers along the border and preparing trainers from the Department of Border Enforcement to deliver mission-focused training to all the members of Iraqi border guards through the newly formed training center in Khanaqin.

Captain Stephen Dobbins and Bravo Troop zeroed in on the objectives of seizing arms caches and raiding enemy safe houses. The local police struggled to maintain order and there weren't enough Iraqi military forces in the area, so the insurgents were able to move from Turki Village to Balad Ruz by using the nearby palm groves and fields that paralleled roads to conceal their movement. In doing so, the Al Qaeda fighters were able to avoid the checkpoints that had been set up by the Iraqi security forces south of Balad Ruz and terrorize the local population by way of kidnapping and murdering civilians. These terrorists also attacked security forces using IEDs and mortar attacks. At first these attacks, according to Dobbins, "seemed like snowballs hitting us." He recalled that these IEDs were poorly placed, "almost like they were the JV squad" setting the explosives.[4] These rookie terrorists were sent to Balad Ruz after just having learned how to place explosives. They'd set pressure-detonated devices in one area, command-detonated in another area and telephone-detonated type devices in yet another location.

Along with slowing the terrorist acts being pursued by the Council, Bravo worked with the police, teaching them patrolling techniques, with emphasis on knocking first before resorting to kicking the door in and walking a beat like cops do in the U.S. as opposed to sitting on a checkpoint. This community policing effort gave the local police force an opportunity to shine in the eyes of the citizens of Balad Ruz. The public needed to know that they could depend on their police to protect them from the terror threat.

Each successive operation built a more detailed and refined intelligence picture. The reconnaissance function gave Bravo Troop the intel it needed to pinpoint the Al Qaeda safe haven, Turki Village. This would drive them towards future battles. The picture that was being shaped by Bravo and Charlie Troops' efforts began to confirm the initial assessment that there was a link, a common thread between the two problem sets. Smugglers were using villages that dotted the border as waypoints for weapons and explosives that they were supplying to Sunni as well Shia terrorist groups.

Lieutenant Colonel Poppas provided clear direction in his orders to Bravo Troop when he said, "Expand the intelligence picture of the Council south of Balad Ruz."[5]

Keeping the pressure up to disrupt the insurgents' attempts to train enemy fighters as well as move explosives into Baqubah and Baghdad provoked a violent enemy response. A more professional enemy began using more advanced explosives. According to Dobbins, these were the "varsity squad kind of guys."[6] The enemy was placing IEDs to strike in between and behind gun trucks because the enemy knew that the paratroopers would be coming back down the road. The terrorists continued to go after innocent civilians to intimidate them. A black trash bag left lying in front of shops at a local market could hide an IED. Instantaneously, dozens of innocent civilians could be torn to shreds and the street soaked in their blood.

Reaching the insurgent base of operations meant moving south past what was known as the Iman Monsour checkpoint. There hadn't been any coalition forces south of this checkpoint for the past 18 months. It was the line of demarcation. South of it there was plenty of potentially deadly uncertainty. Bravo Troop was about to drive into the heart of it, stirring this enemy hornets' nest.

"My driver thinks he just saw a wire in the road," came the warning over the radio. The blast shattered the eerie calm. Heat, smoke and dust consumed the gun truck. "Stop the truck," ordered Sergeant Jeff Loehr, the truck commander, as his gunner, Specialist Greg Voigt, screamed out in pain.

Seconds later, "We've got two guys down, they hit an IED," came the troops in contact report over the radio.[7]

Loehr was able to open the door but was tangled up in the wires, metal and combat lock which he had to struggle with in order to get out of the truck. The blast had blown up through the wheel well. Lying on the ground bleeding and writhing in pain, Loehr watched as Voigt slumped against the back of the truck while the rest of the crew checked the area for any additional threats. They made one pass to determine immediate harm like IEDs and mines. The second pass scanned for and cleared any threats posed by nearby buildings, approaching people and/or vehicles. The rest of the column established a perimeter to deal with any other threats. With rapid precision, the paratroopers secured the area.

The medics found Loehr on the ground with a leg wound that was full of shrapnel. Loehr's gunner, Voigt, had been struck in the jaw. Not only was his jaw fractured, Voigt also had deadly metal pieces in his neck and cheek. Blood poured from Loehr's face, a large piece of metal had pierced his ankle and some of the skin and muscle from his injured leg had been blown off by the blast. The medics began to remove his boot, expose his wounds and stop the bleeding. Even with the administering of morphine, Jeff was still in excruciating pain. The nine-line medic report describing the patients' conditions was transmitted and a medical evacuation helicopter was ordered. A landing zone was set up for the inbound medevac helicopter. As soon as it landed, Voigt and Loehr were turned over to the medevac crew and were on their way to the closest hospital, which was a short flight away.

The gun truck was recovered, and the mission continued almost as if nothing had happened. Everyone knew that this day would come. They were the first casualties suffered by 5-73. They would not be the last.

Once they arrived at the hospital, the medical staff began cleaning the blood away and figuring out how to treat Voigt and Loehr. While Loehr waited to be taken to surgery, he was given a cellphone to call home. There was only one problem: the explosion had rattled his brain and Loehr couldn't remember any of his home numbers. After being moved into the operating room, surgeons began to remove shrapnel from Jeff's body. His leg was so swollen from the effects of the blast that a procedure called a fasciotomy had to be performed in order to relieve pressure that was being exerted on his leg. An incision was made and the site remained open until the swelling diminished. With the leg bandaged and plenty of pain meds, Loehr began the slow recovery process. Bandages were changed twice a day to check on progress and ensure the site wasn't becoming infected; a painful but necessary procedure. When he awoke, Jeff found Voigt was there. With his jaw wired shut and a large incision in his neck from the exploratory surgery to remove shrapnel, Voigt was on a liquid diet.

Loehr finally remembered his aunt's phone number and was able to call her. He left a message to get in touch with his wife so she could email him. It was a complicated effort to access his email and get his home phone number, but it finally allowed him to speak with and reassure his panic-stricken wife. From Baghdad, to Balad, to Germany, Loehr and Voigt were moved in stages closer to home. Loehr couldn't walk yet, so Voigt pushed him around in a wheelchair. Surgeons loosened Voigt's jaw so he could eat some soft solid foods. Loehr headed back to the States first, followed several days later by Voigt. Voigt made it back home and the wheels were greased for him to be transferred to a hospital near where his mother lived in Maryland so he could be close to her. He eventually received a medical discharge.

Loehr returned to Fort Bragg, the 82nd's home, and was reunited with his wife. He was briefly admitted to Womack Army Medical Center. By this time, he'd had plenty of experience with having his wound dressed and knew the best way to approach these twice-daily sessions. A dose of pain meds prior to beginning the dressing change helped him to cope with the discomfort. After a disagreement with a doctor over how to manage his pain, he was permitted to take dressing supplies and a pain med prescription home with him. Daily visits to the hospital were required to ensure he was healing. Loehr appeared determined to return to the fight. In three months' time he was back in Iraq with his 5-73 CAV brothers.

While Bravo Troop was moving south towards Turki in pursuit of Al Qaeda insurgents, Charlie Troop was tasked with training border guards. They found the guards sorely lacking resources: a couple of trucks, always low on fuel, a shortage of ammunition and frequent losses of power. They had 15 guards for each border castle along with only two vehicles and had to cover large stretches of border territory. Iranian border castles were usually situated directly across from the Iraqi castles. The castles were medieval-looking high-walled structures with a turret on each corner that served as observation points. The castles were interspersed along the border. Effective patrolling and interdiction appeared to be a monumental task. Conducting reconnaissance of suspected smuggling routes between Iran and Iraq gave Charlie Troop a better picture of the threats facing them. A disputed border between the two countries created an added layer of tension that could rapidly escalate.

"Charlie 6 [Captain Carson, Charlie Troop's commanding officer] this is Red 1, we'll be reconning out of mortar range," was transmitted.

1st Platoon, or Red 1, was under the command of Lieutenant John Dennison, a young, handsome, charismatic West Point graduate on his first combat deployment. His platoon sergeant was Robert Cobb, a witty, complicated, soft-spoken leader known for keeping his paratroopers on their toes. Never one to raise his voice, Cobb was the kind of person who could succeed at whatever profession he would have chosen. Cobb's opinion always seemed to be valued by his superiors.

Dennison had advised Captain Carson's radio operator that they would be maneuvering out of range of the mortar protection. There was only one problem: the paratrooper monitoring the radio neglected to give the out-of-range report to Carson. Dennison and Cobb along with their four gun trucks and two Iraqi border patrol bongo trucks observed the Iranian guard tower approximately 300–400 meters to their front. Eight hundred meters to the northeast of their position, Iranian soldiers accompanied by tanks watched Dennison and his paratroopers. A lone motorcycle approached their position. Stopping at the Iraqi trucks, he began to converse with the Iraqi guards. Without warning, the Iranians began to move towards Dennison and his gun trucks.

"Lay in on the tanks," ordered Sergeant First Class Donnie Workman, the mortar section sergeant.[8] Workman was a tough but fair leader who was on his third combat tour. He'd arrived at 5-73 just prior to the deployment and was still working on gaining the trust of his paratroopers. The situation was getting tense. Workman and the mortar section could quickly provide the patrol with the protection it would need to safely disengage from the Iranians.

When a fire mission is requested, the mortar is sighted, a round is dropped down the mortar tube and it is immediately fired down range to impact on the target. The mortar is relatively light weight and its simplicity allows infantrymen to move it rapidly and engage targets quickly with a high volume of fire, either killing the enemy outright or suppressing enemy movement so the infantry soldiers can close with and destroy them.

The mortar crew had to determine the distance in order to accurately strike a target with a mortar round. "Range too far," came the response. "Run it again," commanded Workman, thinking that there must be some mistake. After a second attempt with the same results, the range was shifted to lay on the platoon's position. Workman figured that "if they've got to leave, we can at least start dropping rounds so nobody can start following them." Once again, "Range too far" was the heart-dropping response. Quickly checking his map and calculating the range, Workman confirmed that the mortars were outside the 7,200-meter coverage. Workman reported to Captain Carson that moving a kilometer or so further south would put them in range.[9]

The paratroopers took the guns out of action, separating the parts of the mortar and preparing to move them if it became necessary. Even with each 120mm mortar weighing over 300 pounds, the mortar section could have the gun loaded and ready to roll within two minutes. By this point, the Iranian troops were scrambling to move more troops to the nearby border outpost. Both Carson and Lieutenant Colonel Poppas were concerned that any movement could easily escalate an already delicate and tense situation.

An attempt to disengage by 1st Platoon resulted in the Iranians maneuvering to encircle the paratroopers. Shots fired by the Iranians were met with returning fire from Dennison and his troops. The Headhunter gun trucks and Iraqi vehicles quickly escaped what had become an untenable situation. By the time Dennison and his paratroopers rejoined Captain Carson and the mortars, 1st Platoon's gun trucks had the souvenir bullet holes to confirm that the Iranians were playing for keeps.

Following the brief firefight on the border, it was obvious that these paratroopers had narrowly averted an international incident. Had they not quickly sized up the intent of the Iranians there's no question that the Americans would have been involved in a major firefight with the Iranian forces and subsequently accused of a border incursion.

As these attacks grew in intensity and frequency, the amount of human intelligence also increased. The ever-increasing level of violence south of Balad Ruz reinforced the intelligence that Turki Village was the center of gravity for the Sunni extremists. Charlie Troop split their resources, minus 1st Platoon, which would continue their training mission for the Iraqi border guards while the remainder of the troop performed reconnaissance of the area east of Turki Village identifying routes and outlying villages. Conversations with the locals along with multiple shaping operations reinforced the magnitude of the insurgency in the area and led Headhunter to switch their focus towards Turki which appeared to be a "hub of activity" for extremists.[10] The area contained a large network of training camps, safe houses and early warning networks across southern Diyala and provided training for Al Qaeda insurgents from Syria, Jordan and Saudi Arabia.

CHAPTER 4

Turki Bowl I

November 12, 2006 brought the thumping rotor blades of Black Hawks carrying Lieutenant Colonel Poppas, along with most of the 5-73 CAV leadership, performing an aerial reconnaissance over the area in and around Turki Village.[1] One could not help but wonder what its history held. This fertile land contained rich green fields and palm groves with irrigation canals crisscrossing the landscape: a peaceful agricultural scene. In stark contrast was the sectarian violence that Al Qaeda was fomenting.

Turki had been untouched by coalition forces for quite some time. Intelligence documents had described an earlier effort by special operations forces that had executed a mission to capture or kill enemy leaders. The goal had been to loosen the Council's insurgent grip on the region. A 10-hour firefight had erupted during which the enemy used the canals for cover and concealment. When it was over, two special operators and 20 enemy fighters had been killed.

A major feature of the area was a system of irrigation canals, 15 to 30 feet deep, just wide enough that vehicles couldn't cross, filled with water and thick grass. Much smaller splinter canals ran from the larger feeders. The land south of Turki Village was covered with crops and farm buildings. The village had hundreds of buildings, one- and two-story mud structures, most of which were surrounded by an outer wall that formed a courtyard. Moving from north to south, a dirt road would allow access for the squadron's gun trucks. From east to west, the canal system was going to severely reduce their speed of movement.

Poppas had the Black Hawk pilots make numerous descents in an effort to detect any enemy movement. By midafternoon, they had been in the air for hours and nothing of any consequence had been noted. Suddenly, something appeared out of the corner of several pairs of eyes. "It's a fucking huge hole," Captain Carson told Major Sylvia.[2] Several others, including one of the helicopter crew chiefs, observed a glint of light. Before anyone could transmit over the net, they'd already flown well past it. The search for the source took 10 minutes to accomplish. While approaching the site for the second time, Lieutenant Colonel Poppas transmitted that they'd found what looked like a white Nissan truck hidden in the tall vegetation. At the same time, the power of the Black Hawk's rotor wash forced something out of the

Turki Bowl I (Josh Andrews)

berm: it looked like a door or a hatch. The canal system was the perfect place to camouflage the enemy and their implements of war. The hole turned out to be the entrance to a buried 20-foot shipping container.

After landing to investigate further, Poppas looked at Sylvia and asked, "What do you want to do Brett?"

The paratroopers were right in the middle of some deep shit. There wasn't help anywhere close and the main force wouldn't reach Turki for hours.

"We were going to attack into this area and clear it in a few months anyway, I guess the fight starts today," Sylvia declared.[3]

It was going to either go like clockwork or we were going to get fucked up, thought Captain Few.[4]

For now, a deliberate reconnaissance was in order. At that, Major Sylvia pulled out a map along with some blue 3x5 note cards and began to formulate a course of action. The reconnaissance would precede the pending operation, which was expected to take place within weeks. Its goal was to secure Turki Village. Turki had to be secured otherwise the enemy would always be in the squadron's rear biting at them while they attempted to clear, hold and build the rest of the province. The recon would give 5-73 the necessary intelligence to decide how to proceed. Going to work meant bringing the entire squadron to the battlespace. The squadron—Alpha, Bravo and Charlie (less their 1st Platoon) along with the forward support company—were alerted for the operation.

This is the big one, thought Sylvia.[5]

In the meantime, Poppas, along with eight of his subordinates and his security detail, remained on the ground to maintain a foothold on the site. Alpha Troop's first sergeant, Tim Metheny, pulled off his kit and body armor so he could fit through the hatch, drew his 9mm pistol and cautiously entered the container under the watchful eyes of Cobb and Dennison. The container was filled with enemy weapons, munitions, IED-making materials, documents, and even human remains.

They remained on the ground for hours awaiting the arrival of the remainder of the squadron, the whole time being probed by the enemy. Motorcyclists were the enemy's recon element. Unarmed riders were left unmolested by the paratroopers since there didn't appear to be hostile intent. According to Metheny, when the lead motorcycle got 20 meters from the white pickup truck that had been seized by the paratroopers, the rider "became spooked, turned around, and headed north."[6] The truck contained IED-making materials and 1,400 dollars in new U.S. 100-dollar bills.

Sylvia transmitted a situation report back to the squadron headquarters while en route by helicopter. He needed a dry erase board and markers ready when he landed. Brett formulated the operations order for the commanders while in flight and delivered it immediately after landing. The operations order gave all the principals a clear understanding of how an operation would be accomplished. In turn, the key leaders disseminated the mission details to their subordinates.

Preparing 300 paratroopers to move into battle, drawing sufficient food, water, fuel and ammunition for three days was a monumental effort. In addition, enough assets were needed for the ground assault convoy from Caldwell to Turki over roads and terrain that were both treacherous as well as unimproved. It took time to reach Turki due also in part to the fact that the road could be mined and there was always the risk of an enemy ambush. It was a huge task to obtain the necessary helicopters to move a portion of the squadron, along with making sure fire support in the form of air force fighters, attack helicopters and artillery was available. The squadron's mortars provided close-in fire support. Tactical satellite radios, both voice and digital, were essential. This system also had a laptop that could be used to transmit email which facilitated communications with the squadron headquarters as well sending battlefield update briefings to higher headquarters.

After the returning aircraft refueled at FOB Warhorse, they returned several members of the original recon party to FOB Caldwell. Captain Few briefed his Alpha Troop subordinates and collected some gear for Lieutenant Colonel Poppas, including his cigars and coffee pot. Having been up since zero dark thirty, Alpha Troop grabbed a few precious moments of sleep. You grab rest when you can. It was shaping up to be a long couple of days.

Bravo Troop, led by Captain Dobbins, arrived in Turki with gun trucks around 7:00 p.m. The cache site could only be reached by driving through Turki. As the convoy traversed the village, it appeared that every adult male was outside giving the convoy a stare of hate-filled contempt. With their arms crossed in angry defiance, their body language was telling of the battle that was about to unfold.

Bravo Troop was immediately tasked with an air assault mission to surprise enemy fighters trying to recover weapons from a cache about 10 kilometers from the original landing zone and first cache location. The lift helicopters landed and the paratroopers began to move north through Turki. While maneuvering towards the cache objective, information was received from a Predator drone about a reported nearby insurgent safe house with enemy fighters in it. Bravo Troop received the change in mission to investigate the report. The drone observed what appeared to be three enemy fighters attempting to escape from the safe house but couldn't confirm if the suspects were armed, so the paratroopers pursued the suspects and detained them. When it was time for Bravo Troop to be picked up the lift helicopters weren't able to make it in due to the weather. The paratroopers would be stuck out there all night, cold, wet and hungry.

The next morning 5-73 began to move into the villages. The battlespace was shaping up to be approximately 15 by 15 kilometers. There were a series of villages on the west side in a row about five kilometers in length, then off to the east and northeast there was a palm grove. The usual irrigation canals checkered the landscape.

The paratroopers entered each village, going house to house, knocking on every door, seeing every face, taking pictures and writing down names of villagers. The goal was to build the profile of Turki and the surrounding area. The civilian population wasn't above suspicion. One woman said that her husband had been gone for years. Problem was she had a baby that was only a couple of months old. So, who is the dad if your husband has been gone for years? There were women, children and old men. All the military-age males had vanished. The assumption was that they had become radicalized and were prepared to fight and die for their cause.

The technique used by the paratroopers to enter and clear a building had been practiced until the skill was automatic. The difference now was that this was the real deal and that the next step could be deadly. Through each door, around every corner, down each hallway there was the constant potential for violence. Were they just innocent civilians or Al Qaeda terrorists? Was the place rigged to explode when a door was breached? This clearance went on for the next two days. The danger of IEDs continued to take its toll. One of the Iraqi army vehicles hit an antitank mine, setting the truck on fire and killing an Iraqi soldier. After that Sergeant First Class Willie Lillie recalled that it started to get real: "You know we're getting closer and these are their defenses. This guy I had just had breakfast with, I had just worked on the mission before, they did alright. You know now he's dead."[7]

All at once, there was a dramatic turn of events.

CHAPTER 5

First Blood

Charlie Troop had been given the mission to "knock and search" the town of 30 Tamooz, a small village located next to Turki. The night of November 14 the squadron had identified, engaged and killed 27 enemy fighters that had massed south of 30 Tamooz. Captain Carson remembered that the village "was about 2km long and about 600 to 800 meters wide and normally they would have about, I'd say about 5,000 to 6,000 people in it."[1] Charlie Troop found that the village had been swept clean by the enemy. No enemy fighters, no suspects, no weapons caches. There was a series of approximately 20 to 30 irrigation canals to the southwest of 30 Tamooz that ran parallel to each other that would need to be searched and cleared of any potential threats.

The morning of November 15, Carson pulled in all of Charlie Troop's leaders to give them a battle update brief. As Carson began to brief his junior leaders, he turned to find that Lieutenant Dennison was handing him a cup of coffee.

"Thanks, brother," Carson said. He momentarily thought what this small gesture meant to him then quickly returned to the mission at hand.[2]

Charlie Troop's movement to contact commenced with the sniper section in the lead, followed by the command element with Dennison's trucks covering the column's rear. As the column moved down the road, which sat above the canals on either side, it immediately became apparent that this elevated position that was surrounded by large fields on either side provided good cover for the enemy. The roadside canals were concrete lined and had water in them. The secondary canals were dirt lined and dry until the valves were opened to fill them. The terrain on either side of the canal had chest-high marsh grass interspersed by field-high vegetation with sporadic hedgerow. Turki Village was visible off in the distance. There was also another road on the opposite side of the canal, a bit lower than the parallel road.

Suddenly, in the middle of the road two insurgents were caught digging a placement hole for an IED. They were quickly captured while the remainder of the column began sweeping the area for any other enemy activity and pulling security to defend against an enemy ambush.

John Ryan Dennison (Haley Dennison Uthlaut)

Captain Carson ordered Lieutenant Dennison to take at least a nine-member squad plus some extra firepower, dismount and move into the brush with the objective of locating any enemy weapons caches. Dennison made the decision to be up at the tip of the wedge, taking the position of point. It's an essential part of a patrol formation, providing early warning in the event of any enemy movement. Next in the order of movement is the squad leader, then the platoon leader with the remaining force following close behind. If contact is made with the enemy, the formation can lay suppressive fire down with the lead team and can move the soldiers that make up the rear team around either the left or right to outflank the enemy.

The cornfields, marsh grass, weeds and trees all grew tall which gave the enemy excellent cover and concealment. A small grass hut was located next to a berm covered with date trees and a cornfield along with canal ditches. Once they cleared the trees, there was a cornfield close by and Lieutenant Dennison requested to clear it since it was adjacent to the tree line. Captain Carson gave approval to proceed.

The formation entered the cornfield to clear it. Lieutenant Dennison was on Staff Sergeant Geriah McAvin's right. At the time, McAvin was a section sergeant and lead scout for this movement to contact. Humble and reserved, McAvin took his job very seriously and expected those around him to do the same. As the sweep progressed, Dennison shifted to McAvin's left. As they were reaching the end of the clearance, Sergeant McAvin gave the command to wagon wheel, which meant that the far left stayed in place and the right swept through and came back around, assuring that the entire area was swept. As the sweep progressed, the platoon discovered a hut with a cooking fire nearby.

As they moved closer, a military-age male stepped out, made eye contact with the patrol and immediately raised his arms signaling that he wanted to surrender. Almost simultaneously, another suspect bolted from the hut, running away from the patrol. Within seconds of this contact, the sounds of enemy rifle fire suddenly filled the air. From behind a motorcycle next to the hut an enemy fighter began spraying the column with deadly accuracy. The paratroopers immediately began returning fire, killing the insurgent. A situation report from the radio operator confirmed troops in contact.

"Charlie 6 this is Red 1 Romeo request immediate medevac, shots fired, one enemy killed, one friendly wounded, battle roster number to follow."[3]

The battle roster number would have the casualty's troop letter, initials and the last four digits of the social security number. It was Lieutenant Dennison. Medics rushed to Dennison and began the desperate effort to save the young platoon leader's life. One round had struck Dennison in his side just below the armpit along with several shots to the legs. His wounds would prove to be too numerous to survive.

The sniper section immediately reacted to the contact, threw the detainees from the road into another gun truck and took off in the direction of the contact. As they moved forward, the gun trucks on the road began taking fire. With tracers all around, but unable to return fire due to Alpha Troop bringing up the rear, the quick reaction force moved over the berms at such speed that one of the gun trucks' tire racks was completely torn off. Dennison's gun trucks also made their way toward the cornfield, establishing security around the engagement.

During this firefight, Alpha Troop was attempting to push forward to reinforce Charlie Troop, detaining any enemy fighters moving away from Captain Carson's fight. As Alpha approached from Charlie's rear, they came in contact. First, one of the gun trucks struck what turned out to be a dud IED rigged to an artillery shell. Explosive ordnance disposal techs cleared that round and the column began bisecting several canals that had to be maneuvered around. The canals had to be traversed. Either a crossover needed to be found or some sort of bridging would need to be deployed quickly so the gun trucks could cross at any point.

As Alpha got closer to Charlie Troop's fight, an enemy fighter suddenly popped up, threw his rifle down and put his hands in the air. 1st Platoon's commanding officer, Lieutenant Mike Anderson, gave orders to apprehend him. Sergeant Keeley, Sergeant First Class Gonzales, Specialists Slack and Ventura dismounted and moved forward. They were 25 meters away when two insurgents jumped up, one on either side of the surrendering enemy fighter, and began firing their rifles and throwing grenades at the advancing paratroopers.

Slack and Gonzales were within a few steps of the canal when the rounds began to fly, pinning them to the ground. Lieutenant Anderson's gun truck immediately reacted to contact and began to flank the enemy. Ventura and Keeley were able to use their gun truck as cover and return fire at the entrenched insurgents. Multiple rounds struck the gun truck including one that was a gnat's ass from hitting Ventura in the face. The machine gunner, Randolph, was pinned in the turret struggling to clear a .50-caliber machine gun malfunction.

While Keeley tried to recover from an enemy grenade concussion, Gonzales along with Slack continued to maneuver towards the trench. Gonzales killed two of the enemy with accurate grenade placement, ending the firefight. It turned out that the first insurgent who had surrendered had done so because he'd run out of ammunition. Keeley continued the fight for four more hours with a concussion that was caused by the enemy grenade when it detonated. He finally surrendered to the dizziness and admitted that he had blood coming from his ears.

"Look at that hole," declared one of the Joes. It looked like an animal burrow that upon closer examination was a tunnel entrance that had been dug into the side of the canal. Weapons along with a trailer containing sleeping mats and rice were found nearby, covered by reeds.

In the aftermath of the ambush that killed Dennison, two of the enemy had been killed and five captured. Upon clearing the hut, motorcycles, small arms and grenades were discovered. Afterwards, the scouts cleared and occupied the nearest home in order to determine what, if any, support the enemy fighters had received from the local inhabitants. There was plenty of bedding and food, which made it obvious that these villagers were aiding the enemy.

As evening approached on November 15, Alpha Troop began setting fire to the canals using accelerant to clear the vegetation and flush out the enemy. Tunnels had been dug to conceal enemy fighters and their weapons. Some of these were complex bunker systems that could conceal up to 15 enemy fighters. A short time later, Captain Dobbins gave Sergeant First Class Willie Lillie, one of Bravo's platoon sergeants, a grid for an open field that would be used to establish a patrol base for the night. Lillie was a calm, confident leader who could be counted on to use the strengths of each paratrooper under his command to accomplish the mission. He had ensured that they were ready for any contingency, having spent many hours training and preparing them for combat. Lillie had carefully marked the path with chemlights to ensure that the gun trucks stayed out of the path of IEDs.

The terror came without warning. Unleashed energy reached into the truck and filled it with instantaneous fear. The inside of the truck carrying Captain Dobbins filled with a cloud of dust and the deafening sound of detonation: Dobbins' truck had run over a land mine. Those not injured quickly tried to assess the damage, tend to their wounded comrades and secure a defensive perimeter in anticipation of an enemy follow-on attack.

Lillie was only 10 feet away when the explosion ripped into him. Turning instinctively or by sheer luck, Lillie avoided being struck in the face by the force of the blast, which had peppered him with shrapnel. The metal fragments had shredded the backs of both arms along with the back of his skull. Lillie described the pain he experienced like "that feeling when somebody pushes you from behind and you're not expecting it. It felt like a Mack truck did it to me."[4] Having the sensation of burning from exposure to fire, the wounded sergeant couldn't orient himself to what had happened and fell flat on his face when he tried to stand. Lillie's helmet had been blown off his head and his weapon had been torn from its D-ring attachment on his body armor.

The head wound was producing so much blood that it would soak through four large trauma bandages before he reached the hospital. The excruciating pain mixed with the concern he felt for his paratroopers drove Lillie with a mix of adrenaline and ever-increasing agony. Morphine managed his pain but could not control Lillie's concern for his troops.

If I keep talking and I keep myself awake than I won't die, he thought as the medevac helicopter flew him to Balad.

As the blood ran down his neck, Willie thought of his daughters. *I gotta make it back, you know my daughters ain't going to have a dad. My wife, what is she going to do?*[5]

Numerous others, including Captain Dobbins, had been concussed. Confused and throwing up, Dobbins fought to stay in control. The troop commander's gun truck was a mobility kill, the front end destroyed. Dobbins was able to partially recover from the brain-rattling explosion, insisting that he could continue. He was evaluated and cleared to stay in the fight by the medics. First Sergeant Clemens had been clearing a nearby house when the explosion occurred. He arrived at the blast site to find Dobbins in rough shape. Clemens placed him in another gun truck, re-established communications with the squadron, provided a situation report to Headhunter 6 (Poppas) and got the eight other wounded paratroopers evacuated.

After seeing to it that the patrol base was secure, Clemens began to use a sensor system that had a daytime video camera, thermal camera and laser rangefinder that tied into the weapons in the turret of the gun truck. The attached night vision allowed it to function at night. Clemens also pushed out a platoon with orders to "set up a dismounted ambush just north of that village." The sensor-equipped gun truck was used to overwatch the ambush site as well as the village. Alpha and Charlie Troops were both engaging enemy fighters.

A coalition fighter aircraft reported that "there's a truck behind this building in this village and there are four guys loading stuff into the back of it. It looks like they're loading up either rockets or rocket-propelled grenades."

From his position, Clemens picked out the front end of the truck but nothing else. Striking the truck with a laser, Clemens requested the fighter aircraft provide confirmation. "Roger that," confirmed the pilot. Clemens fired several bursts from the turret-mounted machine gun and tore off the front end of the truck. The fighter aircraft requested approval to finish off the work started by the gun truck. They got the go-ahead and a Maverick missile completed the job.[6]

Armed enemy fighters were also massing in the center of the village preparing to maneuver on the paratroopers. Clemens engaged and eliminated the threat, killing at least 12 of the insurgents. The following day, a battle damage assessment discovered fragments of auto glass and a twisted scrap of charred metal which was all that was left of the pickup truck.

CHAPTER 6

Tactical Surprise

It was just the luck of the draw. How things always seem to work out in the battlespace. Carson was along for the leader recon that carried them into Turki. Since he was committed to remain in Turki while the squadron was mustered, it would fall on the shoulders of the executive officers to assemble the troops. Charlie Troop's was Rhett Schiller. Schiller desired only to lead paratroopers into battle. So, he'd get his wish and bring Charlie Troop forward. After the loss of Dennison, Rhett took over his platoon.

Leading troops was what Rhett really wanted to do. This clashed with the need for the executive officer to keep the wheels of the troop lubricated and turning. It was vital to mission success and that's why Carson had him there. He was dependable, able to ensure that all their needs were met. Schiller wasn't a braggart. He did things that were special and didn't flaunt it. His dad recounted the story of when the family moved to China. When they arrived, Rhett came to him with the desire to learn Chinese. Not only would he accomplish that goal, he would go on to attend West Point, majoring in Chinese.

Schiller was being granted his golden opportunity. As the column moved through that canal towards the aftermath of the destruction of a sizable enemy force that had been detected the previous night, it must have been on his mind that he was so fortunate to be living that dream.

The night hours of November 15 into 16 found elements of Alpha and Charlie Troops being maneuvered on by enemy forces. Night optics captured a possible hostile force of 30 or more enemy fighters maneuvering against Charlie Troop. There were three distinct elements: forward security, main body and then rear security moving in a classic patrol formation. The problem was the signature didn't offer absolute certainty that these images were the enemy, as it was difficult to distinguish any weapons. Not wanting to risk injuring civilians Carson conferred with Poppas to determine the best course of action. Poppas reinforced the need to "identify weapons before we engage" thus confirming that they were enemy fighters.[1]

Rhett Schiller (Bill Schiller)

As he plotted his next moves, Carson decided that his paratroopers would "conduct a movement to contact, set up an L-shaped ambush in the canal and when they move through it we'd positively ID them and light 'em up. Sounds pretty simple."[2] Night movement, unknown enemy, unfamiliar terrain. Complex and dangerous, yes; simple, no. Carson issued the operations order. Red Platoon would have one side of the ambush; Schiller, with the snipers and mortars, would have the other side of the L while Charlie Troop's headquarters element, led by Carson, would have the apex. The movement took several hours and as they reached their objective, Carson requested an update from the surveillance system that was monitoring enemy activity.

"They've gone to ground," reported the surveillance team.

There was no movement. Carson requested Kiowa Warrior air weapons team helicopters to come on station and give identification a try. Carson wanted them to push the enemy into the kill sack. Again, no luck. The Kiowas were low on fuel and returned to their base to refuel.

It fell to the Charlie Troop element to make contact. Captain Carson requested that the F16 fighter jet that was flying overhead attempt to determine any enemy presence. The pilot reported back a short time later that there wasn't any movement and no visual on weapons. The F16 did identify a crossing point and was able to mark it. Schiller moved forward to secure it. As the L-shaped ambush took shape, Carson got a call from Poppas advising him of what he had been waiting for. The Kiowa gunships had their film developed and it had clearly identified enemy fighters with a variety of weapons including rocket-propelled grenades and mortars. All of a sudden, it got real easy. Carson brought Schiller's patrol back to the berm, Poppas gave the OK and the F16 went to work with its 500-pound bombs. Another F16 joined the fight to finish the job with gun runs. This made Charlie Troop's night a bit easier. That was about to change.

First light brought with it the need to gather intelligence and perform a battle damage assessment. Before moving, Captain Carson had to make sure that his gun trucks could be moved forward. To do that, he'd have to send half of the paratroopers back to retrieve the vehicles and move them forward. Poppas was sending a mounted platoon from Alpha Troop up to give Carson some added muscle and block any enemy fighters who might try to escape. The dismounts would include Carson's headquarters troops. Carson told Schiller to move forward to the crossing point that had been marked the previous night.

Just before daylight, Alpha Troop's 3rd Platoon moved into position two canals over from where Captain Carson and his paratroopers were located.

"Blue 4 to Alpha 6, receiving effective enemy fire," came the call to Captain Few, Alpha Troop's commander, from Shane Bates of Alpha's 3rd Platoon.[3]

Enemy fighters using rocket-propelled grenades and machine-gun fire were attacking the paratroopers. Sergeant First Class Bates, 3rd Platoon's enlisted leader, was an experienced NCO who performed well under fire. The insurgents had riddled the side of his gun truck and shattered the side window glass. Two of the platoon's gun trucks were damaged.

The Alpha gun trucks were off to the right, about a half-mile away from Carson and Schiller's patrol. The Charlie Troop dismounts had consolidated at the crossing point. The canal that Charlie Troop had exited was just a huge trench. As Alpha's firefight continued, Charlie 6 transmitted urgent radio traffic,

"Blue 4 Blue 4 this is Charlie 6 break contact, break contact you're firing at us, you're firing at us."

The grenade launcher and machine gun fire coming from Blue Four's gun trucks drove Carson and his dismounts to their bellies. Whatever the intended target, it was about 100 to 200 meters in front of Bates, but all the ricochets were placing Carson and his troops directly in the line of fire. With the sound of battle in his voice, Blue 4 (Bates) ordered Charlie 6 (Carson) to:

"Go to ground, we just made contact, I've got four to five enemy personnel engaging us with a machine gun!"[4]

First Sergeant Metheny, Alpha Troop's senior sergeant, moved forward along with Bates and temporarily silenced the enemy with two well-placed grenades.

After about five minutes of continuous firing, Blue 4 reported that they were still receiving effective fire from the enemy. After determining that there was a Hellfire armed Predator drone above the battle, Carson requested and got approval from Poppas to destroy the remaining enemy with the Hellfire missile. That took care of the entrenched enemy and allowed Carson's patrol with Rhett Schiller in the lead to move forward. As the column moved forward, Carson noticed that Schiller had placed himself forward, so he wasn't, as Carson recalled, "necessarily on point, but he was about two positions back from the point man."[5] They were moving through a decent-sized canal, with a dry trough with vegetation growing out at the base. There was a narrow dirt path running alongside it with berms on either side.

Specialist Austin Honrath was on the inside of the canal on the top portion walking point. Staff Sergeant Rhodes and Captain Schiller were up front as was an Iraqi soldier moving along the center of the trough. Captain Carson, Red Andrews, the air force Joint Terminal Attack Controller or JTAC, along with several other paratroopers were further back on the inside of the canal on the right flank. First Sergeant Coomer and one of the medics, Idi Mallari, were on the outside of the berm.

"Move your ass back a little bit, you don't need to be leading from the front always," Captain Carson ordered.

Schiller gave Carson a "fuck you" scoff. In response to Carson's urging, Schiller let the lead Joe move up maybe another 10 meters in front of him." Not 10 seconds later…

"Man down, man down!"

They had walked into an ambush. Anyone in the canal was immediately placed under accurate and extremely effective enemy machine-gun fire. Struck multiple times, Captain Schiller went down. One round found its mark, entering just above his body armor piercing his chest. Another round tore into his leg, rendering him grievously injured.

"Contact front!"

Led by First Sergeant Coomer, Specialist Honrath, Staff Sergeant Rhodes and Private Lawerence rapidly moved forward, came online and began returning fire. A grenade thrown directly on the enemy position by First Sergeant Coomer destroyed the enemy machine-gun nest. Enemy fire was also coming from further down the canal near a crossover.

From the canal, shouts for a medic sent Mallari running forward. A second medic who was with the platoon also moved forward from his position alongside Captain Carson to assist Mallari. They found Rhett Schiller lying face down. The medics began removing Schiller's body armor so his wounds could be assessed. They inserted an airway and attached a ventilator to help Rhett breathe. Schiller's chest wound was proving difficult to manage. They were also attempting to stem the flow of blood coming from the leg wound.

In an effort to destroy the far target, Honrath deployed two dual-purpose high explosive grenades. At the same moment, screams from the Iraqi soldier sent Honrath bounding down into the canal trough while receiving covering fire from Rhodes and Private Kelly. First Sergeant Coomer moved forward to help the wounded Iraqi. Coomer began initial medical care and with the assistance of Honrath moved the wounded soldier to the casualty collection point all while providing suppressive fire on the enemy machine-gun position. Coomer continued to provide suppressive fire and urged his paratroopers forward without the benefit of any cover or concealment.

While Schiller was being treated Honrath marked the enemy position by firing multiple smoke grenades from the grenade launcher attached to his rifle. Two F16 fighter jets came on station and identified 20 to 25 enemy fighters directly in line with the casualty collection point that was being established to medevac the wounded. The enemy fighting position was marked with smoke so the fighter jets could have a visual.

The air force JTAC Josh Andrews told Captain Carson that he had to provide his initials over the radio as he ordered the strike. This was done to confirm that he knew that it would be "danger close," translation: so close that it was going to put the ground forces in imminent danger.

The F16s began their attack on the enemy positions. The fighters were so low to the ground that as they passed over the paratroopers, they felt the jet wash pick them up. Three low passes were made in an attempt to determine the exact location of the enemy but were unsuccessful. As the enemy fire intensified, a strafing run was ordered using the aircraft's 20mm cannon. Using any other ordnance would have placed the friendlies in extreme danger due to their close proximity to the enemy. A fourth low, fast pass by one of the F16s was made to get a better visual on the friendly and enemy positions. Flying over the target area at 300 feet and 500 knots, the pilot was able to catch sight of both the U.S. troops and insurgents just meters apart. The gun runs, which were so close to the paratroopers that they were showered by dirt and debris, silenced the enemy position.

Two Apache gunships had been flying continuously for over six hours in rapidly deteriorating weather when they received word of troops in contact needing help. There were several wounded friendlies that needed urgent medevac. Upon arrival, the Apaches identified a group of enemy fighters moving through the canal system. The insurgents were attempting to overtake friendly forces. By the time this vital information was relayed to Headhunter and gun trucks were moved into position to block the enemy's advance, the Apaches needed to refuel.

After refueling, the Apaches' efforts to return to the fight were stymied by bad weather. Despite the conditions, permission was granted to fly in whatever weather the pilots deemed safe. They also received the go-ahead to fly an additional hour which meant they'd be headed into their eighth hour of flying without a break. Their 82nd brethren were still in heavy contact with the enemy, low on ammunition, with two mortally wounded soldiers and resupply impossible. Just past first light they took off on their treacherous flight. Air force aircraft that had made the earlier gun run vectored the Apaches into the battlespace due to the zero visibility conditions.

Using their infrared devices, the Apaches were able to pick up heat signatures of the enemy fighters that were maneuvering on the paratroopers.

"Spotted two squirters in the canal, looking for guidance, over." "This is Headhunter 6, if you got squirters in the canal, engage, over." "I understand PID [positive identification], hostile intent, clear to engage," came the confirmation from the Apaches. The lead Apache maneuvered his aircraft into two gun runs with his wingman.

"Clear to fire—engaging," advised the pilot.

The gun camera showed the effects of the cannon fire: pieces of human flesh flying through the air. The battle damage assessment confirmed that the enemy threat had been neutralized. "He's KIA now," reported the pilot.[6]

Moments later, the paratroopers reported receiving accurate enemy small-arms fire. The Apaches switched leads. The attack helicopters received clearance for "danger close fires" due to the enemy being so close to the friendlies. As soon as the nose-mounted chain gun began kicking up dust, the trailing Apache zeroed in and let loose on the insurgents. Two hundred rounds of 30mm cannon fire rained down on the enemy, chewing them to pieces. The assault force moved forward clearing the canal of the remaining enemy fighters.

With the enemy silenced, Carson moved towards the medics working on the wounded. Carson had been told that it was Rhett, but he didn't want to acknowledge that his close friend was lying mortally wounded.

"Come on XO, you can make it," Coomer demanded.[7]

In an instant Carson realized that he'd lost "Dennison who was my son and Rhett who was my brother."[8] The helicopter that had been dispatched to help save these wounded soldiers was struggling to get in the air due to poor visibility created by high ground winds kicking up sand.

The medics worked on Rhett Schiller and the Iraqi for almost 40 minutes until the aero medevac arrived to transport them to the combat surgical hospital. Rhett seemed to have stabilized so as he was loaded, everyone was optimistic. However, a short time later Lieutenant Colonel Poppas gave John Carson the grim news that Rhett had died from his wounds.

His loss palpable, Carson could not hide his grief, which was mixed with a heavy dose of anger. Grief turned to rage when a senior officer appeared. To encourage the troops, he began to extoll their bravery and spur them forward. When he handed out commander's coins to some of the troopers including Carson, it was just too much for John to bear. Walking away and out of sight, Carson threw the meaningless piece of metal as far as he could, in a show of contempt for this futile effort that gave no recognition and appreciation for the tremendous losses they had suffered.

The fighting in and around Turki continued to intensify. Clearing spider holes dug into the side of the canals was reminiscent of combat in Vietnam. The enemy had their weapons and their Korans. Blood chits were also found. These messages encouraged the insurgents to destroy the invaders, giving their lives to defend their religious extremism. Bringing the gun trucks on line and spraying the canal banks with machine-gun fire and using grenades to clear these entrenched enemy fighters was the only way to ensure that this enemy threat was destroyed.

Towards the end of the day, the commanding general responsible for the region flew out to observe the progress of 5-73. Landing in the middle of a still raging battle, his team had apparently not noted attempts to wave them off.

"Who the fuck is that?" the ground troops wondered out loud.

Poppas and his command element were astounded and roaring with laughter at how ridiculous it was as the scene unfolded before them. As the approaching helicopter landed, the last of the canals was being cleared and enemy fighters continued to be engaged and killed. The general and his entourage approached Poppas and his staff.

"Why didn't you throw purple smoke?" the general demanded.

Poppas looked puzzled by the question and had the look of "I must not have gotten that memo." During the apparent dressing down, small-arms fire and grenade explosions drove the general and his staff to ground. Poppas and his team looked at one another with hidden pleasure that these rear-echelon types did not seem to comprehend the reality of combat.

The general wanted to know about enemy dead. Alluding to the preoccupation with enemy body counts during the Vietnam War Poppas told him "we counted the feet and multiplied times two."

That didn't go over very well. The general asked Poppas how much longer he could keep the 5-73 forces in contact. Poppas defiantly made it clear that staying wasn't an option.

"What do you want us to achieve, sir?" Poppas inquired.

The general went from five days to one day to finally 12 hours. Poppas agreed and the last hours were spent continuing to clear the canals of enemy fighters.[9]

A plan was already being formulated to both deceive and draw the enemy leadership back into Turki. Poppas wanted the opportunity to destroy them and the next month would be used to shape this battlespace for a return engagement. Poppas wanted to return in two weeks; however, another brigade-level mission would take precedence and the necessary assets wouldn't be available until January. They would be fighting there again during the coldest and wettest part of the year.

The paratroopers of 5-73 had bloodied the enemy. Seventy-four enemy fighters were killed. Five large caches had been discovered and eliminated. In the course of heavy sustained combat, 5-73 had lost two of its junior leaders in Dennison and Schiller along with suffering 11 wounded. Over 20 valor award narratives would attest to the ferocity of the battle. It would be just the beginning of a tough fight for these paratroopers. As if foretelling what the future held for this battlespace, as the squadron was leaving, two enemy fighters pursued them on foot firing AK47s. The two were killed by helicopter gunships flying overhead. The insurgents were willing to defy any and all who challenged them.

As Captain Few would later describe, "in attacking Turki Village by initial air assault followed by ground maneuver," 5-73 had "achieved tactical surprise." This "basic tenet of warfare" was not a maneuver that U.S. ground forces were pursuing in Iraq during the fall of 2006.[10] Headhunter had chosen to take a different approach. It was the opening chapter of what was to prove to be a tough, violent campaign.

CHAPTER 7

Stairway to Heaven

It fell to Chaplain Craig Honbarger to lead the squadron through the painful grieving process. These were the squadron's first losses since arriving in Iraq.[1]

Craig's spiritual journey to military chaplaincy had taken several twists and turns. After his first enlistment had ended, living as a civilian wasn't working so he re-enlisted. A friend convinced him to attend a local church. Craig didn't even make it through the front door before being greeted with a hug and greeting of "I love you" by one of the parishioners. Honbarger recalled that "I didn't know whether to hug him back or to hit him." With baptism came a sense of being called to serve God, which kept him awake at night. Eventually, a pursuit of the ministry brought with it thoughts of returning to the army. Soldiers could use someone with his background, he figured: "I had seven years in the army already, I knew the language."[2] His military experience would serve him well and help to build a strong ministry.

The September 11 attacks motivated Craig to pursue a clinical path that took him to the burn ward at Brook Army Medical Center in San Antonio, Texas. Serving these critically injured patients required a special skill set. Frequent debriding of burned skin in preparation for skin grafting or other procedures was extremely painful, despite the administering of pain meds. "I'd want the chaplain too if I had to go in there and get scrubbed," observed Honbarger. It was a comfort for patients to have the chaplain there to read scripture, hold their hands or just spend some time with them while they were in acute physical as well as psychological pain.

After his ordination, Craig recalled that as soon as he arrived at his first assignment with the 82nd, soldiers were "already lined up before I even moved into the office waiting for counseling." As 3rd Brigade prepared to deploy, there was a sense that the chaplains were considered "good juju, or good luck charms."[3]

As he prepared for the memorial service, Craig quickly realized that saying goodbye to John Dennison and Rhett Schiller was going to be tough. Their soldiers as well as their peers loved them. Craig had been close to both, and they had attended church services regularly. Everybody was pulling together to support each other.

Dennison and Schiller Memorial Service (John Ferrante)

The "Stairway to Heaven" had to be completed to standard. The memorial box would hold the U.S. and regimental flags, helmets placed on the overturned stock of the rifles, combat boots facing outward at the rifle's base, and dog tags strung over the rifle's grip. The regimental crest was painted on the front of the box. In the midst of this grief and preparation, the brigade chaplain had shown up to make certain that everyone knew what the brigade sergeant major would be expecting. Their grief turned to anger, insisting that "we don't care" what brigade wants, "this is our memorial."[4] The squadron was being drawn closer together by this loss. These guys were part of their family and they'd have the remembrance their way.

The mess hall manager put up a cross and had John and Rhett's photos alongside it with candles lit in their honor. The "Fallen Soldier Table" was set up in the mess hall. The small round table signifies everlasting concern for the fallen. The table is covered in a white tablecloth symbolizing the purity of motives when answering the call to duty. A place setting complete with a bread plate is set. A single red rose represents the lost service members and those left behind to grieve, an inverted glass represents the lost service member's inability to share in the toast, a slice of lemon is set on the bread plate to symbolize the bitter taste that the loss leaves, while salt is sprinkled on the bread plate representing the many shed tears, and an empty chair symbolizes the lost service member.

Honbarger struggled with the losses, observing that "I'm a Christian and I believe that God is sovereign," but Dennison and Schiller had such potential. To take good young Christian men who could have had such a positive influence on so many "certainly greater than myself. I don't know that it's right, that I have the right lane or authority to question God." He could only pray that someday God would show him why they had been taken so he could make some sense of this painful loss.[5]

John Dennison was the "All American" guy. If you could roll up Captain America and the varsity quarterback into one that would have been John. As vocal and as noticeable as he was, he was also humble. Matt Miller, a close friend of John's and Bravo Troop's executive officer at the time of John's death, believed that "everybody has a source of humility in their life, and I think John was my source. He succeeded big, and he got into trouble big. He was always on everyone's radar, because that's who he was. Because everyone knew him, everyone liked him. I don't think there was one person who disliked John."[6] The platoon's sense of loss was palpable. Although it would be essential to mentally survive this hardship and block the memory of losing such a treasured leader, Dennison's soldiers were none the less devastated by his death.

John Dennison was known for his quick wit and ability to put a positive spin on a situation. In a hide site, rain-soaked in the dead of winter, Dennison sat smiling. Captain Dobbins looked over at him and asked, "What's so funny?" John jokingly replied, "Puppy dogs and Christmas sir, they can't take them from us." "What drugs was this lieutenant on?" wondered Dobbins. He soon realized that Dennison "embraced everything in life this way." Dobbins would later remember John as being "selfless," a humble person who "fully accepted criticism in order to improve himself and his platoon."[7] Dennison's platoon sergeant Robert Cobb remembered him as "one of the best men I have ever met in my life. He always had a sunny outlook on life, a love of God and his fellow man. I know God took him home because his soul was too beautiful to be here on Earth with the rest of us. Now I know heaven will be a better place because Ranger Dennison is on point and is there to look after things."[8]

John's wife Haley would receive the tragic news while deployed to Afghanistan as part of a combat engineer battalion. The young officer had met her future husband while they were both cadets at West Point. They'd fallen in love and married immediately after her graduation. Many affectionately referred to them as "Barbie and Ken" due to their strikingly good looks. Quickly going their separate ways, Haley attended Officers Basic and Ryan (Haley was the only person who used John's middle name) received an assignment with the 82nd. Finally, they were together at Bragg for a mere six months before deploying. The war would ultimately keep them apart forever.

When summoned to her commander's office, Haley entered to find her boss standing alongside the chaplain. Suddenly, it was all too clear that tragedy had struck and that her wonderful life with Ryan had ended. The war bride was now a war widow. In the midst of her grieving, a letter arrived from Ryan. In it was a poem equating their love to the seasons, "likening our love to a tree and the different seasons that our love goes through. There would always be a spring for us." They'd sign their letters "Together we are strong." Despite Haley's dislike of tattoos, Ryan had several. So, to honor and remember him Haley got one of a tree with those poignant words. Bringing him home would be her final act of devotion to the young warrior who would be laid to rest in Arlington National Cemetery.[9]

When the time came to write the condolence letters to the families, Carson had an especially difficult time crafting Rhett Schiller's. After all, there's nothing easy about describing the death of a soldier to a loved one. The army has a very exacting regulation regarding the process. However, Captain Carson was driven to describe the details in his own words and style. Carson felt that "it showed what a relationship Rhett and I had and it was personal."[10]

He wanted to get out more than he was allowed, to command troops in combat. Carson told Schiller's dad that Rhett was always asking to go out with the troops. He jumped at the opportunity to lead. Just before 7:00 a.m. on the day of his death, Rhett was sitting on the side of the canal laughing about the machine-gun rounds that had been flying over their heads a few hours earlier. One of the paratroopers noted that something didn't feel right and that maybe Rhett should drop back a bit. Rhett told him, "Don't you think that's going to keep me from being up front with you."[11]

"You can't send this," Poppas told him. "It has to be an official fucking letter from the army." Carson sent both letters. He believed that Rhett's parents needed to know "what kind of person Rhett was in the army, what kind of soldier as well as a friend and brother" to Carson.[12] As John Carson shared the events of this day, there was a sense that the death of Rhett Schiller would have a lasting impact on Carson's life. He could not bring himself to open the emotional wounds any further. There was a brief glimpse of the enormous impact, just enough to respect the sense of loss and the tragic consequences it has on the human soul.

Carson would also deliver his friend's eulogy. Rhett Schiller was a "courageous man with a gentle smile and a big heart." His wry smile lightened their hearts and brightened even the most difficult days. He exuded pride in being a paratrooper, in having had the opportunity to earn his combat patch while serving with the 82nd, and in how hard his paratroopers worked to accomplish the mission. Rather than Carson teaching Rhett, Rhett was demonstrating to everyone how to be a better human being: spiritual righteousness and the meaning of sacrifice.[13] Schiller had just celebrated his 26th birthday on November 7.

Rhett's life had been idyllic before this fateful day. After graduation from West Point, he had been assigned to the 82nd as an infantry officer. It was everything he had hoped and worked towards. Then his best friend Brian Ray was introduced to Rhett's sister Renee. Soon afterwards, they began to see each other every weekend. Rhett was furious to have lost his favorite weekend skydiving partner when Brian chose to spend the time with Renee instead.

When Renee decided to move to Fort Bragg to be close to Brian, Rhett called her in the early morning hours to tell her that she was being ridiculous. Two weeks after arriving at Bragg, Brian proposed to her. With the possibility of a deployment looming, Brian and Renee decided to get married a mere week after their engagement. A witness was needed so a call went out to Rhett and he arrived all decked out. The bride and groom showed up in shorts and flip-flops with Renee carrying a bouquet of broccoli that had come from their refrigerator. Rhett made sure the ceremony was videoed. The next two years at Bragg were wonderful for Renee. She got to see Rhett at social functions, and spending time with him was always lots of fun. Renee also introduced Rhett to a young woman by the name of Tiffany. Dating led to their engagement prior to the Iraq deployment.

In preparation for his possible death on the battlefield, Rhett had told his dad what he wanted to leave his brother, sisters and fiancée Tiffany. He wanted to be buried in his uniform, have his West Point graduation ring on and a small cross that he'd made for Tiffany placed in his breast pocket. Making sure that his brother Ryan, a Marine aviator, escorted his remains home to Wisconsin was a detail that Rhett's dad discovered during a long-distance phone call with his son-in-law Brian Ray, who was also with the squadron in Iraq. Rhett was definitely a planner. The only detail he didn't share with his dad was where he wanted to be buried. He was killed on his 100th day in theater. He had called home three times during the deployment and his dad missed all of the calls. It was devastating. His sister Rhonda spoke to him on one occasion and asked how it was over there. "It's dangerous," Rhett replied succinctly.[14]

Karla, Rhett's mom, was home by herself when the casualty notification arrived at the door. Their shock turned to action with a quick decision to drive to Fort Bragg in Fayetteville, North Carolina, from their home in Wisconsin. A casualty affairs officer was assigned to the family at Bragg. When Rhett was brought home for burial, the 82nd assigned an honor guard, chaplain and a general officer to provide the funeral detail.

A black stone, about four feet high, marks his grave. The stone has an engraved Bronze Star medal, Purple Heart, Parachutist Badge and Combat Infantry Badge. These symbols tell the story of this warrior. On the back of the stone, there is a bronze plaque that the Veterans Administration provided, which included being in the West Point Class of 2003.

The loss of Rhett reached beyond the grief of his immediate family. Renee called her mother-in-law with the tragic news. She was shocked into silence. The remainder of the deployment was agonizing and it got to a point where Renee found it virtually impossible to speak with her mother-in-law. It always seemed to lead to a worried conversation about whether Brian was OK. Renee's grief over the death of Rhett was compounded by the panic that Brian's mom was experiencing when she didn't hear from her son. Renee referred to it as "the agonizing anguish."[15]

"You should never lose a kid," Bill Schiller, Rhett's dad exclaimed, as his voice quivered with sadness. Rhett's mom Karla's patriotic side knew that he'd given his life for our freedom. She's very proud of him. But "it sucks" to have to cope with the loss. You never forget.[16]

CHAPTER 8

The Lost Boys of Alpha Mortars

Immediately following Turki Bowl I, Captain Hercik, the squadron's fire support officer, had headed to Baqubah with a squad-plus element built around Sergeant First Class Workman and his mortar troops. Under the guise of serving as a military transition team, they were tasked to monitor an Iraqi military police company that was suspected of acting as a death squad, executing local villagers on the orders of an Iraqi army senior officer.

Constantly monitoring the Iraqi radio traffic would lead to getting up in the middle of the night and attempting to find out what the Iraqis were up to. According to Hercik the Iraqi army patrol brief would amount to "get in the truck, we're going somewhere."[1] Maintaining a Readiness Condition 2 or Red Con 2 status the entire time, the trucks were fully loaded, all the radios and blue force trackers were on, all of their kits were on the vehicles and pre-combat checks completed.

Baqubah was infested with terrorists. Their bullet-riddled gun trucks were a constant reminder of the danger these paratroopers faced. Hercik recalled that "every day sounded like World War III."[2] Any given block to the left, right or front of the paratroopers sounded like all hell was breaking loose. On one mission Hercik received a report of an execution that had occurred right down the street. They arrived to find a victim who had been shot in the face. Another body was found close by. When they turned left out of the market, a third body was lying in the median. Making a U-turn they found two more bodies lying side by side on the sidewalk.

Hercik noticed that there were people on the rooftops and as soon as he alerted his crew, the paratroopers began receiving enemy fire. Workman remembered that he was on the .50-caliber machine gun mounted in the turret and "started laying on the trigger and we're hauling ass and how we made it through without stopping, because the market was packed, and I'm just shooting up there and I can see people running to the sides of the rooftops shooting at us with AKs. And I'm just bursting back and forth from each side just shooting the .50 cal."[3] Fortunately, the enemy fighters hadn't tried throwing a grenade in the open gun turret. After that,

Abrams tanks assisting (Donnie Workman)

HESCO wire was draped over the top of the turrets and camouflage netting over that to protect against the grenade threat.

A different unit owned the battlespace and that made it difficult to maintain situational awareness. So much of the violence was sectarian in nature and seemed to be everywhere. The sound of gunfire could be locals shooting at each other or someone protecting their home from an insurgent attack. The paratroopers had to contend with the possibility of being left alone if they were attacked.

The call came in alerting the Iraqis that a local hospital was under attack. With three Iraqi trucks and three of Hercik's gun trucks following, they sped down Route Victory. Suddenly, the column came to an abrupt stop. The Iraqi sergeant informed Hercik that they didn't know where they were going. While urging the Iraqi sergeant to confirm the location by radio, Hercik also found out that the Iraqis believed that they had just passed an IED prior to stopping. Dismounting from the gun trucks, Hercik's paratroopers pulled security while he tried to turn this Iraqi cluster fuck around.

"I've got movement between two and three o'clock," Workman's turret gunner reported.[4]

Carrying a Kalashnikov assault rifle, the lone attacker maneuvered on the column. The gun trucks began to engage the enemy fighter. At about the same moment, an Iraqi police convoy appeared headed straight for Hercik and his troops. The insurgents were known to steal police trucks and begin shooting unsuspecting friendly forces as they rolled through checkpoints. The Iraqi troops attempted to slow them down by firing warning shoots to get their attention. The scene was becoming increasingly chaotic. The Iraqi cops pulled up parallel to the American gun trucks, sprang out holding their weapons and began a stare-down with the soldiers. The police clearly outnumbered the Americans and their Iraqi counterparts. Workman began to calculate, "I'm going to shoot that guy that's right there in front of me and out of these three guys I just wonder which one of those is going to be the one to kill me."[5]

Captain Hercik quickly got on the radio with the local police chief in an effort to calm the standoff. The chatter from a Kalashnikov assault rifle coming from a nearby apartment rooftop brought the standoff to an abrupt end. One of the Iraqi cops was immediately struck by gunfire.

About 20 minutes into the firefight and soon after a column of Bradley Fighting Vehicles from another unit had sped by without offering assistance, two Abrams tanks lumbered up and came to a halt just parallel to the gun trucks. The tanks oriented their 120mm main guns and joined the fight. Being in close proximity to the tank when it sent a round down range was a combination of a near deafening concussion, a small dust explosion, a blast of heat from the gun tube and a shock wave that momentarily froze any movement. At one point, one of the tanks struck an enemy rocket-propelled grenade team that was maneuvering through some tall reeds, which obliterated them. It was just another fun-filled day in Baqubah.

Eventually, Workman told Hercik and Sergeant Major Edgar that they were fried. "I can't keep putting my guys into this situation, we're not getting any more information, we haven't proven that they are a death squad, we can't even keep up with them," as Iraqis raced out of the base on some unknown mission. "I've got a 20-year-old kid who looked like he was 16, who now looks like he's 45." The constant threats left everyone with a sense of impending doom. According to Workman, the consensus was "you're pretty sure you're going to die" in this hellhole.[6]

Workman and his paratroopers would move on to provide security for a provisional reconstruction team. Despite the stress and strain of these missions, the 5-73 paratroopers began to realize that they were making their mark to counter the terror threat. Workman noticed that the regional governor's security detail was wearing the 82nd patch on their uniforms. The airborne tab had been replaced with a Special Forces tab at the top of the "circle in the square," the double A at its center signifying the division's "All American" nickname. When they were asked about it, the Iraqis explained that "the insurgents are scared of the square patch with the circle in it. Do not attack the square patch with the circle because they will fight back."[7]

CHAPTER 9

Turki Shaping Operations

Headhunter had been bloodied in Turki. The loss of Dennison and Schiller had brought them face to face with the stark reality of death in combat. A couple of days refitting and mourning the deaths of their comrades was all the time 5-73 CAV had before they began preparing for a return to Turki. The shaping operations would be a series of raids on 11 squadron- and troop-level targets of recent enemy activity. Each of these would be initiated using troop- and squadron-sized air assaults with paratroopers flying in by helicopter. The goal was to either capture or kill as much of the enemy leadership of the Council as they could, as well as to deny potential safe houses to those insurgents and to gain additional intelligence for future operations.[1]

In part, the decision to use this shaping tactic had been the result of higher headquarters wanting to run an operation in nearby Baqubah first before committing any assets to the Turki operation. It was decided to use this operational pause to shape the battlespace. According to Major Sylvia, these shaping operations would give the enemy the impression that the Americans were afraid to go back "into the teeth of the AO" (Area of Operations).[2]

As he developed the course of action, Major Sylvia needed to fine-tune his knowledge of how to deploy troops using helicopter insertions. So, he went to the source: the Gold Book, the bible for lifting troops into combat. Sylvia and his small staff would frame the operations orders and the logistics that went with it. He reached out to Frank Tate, the commander of the Black Hawk helicopters that would be used for these missions. Tate helped Sylvia figure out the aviation details and got an aviation planner temporarily assigned to the squadron's staff. Headhunter would be raiding villages on the outskirts of what would be the engagement area for the operation that would become known as Turki Bowl II. The goal was to push the Al Qaeda insurgents back into the kill zone in that area. The enemy had the false sense that they had complete freedom of movement.

One of the issues that quickly became apparent was the need to change the amount of time that it took to plan and execute an air assault operation. The Gold Book goes through an extremely deliberate, detailed planning process. It lays out a

IED damage (John Ferrante)

scenario beginning with the 72 hours it normally takes to initiate the preparation for an air assault operation to when the operation is executed. Detailed planning and analysis of locations to land helicopters are identified and the five phases of the operation rehearsed several times.[3] Prior to the fight in Iraq, anytime an air assault was planned, the Gold Book was pulled out.

In Iraq, the enemy seldom stayed in one safe house for more than 24 hours. Executing a mission to maximize the impact on the enemy required reducing the 72-hour window to 24 hours or less. This was accomplished by developing a template of how the air assault would be executed. Basic packages were identified of how many aircraft, type, and the responsibilities of which aircraft would be used for a mission. Planning also detailed the method of landing on an objective and using a cordon insertion. This meant establishing an outer perimeter around the objective and sealing it off so the enemy couldn't escape or "squirt." Once the enemy squirters were confined, the area was searched. The template would be adjusted to account for terrain.

In general, all the pilots flying lead would fly past the objective and land on the far side. The second lift of aircraft would land on the left side, based on flying into the wind, and so on. A one-page planning sheet was put together that laid out the "no kidding" things that aviation had to know from the ground force that was going to be inserting, in order to be able to give them the support they were going to need. Aviation focused on getting that information, rather than focusing on everything that was laid out in the Gold Book. If there was time, the Gold Book details would be obtained. If there was a possibility of missing out on an enemy force, planners would burn through the single page, apply the template and execute within 24 hours. Having planners from the aviation side set up shop in the 5-73 CAV operations center further facilitated the planning process. The two groups grew quite comfortable with coordinating the ever-increasing use of air assaults by Headhunter.

The aviation and infantry plans had to accommodate approaches, proximity of landing zones to objectives, surface conditions, and terrain/physical features. Trees and wires were common hazards to negotiate and rotor strikes on buildings would destroy the aircraft's ability to remain airborne. Another problem for the aircrews was the different types of sand. Sand that's like talcum powder is extremely difficult to land in. Heavier sand was somewhat less hazardous but was still a challenge in the down draft created by rotor wash. Ground ruts could overturn a Black Hawk if a wheel settled in a rut. Even farm animals could create a hazard if they were too close to the aircraft or obstructing the landing zone. Of course, the possibility of enemy ground fire was always present.

Flying at night created its own set of hazards. A pilot looking through night vision goggles would liken the experience to flying inside a ping-pong ball as sand was kicked up during landing. The night vision reduced color to white or green with no visual references. Once a pilot lost visual references the helicopter was apt to begin to drift one way or the other. Night flying proficiency is critical. If a night landing on an unprepared landing zone was planned, "varsity" crews, the most experienced pilots, flew the mission. To develop this level of expertise, pilots would fly many hours on safer missions. Slowly, they would be introduced into the varsity and become familiar with dust landing techniques. Eventually, they would be matched up with seasoned instructor pilots. If the less experienced pilots showed enough aptitude, they would ultimately become a member of a varsity crew. The best pilots and crew chiefs worked night missions the entire 15 months they were deployed.

Missions lasted up to six hours under night vision conditions with the possibility of a one-hour extension by the company commander and a two-hour extension by the battalion commander. Whether it was extracting troops at the end of a mission or providing several additional hours of gunship support, pilots and commanders were given the latitude to extend a mission in order to provide lethal fire as well as getting the Joes back safely.

Another critical piece of the aviation equation was fuel. The ability to leave the battlespace, fly to a forward arming and refueling point (also known as a FARP) and return to the fight as quickly as possible could mean the difference between life and death for the paratroopers. There was about a two and a half hour flying window for pilots to remain on station before they'd have to go find fuel. A round trip to existing refueling points would take too long when a firefight was raging. To solve that problem, a team of aviation fuel handlers was sent to establish a refueling point closer to 5-73's battlespace. The Delta Troop forward support paratroopers had fuel tankers and handlers for the ground vehicles. The trucks for aviation fuel required that the containers be aqua glow tested and certified to carry aviation gas. Several of the 5-73 fuel trucks were certified and maintained for that purpose, so resources were readily available when the refueling point would open for business. This only occurred when a major operation was planned.

There was a need to have a planner with aviation lift expertise working in 5-73's operations center. Captain Ford Peterson walked into the planning meeting not really knowing what to expect. As an aviation assistant planner and experienced pilot, Peterson had a keen awareness of the inner workings of helicopter operations. Now he was among "ground pounders," infantry and cav scout types who didn't speak his language, or so he thought. Worse yet, he didn't speak theirs nor understand much of what they were about to say. It was going to be awkward at best and unproductive at worst. But Peterson would soon learn that these guys were smart and easy to work with. Peterson had a direct link to the aviation units that in turn would be supporting the squadron with Black Hawk and Chinook helicopters to air assault the paratroopers.

Before the mission could be executed, the plan had to go up the chain of command to the division headquarters. Once the plan was approved, the assigned aviation unit would be formally advised to prepare for the mission. The approval process could create the potential for a missed opportunity to surprise the enemy due to the amount of time it took up at the higher headquarters. However, having the aviation planner on the 5-73 staff allowed aviation to have helicopters standing by ready to provide an expedited air assault. This was how 5-73 was able to catch the enemy off guard.

The various elements of the squadron would form up during the late-night hours, in total darkness. The procedures were the same, each mission similar, so it was important for everyone to stay alert and not to become complacent. They'd run through their pre-combat checks and pre-combat inspections, review their piece of the operations order and wait. The signal would be given and in unison the troops would move forward to board the waiting aircraft.

The task of approaching and boarding the helicopter is a simple one, but fraught with danger. The result of coming into contact with the spinning rotor blades is either serious injury or death. The crew chief made certain that this deadly occupational hazard didn't become a reality. With 60 or more pounds of equipment, the weight of each paratrooper's kit made any movement awkward. Settled into their seats, weapons were stowed muzzle down, a round in the chamber and safety on. Quick-release belts that secured them to the bench ensured that falling out wouldn't be an issue. Rotor noise and the reciting of pre-flight checklists punctuated the airwaves.

The pilot advised to prepare for takeoff. There was little if any light in and around the aircraft. With the flight instruments dimly lit the pilots used lip lights attached to the microphone boom of the flight helmet. The exterior was completely dark. There aren't any aircraft anti-collision or navigation lights lit; only infrared strobes and formation lights that are visible only with night vision goggles. The crew chief and door gunner took their seats, swinging their weapons into place, ready to engage targets as needed. The rotors' rotation picked up pace, the mechanical beast shook in a fight to escape and defy gravity; the engine spewed greater effort. The stress, energy and physics collided. Gravity, in a last effort, refused to adjust. More throttle applied, fuel to the spark to turn the rotors, lurching forward ascending into the air. The magic and science of lift coming together, surging into the night sky.

In the back, checklists and timelines occupied leaders like Lieutenant Sal Candela. As part of the plans team, Candela went on most of the air assaults. The flights were generally no more than 10 to 15 minutes, so the majority of the time was spent on the radio or looking at execution checklists. Sal's preoccupation with the plan didn't eliminate the thought of running into trouble. There was also the concern of a coordination piece going wrong. The eerie feelings of a night insertion always stirred a certain amount of apprehension. As paratroopers they experienced the same sense of foreboding as stepping out into the night sky and awaiting the tug of a full canopy. For the Joes it was about getting off what Candela described as a "big, slow-moving bullet magnet" as soon as possible.[4] The fear kept you sharp, attuned to the details. Off in the distance, as if coming from space, there was a beam of light only visible with night vision. Blotches of pure black, empty fields, palm groves or meandering rivers made the entire scene seem dreamlike. The light, an infrared beam being shot from an Apache attack helicopter flying overhead, guided the Black Hawk and Chinook lift aircraft into their landing zones.

As the paratroopers reached the release point, they anxiously awaited the cherry/ice call which indicated whether the landing zone was receiving enemy fire or not. Was the enemy hiding, waiting to pounce? The Black Hawks descended at 200 feet per minute. The door gunners watched intently for signs of the elusive enemy. The pilot had a visual of the front of the aircraft and the approaching ground. The crew chief methodically called out over the intercom, "Dust at the tail. Dust at the cabin. Dust at the wheels. Dust at the cockpit." By the time the aircraft was consumed by these brownout conditions created by the combination of rotor wash and sand, the pilot needed to have it on the ground. It was a deadly dance.

Filled with a mixture of gut-wrenching anxiety and anticipation, the paratroopers stepped from the aircraft, lost in the wall-like cloud. It was as though they had passed through some mysterious time portal.

Out of the 11 air assaults and various ground assaults there were several that proved noteworthy. The first raid target was identified through human intelligence gathering and determined to be a possible enemy safe house. Charlie Troop conducted the mission by ground assault and they detained three insurgents. The next mission was a squadron-level air assault to exploit two separate targets simultaneously. Although the primary high-value insurgent or HVI wasn't found, several suspects were detained and the intelligence picture for Turki Bowl II refined along with denying the locations as a safe house and training area for the enemy. Several enemy fighters were killed when they attempted to escape carrying weapons, and two weapons caches were exploited. On another mission conducted by Alpha Troop an enemy safe house was destroyed and evidence of a weapons training range was discovered. The troop even unearthed a completely buried vehicle.

In addition to the air assaults, mounted reconnaissance patrols on the northern, eastern and western sides of Turki were to be conducted. There were mounted patrols or movements to one of the police stations or outstations, staging there, and then conducting dismounted patrols at night. Mounted screen lines would attempt to identify enemy movement routes and patterns of lines. The placement of sensors to track enemy movements and establishing hide sites to observe enemy activity were going to be used to help determine where to focus during Turki Bowl II. The covert placement and collection of data from unattended ground sensors would provide information about enemy movement.

Bravo Troop was among the ground elements placing sensors when they received a call that a nearby platoon had hit a mine. Captain Dobbins along with Sergeant John Ferrante's gun trucks reached the site of the explosion, called for a medevac helicopter and a tow for the damaged truck. As the column left the area to return to base Ferrante placed two of his soldiers out front to walk the route looking for the telltale signs of explosive devices, rocks piled and placed along the side of the road warning the locals not to use it or Christmas tree lights that were actually small pressure plates so that when pressure was applied, the activated circuit would detonate the buried explosives. While trying to avoid potholes, the left rear tire of Ferrante's truck rolled over a pressure plate. Instantaneously, everyone and everything including the truck was thrown forward. Ferrante recalled that "all I saw was that big flash, in front of my eye, and I'm getting thrown around in the truck."[5] The truck was picked up, turned 90 degrees and moved 15 feet or so. Everything in the back was thrown out. A storage box in the cargo trunk that easily weighed 100 pounds and took a couple of guys to load was blown clear of the truck.

After the truck came to a stop, Ferrante got out and ran around to check on his driver. Ferrante opened the door to see him staring at him with what he described as that "deer in the headlights look." Yells for help were coming from inside the gun truck. Jumping up on the truck, Ferrante tried to assess the injuries of his crew. A medic appeared as if out of nowhere and was told that they needed to get the gunner out of the truck. Doc unhooked him from the gunner saddle, pulled him out and moved him clear of the blast site. Ferrante immediately began quizzing the disoriented paratrooper:

"What's hurting, what's wrong, where are you hurting?"

"Shut up, I'm fine, I'm OK. Just take pictures of the truck," came the response. Ferrante kissed him on his forehead and began snapping pictures of the damage.[6]

The left rear side and rear hatch were gone. The right rear panel was still intact. It was hard to believe that the entire crew had not only survived, they'd mostly walked away from it unscathed. The look of amazement on their faces told how close they'd come to a different ending. Recovering the trucks took almost 17 hours to complete. It turned out that the entire area was laced with mines. The recovery truck showed up, loaded Ferrante's truck, turned to leave and was disabled by another mine.

The phone rang at midnight. Danielle Ferrante grabbed for it not knowing what to expect. John was on the other end telling his wife, "I want to tell you before you heard from anybody else. I got blown up." Assuring her that he was OK brought the gut-wrenching response, "How OK, John?"

Some minor cuts and bruises were the extent of the injuries. John's wife wanted to know about the other guys in his truck, and John once again reassured her that they were fine. John had to cut the conversation short telling her that they had work to do and that she should go back to sleep, as if the phone call had never been received.

Needless to say, sleep did not come easy. John had walked away virtually unscathed but what about the next time? Was it only a matter of when the phone call would be replaced by a knock at the door, a visit by the chaplain and a casualty assistance officer? What would she tell their little boy? "Your daddy was a brave soldier, and he gave his life for our country?" How true would that ring? Being without John to raise their son and grow old together, she fought to put all these negative thoughts out of her mind, but it was so difficult to cope with the reality of the job he was doing, a dangerous job in a far-off land filled with uncertainty.[7]

Another means of tracking the enemy was to insert troops to establish hide sites to determine the whereabouts and movement of enemy fighters. Insurgents were using the palm groves to hide their activities. This solid green wall of vegetation concealed unknown dangers. Each step was filled with the uncertainty of what deadly menaces lay ahead. This isolated area not only had insurgent camps, some were large with obstacle courses and firing ranges. The intelligence reinforced that these enemy fighters were well trained, dug in and knew how to maneuver like soldiers.

Six-man elements were inserted to either gather or confirm intelligence about a portion of the battlespace. Each team was well equipped and self-sufficient for three to four days. They carried in plenty of ammunition for each rifle, machine gun and squad assault weapon, several claymore mines, optics, night vision thermals, radios for maintaining communications with the tactical operations center, rations and cold-weather gear. Each member had a small rucksack or assault pack.[8] Since the area had seen significant IED activity, finding the bomb makers became a top priority.

The team was brought into the area by Humvee gun trucks, then moved to the hide site on foot using the cover of darkness. Stealth was vital to make sure they were undetected by the enemy or would-be informants. The remainder of the platoon, along with their gun trucks, was located 8km south of the team's location, ready to reinforce the team or extract them if they were attacked. A two-room shack was used as an observation platform, overwatching from the windows during the day and moving to the roof during the night. The team observed flashlights piercing the darkness, flashing like tiny lasers. It was easy to assume that they were moving with sinister intent.

Two days into the mission, a 12-year-old boy compromised the site. Bringing him into the hide site, the interpreter tried to explain to him what they were doing. Knowing that the child's family would come looking for him, the boy was released. It wouldn't be long before enemy fighters would target the team. As soon as darkness fell, the paratroopers moved to a house approximately 200 meters away.

The crescendo of enemy small-arms fire broke the night stillness, directed towards the shack the team had recently vacated. The paratroopers responded with their precise fires. Suddenly, visibility was reduced to just about zero by fog. It was impossible to detect any enemy movement because the fog made their night vision inoperable. Before long, the enemy began maneuvering towards the team. One of the machine gunners was able to engage an insurgent and the threat was eliminated. A battle damage assessment confirmed that multiple enemy fighters had been killed. The decision was made to end the mission.

In the pitch black of night Matt Guza, one of the snipers assigned to the sniper section of 5-73, set the eye relief on his thermal optic scope and scanned the darkness. For Guza, it was the first time he'd engaged the enemy at night. He had the business end of his sniper rifle prepared to respond to any threat or dispatch any target of opportunity. The rifle had its name etched into the stock by the previous sniper: "Binky." It was the pacifier to keep the enemy quiet. Firing a .50-caliber round with an effective maximum range of 2,000 yards these precision marksmen provide the psychological deterrent on the battlefield, quickly demoralizing the enemy or instantly stopping a vehicle that poses a threat by firing a round through the vehicle's engine block.

Stealth is a key part of the sniper's success. Guza and his spotter slowly moved towards the enemy target, careful not to alert the enemy insurgents to their presence. Landing between midnight and two in the morning, darkness reinforced the element of surprise. Guza explained that, "It's a lot of time to think. There's so many thoughts going through your head," not knowing exactly what you're going to be confronted with as a mission takes shape. The first few minutes are critical because the element of surprise is essential to successfully completing the mission.

Having reached their objective, Guza slowly raised his head and detected movement on the roof of an adjacent building which was only 300 meters away. The snipers moved to a different position to avoid detection. They observed the silhouettes of two enemy fighters running with Kalashnikov assault rifles. As they moved into the palm groves, Guza took the first shot. Breathe, relax, aim, squeeze. Guza remembered that "when the first shot hit, it was a white-hot flash on a soft target. I'll never forget it."[9] Instantaneously, the bullet tore into flesh and bone, creating the splatter effect of blood exploding from the body—and death. Moments later, the sniper received a radio call from a helicopter gunship flying overhead reporting enemy movement. Through his scope Guza registered the movement. Breathe, relax, aim, squeeze. The team killed four insurgents before they were extracted.

Christmas Day 2006 would be the only day during the entire deployment that there weren't any tactical operations conducted by 5-73. Lieutenant Colonel Poppas, Sergeant Major Edgar, and Majors Hedrick and Sylvia circulated among the paratroopers spreading holiday cheer. It would be short lived.

On December 27, 5-73 launched their final mission of the shaping operations. This large squadron air assault ended with finding and destroying three weapons caches and capturing 40 suspected enemy fighters, including one of the top three leaders of the Council.

It was time for the next phase: Turki Bowl II.

CHAPTER 10

Turki Bowl II

As the preparations progressed for the return to Turki, the deaths of Dennison and Schiller weighed heavily on the paratroopers. Marc Adams, one of the medics assigned to 5-73, recalled their desire was to "get down there and finish them off," destroying the insurgents and avenging their comrades' deaths.

Following Turki Bowl I, there was chatter that the Council had begun the retaliation-style execution of Shia males who had lived in the villages surrounding Turki. Not only were 46 Shia men murdered, 600 Shia families were forced out of their homes by the Council. The key leaders of the Council had decided to use this violent approach as an attempt to discredit the coalition forces, leaving the impression that these terrorists had complete control of the people. Jihadist fighters had emplaced homemade explosives and mines to slow any attempt by the coalition forces to regain control of the area. The early warning system was in place along Route Green, which was the only passageway into the region from the north.

Headhunter had pinpointed their enemy. Turki Bowl I had started as an aerial reconnaissance that quickly shifted to engaging the enemy, probing their capabilities to determine their strengths and weaknesses. It had been limited in its scope. Raids, intelligence gathering and data mining followed, interwoven with the use of information deception. This approach had allowed 5-73 to use the shaping operations to either capture members of Al Qaeda or push them back towards Turki. All the imagery came back saying that the enemy had started to set up defensive obstacles to prevent 5-73 from getting through. The insurgents appeared to have a sense that the fight wasn't over. It was going to be a classic linear battle.

The centuries-old regional trait of spreading information by word of mouth and rumor was also effectively used by 5-73. The perception that the enemy had was that they were safe in Turki. The Americans had no interest in returning. The reality was much different. The purpose was to deny Al Qaeda and other insurgent groups a safe haven in eastern Diyala. The desired end state was that the Council leadership would be destroyed, thus defeating the insurgency in the area. It would

Ace's Bradley (Sean Ventura)

begin with a fundamentally linear fight against an asymmetric foe. Iraqi army forces were preparing to ultimately lead security operations in the vicinity of Turki Village thus bringing stability to the province.

It was time to unleash the full force of a combined arms attack. The operation was designated a division main effort, so all sorts of firepower was assigned in support. In addition to 5-73's troops (Alpha, Bravo, and Charlie along with the Delta support troops and squadron headquarters) were a company of airborne infantry riflemen, four companies of Iraqi troops, a platoon of four Abrams Main Battle Tanks providing traditional armor support, a mechanized rifle platoon equipped with Bradley Fighting Vehicles, an armored troop carrier with a 25mm gun in its turret, and Paladin self-propelled tracked artillery. The operation had a heavy force arrayed to provide a powerful punch both close in and at long range.

Additional firepower was needed that the organic up-armored Humvees didn't offer. Two of 5-73's troops had experience with armored vehicles. The scouts had trained with the Bradley and several were assigned to the squadron. These assets were positioned at the far end of the canals to provide continuous surveillance to ensure that that the enemy didn't attempt to reoccupy them after the canals had been cleared. The western escapes from Turki had to be blocked to ensure that the enemy didn't slip through them.

The self-propelled 155mm howitzers, nicknamed Paladin, provided long-range (up to almost 15 miles' distance) heavy artillery. Detonation of a round resulted in the delivery of thousands of deadly fragments on an enemy target. These tracked vehicles had the ability to fire on a target, then immediately move to another location to avoid the enemy attempting to fire on their position. In order to speed their movement into the staging area, the Paladins were put up on trailers and brought in from the southwest. This kept the element of surprise with friendly forces. The howitzers ultimately provided the fire support from a location that avoided direct enemy contact. They proved invaluable, firing so many rounds that they would "go black" several times, running completely out of ammunition. More shells were hustled forward from various stores by the forward support Joes from Delta Troop.

The fight for Turki couldn't be won without the support provided by the Delta Troop paratroopers. Even before the operation began, Delta was looking for ways to make it easier and safer for their fellow paratroopers to defeat the enemy fighters occupying Turki and the surrounding villages. Delta's commanding officer, Captain Jake St. Laurent, recalled that, "I had very enterprising soldiers. They would identify a need and next thing you know it would be fabricated."[1]

Knowing that a major challenge in the fight to retake Turki was going to be the trench warfare, Delta took cargo pallets, metal platforms that serve as the base for securing cargo that goes on military airlift aircraft, and began to figure out if they could be used for crossing the canals. The pallets were placed across eight- to 10-foot-wide concrete culverts, and an up-armored Humvee was repeatedly driven over them. Next, a Bradley Fighting Vehicle was driven over the platform repeatedly to ensure that it would support its weight.

Each troop was assigned a fuel truck that carried five sections of bridging material strapped to the top of it. There was one site that required bridging before the grunts could proceed. A 20-foot flat rack from a palletized loading system was dumped across a canal that had been compromised at one end. The gap was 15 feet across a swift running current.

A mine roller was designed for the gun trucks, modeled after the tank mine rollers. The roller stood off the front of the Humvee about 10 feet and consisted of the road wheels from an M1 tank. Two of the rollers went out to the troops that were going down the road; the other two went in from an off-road direction and it wouldn't have helped them to maneuver easily. So the motor pool ended up cutting two in half and welding them together so that they could be attached to the route clearing equipment, which was an M88, a tank-like wrecker. According to First Sergeant Doug Yates, Delta Troop's senior sergeant, the M88 "would be the lead the vehicle driven by the mechanics when combat logistics patrols went out to deliver supplies, refuel trucks or return enemy detainees to the holding facility."[2]

The maneuver plan indicated that the operation would last at least seven to 10 days. A refueling plan would be essential. This would be the first time that the troops would have the refueling trucks assigned to them for the entire operation. The same two or four fuelers would rotate out. There were eight fuel guys along with water resupply or water dogs rotating out. The fuel trucks stayed with the line troops and resupply missions were run every two to three days. A fuel truck went out and was exchanged for the empty one.

Any resource needs or parts requests were received by Delta Troop and a combat logistics patrol was organized. There was a lot of communication not only with the line troops but with the intelligence folks. It was important to know the face of the battlespace each day. Friendly as well as enemy disposition, tactical situation and current threats were all part of maintaining situational awareness.

About two weeks before the operation was set to kick off, Delta did a lot of work with the 25th Combat Aviation Brigade to establish a landing point at Caldwell. The landing zone would be located 100 meters from the squadron headquarters. Two M88 wreckers dropped their plow blades and cleared a football field's worth of space that could handle two Black Hawks, three Apache gunships and a Chinook heavy lift helicopter. Delta's fuel trucks were used and the fuelers processed the fuel. The aviation soldiers gave added support to the operation, running it day and night. Nightly supply aircraft worked to resupply the fight. The aircrews were flying in some marginal weather conditions to get the grunts badly needed supplies or to perform medical evacuations.

The squadron logistics officer, Captain Jon Grassbaugh, was the linchpin coordinating the flow of supplies. Grassbaugh received his commission as a Second Lieutenant through the ROTC program at Johns Hopkins and had served his platoon command time in Korea as well as a previous tour in Iraq. His amazing talent for multi-tasking and going beyond the normal supply needs of the paratroopers, along with pitching in and getting dirty whenever necessary, made him a vital squadron asset. It was not unusual to see Grassbaugh making the runs himself or personally loading supplies on an outbound helicopter. Replacement parts for the Humvee gun trucks were quickly grabbed from the motor pool and hustled down to the airfield so they could be put on an outbound supply helicopter. Pallet after pallet of water and rations were loaded until it was doubtful whether it would all fit.

Captain Grassbaugh's creativity and desire to keep the troops supplied went several steps further than the usual combat meal provisions. One night, Grassbaugh even made a massive pizza run from Balad to the troops in Turki. Arrangements were made to have the food service contractors prepare roast beef, egg and cheese sandwiches each night to be loaded on the resupply bird for the flight out to Turki.

The Delta paratroopers had responsibility for security at Caldwell as well as transporting enemy detainees. They were juggling roles and filling many voids that were created by the operation in Turki. Any vehicle damaged during the fighting had to be recovered. The convoy received a grid, recovered the truck, and returned it to be repaired. A replacement truck was brought along so they could continue to fight. Returning from a combat logistics patrol, Delta could turn their trucks around in a matter of hours in preparation for the next mission.

The Joes in and around Turki were running out of dry socks and t-shirts. So, every other day the clothing collection plate went around. Guys were pulling their last couple of socks out knowing that the scouts and riflemen in the fight needed them. Pretty much everybody who was back in the rear wanted to be part of the fight, to contribute.

Captain Steve Magner, who would take command of the Delta "Demons" just as Headhunter was preparing to enter the Diyala River Valley in early 2007 following Turki Bowl II, described these paratroopers in his best Bostonian lingo as "hard working muldoons." Officially, they'd been attached to 5-73 CAV but to Delta "the squadron was their squadron." Magner spoke for all his paratroopers when he said, "They're our fuckin' boys out there."

These support paratroopers were a bunch of characters. Unlike the other troops where everyone was either an infantry rifleman or a cavalry scout, Delta Troop had, according to Captain Magner, "every walk of life." Cooks went out to the patrol bases making sure the line troops were well fed and maintenance support teams were there to care for the gun trucks and other mechanical systems. But when need be, cooks were lying in ambushes, and fuelers were walking dismounted patrol. Magner described a truck driver, a big old farm boy who "could probably throw hay a mile"; his only desire was to "gun and help with security."[3]

The squadron needed a point to stage, organize and maneuver into the battlespace. An Iraqi army patrol base was designated for the squadron's mortar section to secure this passage of lines and establish a firing point for the 120mm mortars. The location gave the mortar section a good firing position.

Not long after arriving the day before the operation was to begin, the base began to receive enemy mortar fire: the insurgents were aware of their presence. The mortars effectively suppressed the enemy position. Several minutes later, the patrol base was hit for the second time by enemy indirect fire, this time from a different location. The 5-73 mortars fired a second volley and destroyed the enemy position. The mortar barrage had given the paratroopers and their Iraqis counterparts a taste of what lay ahead, an enemy that was still willing and able to fight.

CHAPTER 11

Tightening the Noose

As the sun rose three hours into the battle, the helicopter carrying the command element landed behind Bravo Troop. The aerial lift had involved enough Black Hawks and Chinooks to deliver troops to nine landing zones. The helicopters flew from both the Warhorse and Caldwell bases in an effort to maintain operational security. If 11 aircraft took off from a small base like Caldwell, the enemy would have known that this massive air assault was meant for them.

H-hour, the time when the operation commenced, was 4:00 a.m. The earlier air assault missions that took place during the December shaping operations had been able to determine when the enemy and the inhabitants began stirring. Headhunter wanted to ensure that the area was isolated before they began the clearance of the villages. They needed to be able to stop any enemy squirters from getting out of the trap that 5-73 was setting.

The battlespace limits ran south to Turki and it was approximately the physical size of Baghdad. The battle plan followed a deliberate clearance of the area from north to south while blocking any escape in the east and west. Bravo Troop was the center ground maneuver element, the tip of the spear. Bravo also had the local troops from the Balad Ruz area. Alpha Troop had the Kurds and covered the western side of the engagement area. Charlie Troop had gone in by way of both an air assault and convoy, establishing blocking positions to the east. The attached mounted troop with their Bradley Fighting Vehicles blocked the southern side of the engagement area along with the airborne infantry company that had also been attached for this operation.

Everyone moved in a synchronized fashion. Trucks moved in from the west, north and northwest. The troop commanders made sure everyone reached their phase lines at the same time. All egresses were covered. Within five minutes of kicking off the operation, the first of many land mines was struck. The truck was destroyed, torn to pieces, a mobility kill that set the tone for the southern approach to Turki by Alpha and Bravo Troops. They'd hit three mines the first day. Josh Kinser, an Alpha Troop section sergeant, recalled that, "You couldn't spit without hitting an IED."[1]

Bad weather during Turki Bowl II (John Ferrante)

As Alpha Troop began their clearance assignment, it became apparent that the military-age males had vanished again. The story was always the same, "Oh, he's working in Baghdad." Family members had this look of resentment etched on their faces. Everyone knew what it meant. The canals were teeming with jihadists ready and willing to exact their brand of fanaticism upon the paratroopers and their Iraqi partners.

As the first day ended, a house off in the distance seemed to be a good place for Alpha Troop to set up a patrol base for the night. It offered good fields of fire and allowed the gun trucks to circle up forming a defensive perimeter. After the house was cleared, an irrigation point that was being fed by an adjoining creek needed to be made passable for the gun trucks. If not, the area would quickly become a quagmire of mud. While security covered them, a detail of two paratroopers began placing logs and rocks to deal with the potential flooding. In the meantime, Iraqi troops pulled up to reinforce the position.

Suddenly, one of the gun truck turret gunners observed movement in the high reeds. Two military-age males were neck deep in the creek water and were attempting to ambush the paratroopers working in the creek. Just as the enemy fighters were moving out of the water, Iraqi army troops sighted in on them, and the insurgents tried to return to the assumed safety of the water, firing their weapons at the same time. Surprised by the gunfire, the paratroopers were unaware of the potential death trap. While trying to return fire, however, one of the paratroopers slipped in the mud and fell in the water.

When the enemy fighters were pulled from the creek, they turned out to be teenagers clad in tactical vests, armed with assault rifles and grenades. They were willing to stay in the frigid water for who knows how long, unconcerned about their fate. They were no more than 10 to 15 meters away from the detail working in the creek. Not only were they going to ambush them; a grenade attack on the gun truck had also been part of their plan.

Soon after the tactical questioning began, the younger detainee broke. He was petrified and began crying. He mentioned Sami Kareem, one of the Council leaders. Kareem's name would be constantly thrown around in an effort to confuse Headhunter concerning the intentions of Al Qaeda and Kareem's whereabouts. The detainee mentioned that more enemy fighters were to move into the area the next day. Al Qaeda did have prior knowledge that the operation was going to be conducted due to an ongoing psychological operations effort of broadcasting and dropping leaflets. It dared the enemy fighters "to come out and meet us. If you are a Jihadist, then you'll be killed."

The older detainee looked at the interrogator and dared him to "do whatever you want to with me but you're going to die in hell with all the other infidels" and spit right in the interrogator's face. This guy was just not scared. He didn't care. Even after hours of tactical questioning, he dared his enemy to "bring what you got on." The enemy fighter's eyes showed that he wasn't about to give anything up.

The detainees seemed to be following the Al Qaeda Training Manual to the letter. As if on cue, giving some piece of a story, "Sami Kareem is our leader," believing that if some information was provided the questioning would end. They'd be handed over to the Iraqis to pursue a court case, treating them like criminal suspects rather than enemy combatants. Any allegations of torture by detainees, often with references right out of the Al Qaeda chapter listing the top 24 torture methods, would make any and all evidence obtained during tactical questioning inadmissible. The cunning and violence of these terrorists knew no bounds. Evidence of how Al Qaeda tortured kidnap victims had been found in one of the buildings during the clearance. Blood-splattered rooms, gallows of some sort and two bloody nooses told their own horrific tale of the insurgents' cruelty.

The squadron began efforts to connect with the villagers who remained, locate the village elder, and figure out their needs. The military-age males, husbands, fathers, and sons of the village were either being detained, had been killed or were nowhere to be found. The women of the village hissed at Americans with contempt, "their eyes full of hatred" as they quickly returned to their homes, dragging their children.[2] One of the interpreters reported that the women said that the paratroopers would "burn in hell with the rest of infidels" for zip tying and interrogating their men in front of their wives.

One of the presence patrols came across a taxi driver from Baghdad who claimed that he had been "on vacation" when the fighting had started. His car had been destroyed and he had no way of getting his family back to Baghdad. He found and brought the village elder to speak with the paratroopers. He claimed to be fed up with the violence and said he didn't take sides. He wanted assurances that the Americans could "keep the mujahedeen from coming back."

Later, some background files were reviewed and the village elder was found to be "listed as a financier and linked to Syrian weapons dealers."[3] One paratrooper observed that it was difficult to believe "anyone down here is who they seem unless they all seem to you they are the Al Qaeda, the same type of man who flew a plane into those buildings, the same enemy who will never give up, the same fanatic who will fight me until the end and relish his end as a martyr."[4]

Women, and a few children shyly peeking their heads around the adults, occupied the next house they approached. "We haven't seen nor heard from the men since the fighting that had occurred in November," one villager noted, referring to Turki Bowl I. The men had fought and everyone in the village assumed they were dead. An elderly woman inquired about whether there was a doctor available. The medic stepped forward and the woman's grandson was brought out.

The child wore a heavy purple and green girl's coat, torn sweat pants and multicolored shoes. A heavy bandage covered his tiny right hand. When the fighting erupted in November, the children had been out in the fields. All the children returned safely except little Ali. His mother and aunt went in search of him. As they approached where he'd last been seen, they could hear his screams. He was found holding out his arm with his hand limp and bloody, dangling from his wrist. A stray round had entered between his index and middle knuckles, splitting his hand. The bullet was lodged near his wrist. His index finger was gone and the middle one as good as gone.

The wound had healed but it appeared that a piece of the bullet remained in his hand. The wound was painful, and Ali guarded it, knowing that if it was disturbed it would make him cry out in agony. He hadn't spoken since being wounded. The hand was scrubbed clean and antibiotic ointment was applied along with a new dressing. There wasn't much else that the medic could do for him. The injury had left him unable to use the hand. The little boy was in constant pain, and the hand was only going to become more contorted.

To distract Ali and ease his pain, a box of animal crackers was found on one of the gun trucks and presented to him. Digging through the box Ali discovered a lion-shaped cookie that he set aside. He continued to eat the other cookies but each time he came to a lion he would put it with the others. All the children appeared to have been sickened from having drunk water straight from the canals. Bottles of water were handed out to stem the spread of diarrhea and rehydrate the kids with clean water.

Continuing their patrol, the paratroopers arrived at the home of a schoolteacher and his family. They were extremely polite and pleasant. Chai was brought out and offered to the soldiers. A young boy who couldn't have been more than 10 commanded a presence and charisma far beyond his years. He was missing his left eye. There was only a portion of the eyeball remaining, leaving a red empty socket. His father explained that during a firefight between Al Qaeda and coalition forces their home had come under fire. An enemy rocket had hit the side of the house and shrapnel had struck the boy and destroyed his eye. Eventually, he would be able to be fitted for a prosthetic eye but he would have to wait until he was older. Another casualty, courtesy of Al Qaeda.

The next morning, every vehicle needed fuel before beginning the clearance of the next village. The fuelers had linked up and established a refueling point not far from Alpha Troop but on the other side of the canal. Several gun trucks and the Bradley moved forward, reaching a choke point that would serve as a crossing between the two canals. The Bradley was providing extra punch for cordons and security when maneuvering. The first truck made the crossing, made a U-turn and proceeded towards the fuel truck. The second truck followed suit. The third truck moved forward following the same route.

With a sudden shudder, the truck disappeared. It had hit an anti-tank mine and the force of the detonation had blown the front end completely off. The shock wave went through everyone in proximity to the blast. Sergeant Adam Jeter, Bravo Section Leader, 3rd Platoon, maneuvered his Bradley to prepare for an enemy ambush and to recover the injured. The former Marine with nine years' service had re-enlisted in the army and had been a cav scout since 5-73 had been stood up. Jeter knew exactly how to respond.

Was the explosive command-detonated? If so, insurgents could very well be following on with small-arms fire. The Bradley spun around and dropped its ramp. Out of the cloud appeared the gunner. He wasted no time rushing into the safety of the Bradley. The driver was in a post-explosion daze and couldn't figure out how to open his door. Using a combination of hand signals and hollering at him, Jeter was able to get the disoriented paratrooper to climb out of the truck by way of the gun turret.

Jeter's platoon sergeant was on the ground for a second. He stood up for a moment, rested on a knee momentarily, stood a second time, took three steps and collapsed. As Jeter watched in horror, he got on the radio and began calling for any available medics to move forward to start treating casualties. Fortunately, there weren't any serious injuries because this type of mine blows straight up so the Humvee absorbed a lot of the blast; the outward force is the shock wave. It's hard to imagine that everyone doesn't suffer from a traumatic brain injury after that kind of exposure to a blast.

The Delta wrecker came in to recover the truck, the medic had moved up to check for injuries and a group of Joes had gathered around the blast site, inspecting the damage to the gun truck and assessing the size of the crater. The decision was made to continue refueling the other trucks. The platoon sergeant's truck had maneuvered to the rear and to the right of the site along with Jeter's Bradley. Bomb techs came in with their robot after they noticed two strange dig holes and found two more mines. After that, an infrared scan was done, but nothing else was detected.

The gun truck being driven by Mario Mendoza began backing up. It was tight, so a ground guide was needed to make certain that they didn't end up in the canal. The gun truck had moved about five or six feet from the site when the ground guide heard a "pop" that sounded like a soda bottle being run over, immediately followed by an explosion.

The mine detonated directly under the driver's side wheel and Mendoza appeared to have had both his legs broken. The force ruptured every blood vessel in his legs. He looked as if he'd been severely beaten: purple, bruised and unable to move his lower limbs. The steering wheel separated from the chassis, striking him, breaking his jaw on both sides and partially severing his tongue. Mendoza was evacuated to Germany that night. He recovered from his injuries and returned to 5-73 to finish out the deployment.

As the battle continued, cellphone intercepts were being monitored by the paratroopers. Messages revealed that the insurgents were concerned about being surrounded and that many had moved from Turki to the nearby village of 30 Tamooz in an effort to escape capture. Based on intelligence gathered during the continued clearance of various villages, it was learned that the enemy's plan was to use the canal complex as an engagement area. As Bravo Troop questioned a number of detained military-age males, two of them claimed to have information on the location of Sami Kareem and Mohammed Bender, prominent insurgent leaders.

Bender was preaching hate in 30 Tamooz every Friday. Bender stood 5'8" to 5'10" tall and was 30 to 35 years old, with no beard and wearing a black and blue robe. Bender moved around the area using fear to secure the loyalty of the inhabitants. Five of Bender's henchmen remained in the town to enforce Wahhabi practices among the populace. Charlie Troop was able to capture two of them. The people of the town had obeyed Bender out of fear. A lack of a friendly presence in the area had left the locals with no other choice but to comply.

As the insurgents travelled along the canal roads on motorcycles, their movement further reinforced the probability that the enemy was using the canals to make their stand. Along with the clearance operations, blocking positions were established to inhibit enemy movement and in turn lead to the capture of the insurgent leaders. During Turki Bowl I, insurgents had been discovered in spider holes in the canal network. Headhunter had performed a Vietnam-style search and destroy mission to eliminate the enemy force hiding in the canals. In an effort to avoid having to perform an "enter and clear" mission, a preparatory airstrike was executed to soften up the enemy stronghold.

Two giant B-1B Lancer bombers were used to destroy the enemy as they lay waiting. Flying thousands of feet above the battlespace, the B-1Bs released their payload of 33 huge 2,000-pound air burst munitions that minimized the destruction of the canals. There was no warning of their approach. Suddenly, the ground quaked and there was a rumbling sound. It was as if thunderclaps had been released from the earth.

A cordon was set to prevent ground forces from becoming casualties of the airstrike. It also ensured that there wouldn't be any enemy squirters escaping. The first pass delivered ten 2,000-pound bombs just before daylight. The second pass was completed after daylight. A chorus of, "Fuckin A, killum all! Fuckum up!" arose from the distant friendly forces that heard and watched the bombing runs.

The hope that this massive airstrike would have eliminated the enemy threat posed in the canals was short lived.

"Hound 52 from Brewmaster 46, troops in contact."

The urgent call came from the air force JTAC to the lead air force fighter jet. Two F16 Fighting Falcons had just tried to provide a battle damage assessment following the earlier B-1 strikes. The cloud deck wouldn't allow them to safely complete that assignment. Now Headhunter had begun to maneuver towards the canals to finish off the enemy fighters that might be left. Lead pilot Mike Wilburn recounted that the two pilots quickly conferred and the decision was made to "get through the weather and support our guys!"[5]

The JTAC, call sign Brewmaster 46, painted a tough fight. The JTAC acknowledged Hound 52 had the lead and added, "Red, this is Scorch," knowing he would recognize the name. Brewmaster 46 acknowledged with friendly banter and the familiar tactical back-and-forth communication describing the battlefield. As the flight descended through 3,000 feet, a small break in the clouds appeared. The aircraft remained below the clouds and rain peppered their canopies as they sped to the battle at over 500 knots.

The image of the battle was surreal. The fields of mud flashed with the tracer fire of .50-caliber machine guns and small arms. At such a low altitude and high speed, the landscape screamed by. The enemy targeted the approaching aircraft each time the F16s passed overhead, and flares poured out of the aircraft to prevent enemy heat-seeking missiles from locking on to the aircraft.

Brewmaster's situation report of the battlespace gave Hound 52 a clear picture of where the friendly forces were located. The paratroopers placed tracer fire on the enemy positions, which gave Hound 52 an accurate location of the insurgents. Using "gun only" due to the low altitude that wouldn't permit the arming of any other ordnance, Hound 52 began his run.

"Hurry because we need it, you're cleared hot," exclaimed Brewmaster.

In an instant the buzz saw-like rotary gun of the Fighting Falcon expended 120 rounds of 20mm explosive rounds down the canal.

"Hound 52 you are cleared for an immediate re-attack," came the second urgent call from Brewmaster 46.

"I'm in from the south," Hound 52 responded.[6]

Putting the jet into what amounted to a bolt-rattling maneuver to return to the target, Brewmaster cleared the aircraft hot. Once again, the fighter's gun expended another 150 rounds into the same canal. As he cleared the target, Hound 52 observed 20mm rounds impacting on the enemy position. The enemy small-arms fire ceased.

CHAPTER 12

Hot Chow

As the third day of the Turki Bowl II operations began some of the Iraqi soldiers were fed up. They'd been promised by their brigade commander that hot chow would be brought to them. There were plenty of field rations and the clearance operations had been going well; the area was heavily mined and the Iraqis were warned not to risk leaving. But nothing could dissuade the Iraqis and the column proceeded to leave.

With an American gun truck in the lead the column cautiously proceeded. Without warning, one of the Iraqi vehicles hit an anti-tank mine. The vehicle caught fire.

By the time the paratroopers reached the site, the vehicle was engulfed in flames and rounds were cooking off. One Iraqi soldier burned to death. It really shook the Iraqi army company. Their commander convinced them to stay in the fight for one more day until another Iraqi company could replace them. Out of loyalty to Hercik and his paratroopers, the Iraqi captain reminded them that while they had been in Baqubah they had fought together. While they had been in Turki the Americans had protected them, staying up at night while the Iraqis slept. The Iraqi officer reminded his soldiers that it was dangerous out here and that Captain Hercik needed their protection. After that, every Iraqi soldier agreed to stay on until relieved.

The next day, the convoy with the replacement Iraqi army soldiers was moving down a road that made a very gradual turn to the left. To the left of the road was a large open field bordered by what was probably an irrigation canal that was covered by reeds. Immediately to the right side of the road, the earth sloped up and ended in an enormous canal that had several feet of swift-moving water in it. The drivers had been warned to drive directly in the tire tracks of the vehicle to their front because of the danger of anti-tank mines. The weather was nice for Iraq. It was a clear cool day with a slight breeze.

Andrew Harriman, the combat medic assigned to the convoy, was driving one of the lead gun trucks. Suddenly, the sound of an explosion followed by a shock wave overtook the gun truck. Opening the door and looking to their rear, an enormous column of smoke and dust could be observed coming from the rear of the convoy.

A mass casualty incident during Turki Bowl II (Brad Rather)

As the only medic on scene, Harriman grabbed his rifle from next to the driver's seat, ripped the aid bag from the back seat and took off running. Debris from the blast started raining down. It was mostly dust, dirt, and smaller rocks.

After what seemed an eternity, Harriman arrived to find utter carnage. Off to his left Harriman found two 5-73 paratroopers just staring in disbelief. The horror transfixed them. They were younger guys, and they were frozen in place with no idea what to do.

There were bodies strewn in all directions. Some of the injured were walking around yelling and screaming, others were walking aimlessly, not sure of what was happening or what to do. There were some uninjured Iraqi soldiers who had materialized from the vehicle that was following the one that hit the mine. They were running in figurative circles, yelling in Arabic and in a mass panic. It was quickly apparent that triage would need to be utilized to determine how many were injured and who would need to be treated first.

Without stopping, Harriman grabbed one of the paratroopers by the sleeve and yelled at another one to assist him. Pointing to an area just outside the blast zone, Harriman began to triage the wounded. He instructed one of the interpreters to tell any Iraqi soldiers that could walk to move towards him. This was an easy way to identify the "green" or walking wounded. They could follow instructions and were moving under their own power. They would also need an area for those tagged as "yellow", the more seriously wounded, and the "red" or critical patients who would die if they weren't given priority treatment and transportation to a surgical hospital. The dead would be tagged "black" and left to be collected after all others were flown out.

The radio call known as a "nine line" was transmitted giving the details of the mass casualty incident along with the request for helicopter medical evacuation. There were 10 patients that had at least one full or partial amputation. Harriman was in the process of applying tourniquets when several more 5-73 paratroopers arrived to help. Combat lifesavers began arriving and Harriman quickly put them to work providing basic life support, treating patients by controlling bleeding, maintaining adequate airways and making sure that the wounded didn't get any worse. The blast site along with the casualties was in the open so the need for security quickly became apparent. The medical report gave a count of 24 patients, 10 urgent surgical, six urgent, five routine/priority, three convenience/fatality (black or soon to be black tags). A confirmation of the number of wounded brought a momentary "holy shit" pause before the traffic was acknowledged. Medical evacuation helicopters were inbound. Only seven minutes had passed since Harriman had arrived.

As Harriman feverishly worked, a Humvee pulled up and skidded to a halt behind him. Glancing over his shoulder, Harriman saw Major/Physician Assistant Brad Rather and another medic, Marc Adams, vaulting out of the truck. It was a welcome relief to know that some help with an advanced skill set had arrived. Marc and Brad both yelled in unison for an update. Harriman gave the initial numbers and pointed out the critical patients as he exposed the wounds of a barely conscious patient. Marc did a quick follow-up and double-checked the black tags, then went off to treat other yellow and red patients.

After applying numerous tourniquets to the amputations, Harriman began to work on a multi-systems trauma patient who was in obvious pain. He had a fully amputated left leg, a mostly amputated right leg, a mangled right arm, crushed chest and was struggling to breathe. With no time to stop and do an IV, Harriman opened the narcotics box, pulled out a carpuject syringe of morphine and injected it into the right jugular of the near-death soldier hoping that it would at least reduce the excruciating pain. As the needle was pulled out, a frantic Iraqi soldier grabbed the medic to help his friend and the carpuject needle, fresh out of the patient's neck and covered in his blood, went right into Harriman's finger. He shook the soldier off, tried to scrub the contaminated finger with an alcohol pad, and pulled on another pair of gloves, surely wondering how much worse this horrible situation could get.

Doc Rather was getting ready to do a surgical cricothyrotomy and Harriman knelt to help him. The soldier was unconscious and blowing a lot of blood bubbles. Brad sliced his neck open and put the tube in. As soon as it was secured Harriman left Brad and moved onto the next patient.

Then it got worse. The gunfire started.

Enemy small-arms fire was coming from across the canal. It wasn't particularly heavy or accurate but in the current state it only required one lucky shot, and someone would be joining the present list of casualties. Turning to Rather, Harriman noticed that he didn't have his helmet or body armor on, probably finding it too restrictive as he prepared to intubate another patient. Harriman shouted at him to put his helmet on, and all he got in response was a middle finger, too busy to yell verbal insults. The returning fire from the gun trucks that had a visual on the attackers was highly accurate and silenced the enemy.

The first set of helicopters landed approximately 100 meters west of the blast, one aircraft at a time while the additional aircraft circled overhead. Trying to get the non-English-speaking Iraqi soldiers calmed down and organized to move the injured to the landing zone was a lot like trying to teach a three-year-old advanced chemistry. Or in military terms, they looked like monkeys trying to fuck a football. The screaming, crying and general chaos made for a confusing scene. After what seemed an eternity, the process of moving the injured began. The first Black Hawk was loaded, lifted off and headed for the combat surgical hospital in Balad. The second aircraft landed, a brief patient report was given and the aircraft lifted off. The second set of Black Hawks came in and the process was repeated.

While walking back to the road from the landing zone, Harriman came across a blood-spattered combat boot. Picking the boot up, a fraction of a second passed before he realized that there was still a leg inside the boot, cut off at mid-calf. The top of the leg had jagged edges and was matted with grass, dirt and debris, wet and sticky with the dead man's blood. The boot and leg were tossed aside. The combination of being pissed off, tired, adrenaline drained and covered in who knows what along with the condition of the limb, the amount of debris in the exposed blood vessels and the overall fact that he had no clue who the fuck it belonged to didn't provide too many other options on what to do with the limb. It would be collected with the other remains.

Wearily walking back to the scene, Harriman thanked the scattered paratroopers who'd assisted with this enormous cluster fuck of a scene. Harriman finally made it back to the road and began the arduous task of cleaning up and collecting equipment. Brad had just shoved all of his shit back into his aid bag and made the genius decision to reorganize it back at his truck. Most of the Americans were making the journey back to their vehicles to the south of the blast and the Iraqis to their remaining vehicles to the north.

Harriman was a short distance from the wreckage and was bent over trying to figure out how to fit the remaining supplies in his aid bag and making sure his weapon was functional. Off in the distance the engine noise of one of the Iraqi bongo trucks, a compact unarmored civilian-style steak-body delivery truck, could be heard starting up and accelerating toward the wreckage. At a glance, it seemed that the Iraqi soldiers were going to use the vehicle to collect the dead and the salvageable equipment and move the smoldering hulk of the truck frame off the road.

Something struck Harriman as odd and ominous. He turned his head away from the wreckage, and a fraction of a second later, a bone-crushing BOOM resonated from the other side of the wreckage. He was thrown several feet from his crouched position and landed facedown. Lifting his face out of the dirt, Harriman was momentarily disoriented and was now looking at the front of the column of vehicles. He saw a handful of paratroopers running back towards him and the explosion with Brad Rather in the lead. As his brain began to process what was happening, a windshield slammed into the ground about 20 feet to his front. Not being able to hear anything except for the loud ringing in his ears, the opening scene from *Saving Private Ryan* popped in his head.

The Iraqi truck had detonated another mine. The cab was destroyed and actively burning. The chaos of a second mass casualty event had begun. Triage identified an additional eight patients. Two had full or partial amputations of the legs and the rest had moderate to severe burns and shrapnel injuries from the blast.

The flight medic from the first helicopter disembarked the aircraft and realized it was the same crew from the first blast.

"I thought you flew all of your patients out already!" she yelled over the deafening roar of the Black Hawk's rotor wash and engines.

"We did. These are the guys from the second blast!" Harriman yelled back.

"Second blast?" she asked looking at him quizzically.[1]

She looked past him towards the wreckage as if needing visual proof that Harriman wasn't busting her chops. When she saw the chaos in progress behind Harriman, she shook her head and waved the litter carriers in towards the aircraft.

All the Iraqis had wanted was some hot chow. What a price to pay.

CHAPTER 13

Clear, Hold, Build

As the clearance of 30 Tamooz continued it became readily apparent that any enemy weapons and ammunition hidden in the village had been moved or destroyed by the insurgents or their supporters. Each household was only permitted by law to have a rifle and a certain amount of ammunition. Some villagers began to volunteer information about the insurgents and one even jumped into a six-foot-deep canal to pull up his cached weapon and ammunition bandoleers.

The insurgents continued to be elusive and used the tactic of feigning surrender, knowing that the rules of engagement didn't permit coalition troops to fire on them. When coalition soldiers approached, the enemy would ambush them. In an effort to elude capture, the enemy moved through culverts and tunnels during the night and attempted to hide in the canals using reeds that grew 10 feet tall.

Every night, roving Apache gunships were killing enemy fighters as they moved out in groups of two and three. The Apache pilots called down to the paratroopers, wondering if they had detected them. Unable to pinpoint the enemy location, the paratroopers watched as the Apaches went to work. The paratroopers found what was left of them. They were all dressed like farmers. They weren't carrying rifles but they all had pistols underneath their clothes and one of them had three forms of ID. Another had a cellphone with the insurgent leader Sami Kareem's number on it.

There was a sense that these enemy cells had been significantly degraded by the paratroopers of 5-73 and their coalition partners. The mayor of Balad Ruz was broadcasting messages each day sharing the successes of the coalition forces and encouraging residents to support the effort to rescue their community. As word spread the hope was that displaced Shia families would return.

The winter weather continued to slow operations in and around Turki. Torrents of rain turned the terrain into a quagmire. Even tracked vehicles were hampered by the results of the monsoon season. The Humvee gun trucks not only lost traction, they found it difficult to stay on the rural road network. The hard pack became unstable causing the gun trucks to overturn. The Iraqi vehicles fared even worse. They were for the most part civilian-style pickups and bongo trucks. Tow straps were hooked

Building clearance during Turki Bowl II (Sergeant Armando Monroig, 5th Mobile Public Affairs Detachment)

Molon Labe, Turki patrol base (John Ferrante)

to the squadron gun trucks to winch them out of the mud. The ground fight came to a grinding halt. Trying to walk in the wet winter sand turned boots into cement shoes that added 15 to 20 pounds to each foot.

These conditions called for a somewhat different approach. A bulldozer operated by a soldier nicknamed Action Jackson, detailed from an engineer unit, would save the day. He built crossing points so vehicles could bridge the canals. He would clear the road; if the road was too muddy and the gun trucks couldn't get through, he'd drive over it with his bulldozer and scoop it out to make the crossing point passable. It appeared that the enemy had used heavy equipment to create the obstructions.

Occupied homes were cleared, the occupants moved, and the owner was paid to use the place. Of course, all the military-age males were gone. A high-level terrorist, a financier, reportedly owned one house that was used as a patrol base. While the search was under way, the women were questioned and reluctant to cooperate. Finally, they were persuaded to disclose where weapons were being hidden. Pistols, rifles and a sniper rifle were uncovered. Several days later, a suspect was found in the cow pen hiding behind bags of grain. He provided some valuable intel that served to pinpoint a large cache. He also admitted to being part of the plot to kidnap the mayor of Balad Ruz.

The battle drills for the canal clearance were modified, since the canal roads had begun to collapse under the weight of the gun trucks. Previous clearance operations had found the gun trucks riding alongside and close to the edge of the canal. Integrating ground and air assets for this dismounted fight to clear the canals had to be calculated to avoid any "blue on blue" or fratricide, injuring friendly troops by friendly fire. Most of the enemy fighters had established fighting positions in the canal system with the thought that they could have free movement using the canals. Unbeknownst to them, Headhunter had the canals isolated thus denying the insurgents the ability to move internally through the canals.

Throughout the day enemy squad-sized elements, numbering as many as 12 in one engagement, continued to maneuver to the north and west of Turki Village on the Alpha Troop patrol base and blocking positions. They were dressed in black *dishdas*, an ankle length robe, carrying Kalashnikov rifles and using Motorola radios to communicate. They feigned surrender and continued to move equipment and maneuver on the patrol base. Eventually, they attempted to escape that night. Each time, the enemy probes were met with withering fire from coalition forces and each time more of the enemy were killed.

Enemy activity continued in and around Turki Village. Surveillance indicated that the center sector under the control of Bravo Troop was becoming the gathering point for enemy forces across the front. Bravo engaged and killed two enemy fighters who were serving as a listening/observation post. Numerous secondary explosions indicated that enemy strong points had been destroyed. In addition to these indicators, Charlie Troop's presence in 30 Tamooz along with numerous firefights by Alpha Troop indicated that Bravo was going to face the enemy in the final phase of the operation.

Headhunter was primed and ready to begin the fight to clear Turki Village. The rehearsals had been conducted to ensure that the Iraqis and Americans were completely in sync for the deliberate clearance of all canals and villages. Throughout the day, the enemy continued to probe the cordon while preparing their defensive positions. Indirect fires from artillery and mortars detonated weapons caches that the insurgents were attempting to get their hands on.

The rain continued for several days before conditions began to improve. Headhunter was entering a window to accomplish this clearance before the next weather front moved into the area. As the battle plan was generated, it was clear that the Iraqi army would be the main force of the Turki Village clearance. They went in first riding Abrams tanks after having rehearsed the techniques for safely riding them. To make sure that everything went according to plan, Lieutenant Anderson along with two of his paratroopers dismounted and accompanied the Iraqi forces. Two platoons from 5-73 would clear the flanks of the village.

Dirt-poor farmers living in mud houses gave up without a fight. The villagers were shrewd. The paratroopers got to one house and the entire town was surrendering. So now, when any more weapons were discovered in the other houses, no one could be detained for it because there wasn't any way to know who owned the place. The military lawyers wanted to pretend that this was some cop drama and that there was a 30-day window to do an investigation. In one instance, rocket-propelled grenades were uncovered at a villager's home and he was detained. When 5-73 tried to pursue prosecuting the suspect, the military lawyer raised the question, "How do you know he was intending to use them?" In utter amazement, one of the paratroopers sarcastically responded with, "You do know it's a rocket-propelled grenade and this is a war, right?"

In another house the paratroopers found a false room that contained food, cooking supplies, bandages, ammunition, a camera, a stack of porn and a box of Miagra, which is a variant of Viagra. In another place that was in the middle of nowhere a mud hut was searched. There was a weight bench, punching bag and a speed bag in it along with a training room that appeared to be used to learn the basics of constructing and emplacing explosives. Even a chalkboard had drawings on it showing details of IED placement along with rations and cooking materials that had been recently used.

These findings corroborated earlier intelligence that enemy fighters had come to the region to train and used these small shacks as a base of operations. Extremist propaganda materials and grenades hidden in cow pens were also discovered, as were large quantities of weapons including rocket-propelled grenades, machine guns, armor-piercing rounds, mortar rounds and a mortar tube. Motorcycles along with an SUV with bulletproof glass were also uncovered.

As the clearance teams moved through the village, they came across one house that had a white surrender flag on it. Alpha and Bravo Troops began to see enemy fighters putting an individual on another building with a white flag. During Turki Bowl I, an individual had faked surrender while the machine-gun position behind him prepared to engage coalition forces. This time, instead of maneuvering up to this position both Alpha and Bravo Troops began to scan the area around the flag. Alpha Troop found two enemy observation posts in the vicinity where armed insurgents were in fighting positions. To eliminate the threat, Alpha Troop called indirect fire on these positions in the palm grove. The jihadist with the flag fled with other enemy fighters into a nearby building.

The clearance team sent in to search the building found 25 military-age males sitting on the floor with their hands behind their heads. They represented a mixture of leadership and foot soldiers in the Council. They were directly responsible for the Shia massacres across this area along with enemy attacks on the Imam Monsoor checkpoint. Cellphone video was discovered showing Al Qaeda fighters dragging civilians into the canals and executing them. The awesome power of the assault had so severely shaken the will of these enemy fighters that they could not bring themselves to resist any further.

The detainees were moved outside so the building could be cleared. Once the evidence, hidden weapons, and documents were removed, the detainees were moved into a large prayer room. They were provided with blankets and a heater. The priority was to ensure the safety of the paratroopers first and the prisoners' comfort second. The suspects claimed that they had been mistreated. Out of all the suspects all but two of them were prosecuted. These two were released because they were considered too young, although they were the sons of insurgents. It was believed that they would be running the insurgency in the future.

The paratrooper who conducted the tactical questioning responded to the allegations of mistreatment asserting that:

> [T]hese men are liars. They lied throughout their questioning. They said they had no idea who two of the detainees were and that they had never seen them. Later I found they were first cousins with them on their mother's side. They said their father was dead. I met him in Turki, and he is now claiming to be the village elder and is implicated in a report as having close ties to Abdul Rahkman, another terrorist leader. Weapons were found in their homes, they claimed they had never seen them. Their entire credibility can be disputed by the lies they have amassed. Several men from this group (most of them brothers) mocked our system and were confident in their detention.[1]

One man stated that he grew tired of the line of questioning that was being used to prove he was an enemy fighter. All the suspects seemed to believe that they would be released within 72 hours.

All the detainees had the same story: "We are simple farmers." "There are no terrorists in this area." When evidence was presented to the contrary, they denied any knowledge of it. Some claimed they had medical issues. Medical personnel examined them. Only one detainee appeared to have a legitimate health concern, and medicine was administered to treat it. The detainee attempted to overdose on it.

In an effort to deny any evidence of their crimes, the insurgents had attempted to destroy an Al Qaeda training manual along with related videos that provided tactics, techniques, and procedures for all aspects of enemy operations along with ways to resist or respond to questioning if captured: you should "claim the Americans abused you and here are some ways you can fake marks on your body so that people will think you were abused." These men were obviously trained to resist questioning.

They used several methods listed in the manual. There is a section devoted to how to effectively deal with our inadequate detainee process and the flaws with our prosecution. On pages 173–4 there are instructions on how to get out of anything you have accidentally given up:

> He should deny all information about him by the prosecution representative. He should claim that the interrogation apparatus has fabricated those accusations and should deny his connection to anything obtained against him.
> Once in the prosecution center, however, he should say that he was tortured, deny all his prior confessions, and ask that the interrogation be repeated.
> He should... ask that evidence of his torture be entered in the report proceedings.[2]

Also listed as common types of physical torture were the use of pliers on fingers/hands and the use of sticks striking the back.

As their minor injuries were evaluated, it was obvious that these small bruises were as a result of artillery fire because they were enemy insurgents who were taking cover from the indirect fire during military operations. These fighters were Wahhabists. One of the enemy detainees "implicated the group in the murders of Shias and the mortar attacks on the Imam Monsour checkpoint." The evidence resulted in the recommendation to hold them over for trial charged with "crimes against humanity."[3]

After 13 years of Al-Qaeda domination it was going to take months if not years to help stabilize this region. Aggressive adjudication would be the first stage. Rapport with the villagers helped ensure that the Wahhabists didn't gain another foothold in this region and that Sunnis and Shia could work towards peaceful co-existence. The mayor of Balad Ruz and the city council committed to bringing this formerly lawless region under their care, protection, and influence.

While Alpha, Charlie and Delta Troops continued to capture suspected enemy fighters and find enemy weapons, Bravo Troop along with an Iraqi army company was given the job of establishing the Turki patrol base they would defiantly name Molon Labe, "Come and Take Them." This was to be classic counterinsurgency doctrine; clear, hold, build. Captain Dobbins, Bravo Troop's commanding officer, assessed that it would "take many more of these meetings and some projects in the area to build the trust to a point where they feel free to share intelligence on the activities of the Council members that may still be in the area."

Bravo Troop's First Sergeant, Mike Clemens, observed that "we established a patrol base just outside Turki Village itself, a company patrol base, which at the time was pretty avant-garde," prior to the Surge. The Surge was President Bush's decision to deploy additional Army and Marine troops to Iraq in January, 2007 "to help restore security and to provide the nascent Iraqi government with the breathing space necessary to secure itself."[4] Continuous patrolling would "keep this thing from spinning up again."[5]

The original patrol base location that was being considered was inside Turki Village. Force protection, making sure they would be safe from attack, wouldn't have been possible. Clemens noted that, "There wasn't any standoff. There wasn't any visual on any of the approaches." A couple of buildings just outside Turki provided good line of sight and the necessary standoff distance. Bravo made a deal with the owner to rent the property. Another suitable place was found for him to live and a final deal was reached after some bargaining. You had to finesse it. Clemens made sure that: "We paid him every month. The canals were kept open as much as we could to let the water go through to his fields and we allowed him to come back to work them."[6]

The base was built from the ground up. The various sleeping spaces were earmarked. The dirt- and rock-filled HESCO barriers were brought in. It took almost two weeks to erect, fill with dirt, and deploy the seven-foot-tall collapsible canvas and wire containers. They were able to provide protection from small-arms fire and rocket-propelled grenades as well as the detonation of car bombs. Triple-strand concertina wire surrounded the perimeter.

Prepared fighting positions were established on the edge as well as at various points within the base. Bunkers were necessary in the event of a rocket or mortar attack. Serpentine points using jersey barriers forced approaching vehicles to reduce their speed or risk colliding with the concrete walls. Sandbags were filled and guard towers were placed on top of the buildings. The building had a nice wall around it. There was a lot of farmland so a front-end loader was brought in and flattened it down to improve fields of fire. Chainsaw-wielding work details were assigned to cut down trees to further ensure a clear line of sight. One platoon was working on building up the patrol base, one platoon was on security and patrols and the other platoons were on refit, and that's how Bravo Troop rotated for weeks until the base was constructed.

While the initial steps were being taken to provide a long-term coalition presence in and around Turki, there was also a personnel matter that had to be addressed. Major Rather looked at Sergeant Willie Lillie in utter amazement as he stood in doorway.

"What the fuck are you doing here?" Rather exclaimed.

Lillie had returned after being wounded during Turki Bowl I. He still had open wounds on his arm and his head wounds were still scabbed up. Lillie recalled that "if you would have ripped one of the scabs off of my head at this point, there would be a hole there."

Major Rather looked at his ears and gave him the once over.

"You're going to see me once a week and you're not leaving [the patrol base]," Rather ordered.[7]

Lillie's ears had been completely perforated, two holes in each ear. Despite the admonishment by Doc Rather, Lillie was glad he had returned to support his guys. After all, they were his second family. Lillie remembered that "their spirits were lifted to see me back."

In the meantime, Willie's wife was pissed.

"What do you mean they're not sending you home? Tell them the truth, tell them that you can't hear good and all that stuff," his wife insisted.

If the doctors really wanted to, they could have sent Lillie to Germany. But he had the doctors convinced that he would heal quickly and be able to return to the fight. As Willie remembered, "Yeah, but my wife, she was not happy to say the least."

It wasn't long before Sergeant Lillie had connived his way into going through the wire and patrolling. He assured Rather that he would wear earplugs and a Peltor headset to protect his damaged ears. After about week seven his head wounds were closed which allowed him to wear a helmet. The injury to his arm was really tender. Lillie admitted that "it hurt for me to pick up my body armor and put it on, it was bad. Now thinking back on it that was stupid, but I did it."[8]

Turki was secured. Some of the Council leadership had been captured or killed along with many enemy fighters. Now it was time to prove to the people of Turki that their peace and security could become a reality. Major Sylvia observed that "their will to fight had been broken." Sylvia said that this operation had "forced the enemy to fight a linear fight against us and lost. We forced them to come out against our strengths" and the insurgents were defeated.[9]

CHAPTER 14

Operation 300

Following Turki Bowl II, Charlie Troop had gone back up to Khanaqin on the Iranian border to continue their mission with the border authorities. Alpha Troop pushed a bit further to the west to control some of the routes that were feeders into the Turki area so they could bypass routes already patrolled. They moved into another town halfway between Turki and Baqubah, half Sunni and half Shia. One week later, they got a change of mission and went back to the Diyala River Valley.

The unexpected change of mission tasked by a higher headquarters was given to 5-73 to move into the Diyala River Valley to disrupt the lines of communication of Al Qaeda in Iraq between Muqdadiyah and Baqubah. The mission called for a squadron command and control, two troops, and one infantry company to assume additional battlespace for 30 days beginning on February 26, 2007.

While needing to provide the required level of force for the Diyala mission, named Operation 300, the squadron had to simultaneously maintain a presence in the Headhunter area of operations. A revised task organization for the squadron kept Bravo Troop there, continuing to work with the Iraqi army to transition the Turki base to the Iraqis. Alpha and Charlie Troops relocated to the Gadsden area of operations, becoming Task Force 300.

The lack of a coalition presence had allowed the enemy to turn the area between Muqdadiyah and Baqubah into a sanctuary. Weapons caches had been established. Sunni extremists had forced all the Shia families up and down the valley out of their homes. The terrorists of Al Qaeda in Iraq were determined to exterminate anyone who got in their way and dominate this region. The densely vegetated palm grove terrain along the Diyala River was being used as an enemy training area. There appeared to be a well-worn path heading south to Baqubah. The main supply route, known as Blue Babe, was laced with IEDs. These explosives were a constant source of danger to convoys.

Consequently, there was a significant increase in instability throughout Baqubah, preventing coalition forces from successfully conducting clearing and holding

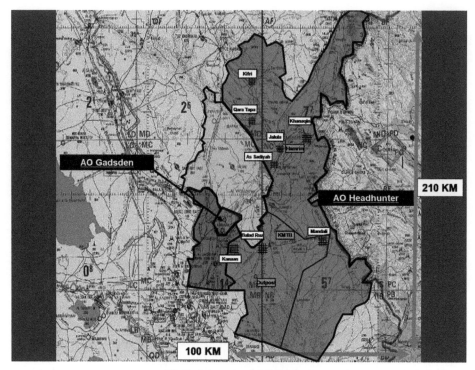

AO Gadsden map (Nick Bajema)

operations. Al Qaeda in Iraq had signaled its intent to establish an Islamic caliphate. Diyala Province, specifically Baqubah, was going to be the initial extremist capital. The task of disrupting Sunni insurgent activity and the logistical network sustaining them was given to 5-73. In turn, 5-73 translated this task into a clearance of the Al Qaeda haven in the Diyala River Valley.

The intent of Operation 300 was to eventually turn over the responsibility of this area of operations to the Iraqi army and police forces after establishing permanent patrol bases as well as identifying and destroying insurgent leadership, caches and safe havens. The end-state for this operation was ultimately denying the Diyala River Valley to the Al Qaeda terrorists, as well as ensuring that convoys could travel safely on Route Blue Babe.

With its heavy vegetation on both sides of the roads and jungle-like palm groves the terrain reminded many of pictures they had seen of the jungles of Vietnam, lush and so thick you could barely see a few steps to your front. There seemed to be plenty of places for the enemy to initiate an ambush. Dense undergrowth with bushes, vines, briars and grasses along with trees that restricted field of vision made it difficult to use fire crew-served weapons, including mortars and trapped signal smoke, and made casualty extraction and air medevac extremely challenging.

The move back to Diyala left squadron leaders with a sense of frustration. The region was bordered on either side by two other cavalry units. Why not let them handle it? Poppas and his staff believed the training of the Iraqi forces in the Headhunter area of operations was the priority. Since there was an interesting historical parallel with the unnecessary land grab that had taken place leading up to the Gadsden Purchase in 1854, the new area of operations would carry the same name. The jab at the decision sealed the name Gadsden.[1]

The Headhunter area of operations, which was located in and around Turki, would have to be built back up by Bravo Troop, which placed a further strain on available forces needed to clear each of the villages in the Diyala. It seemed completely preposterous that they were going to be holding such a large area with eight platoons.

Placing a further strain on how many of the squadron's paratroopers could be committed to this operation, Alpha Troop's mortars along with the fire support officer Andy Hercik were assigned to a security detail for a Military Transition Team. Alpha Troop's 2nd Platoon was handling a Provisional Reconstruction Team security mission.

Before a campaign plan could be formulated "the intelligence picture needed to be built."[2] Alpha Troop had spent the first three months in Diyala in the reconnaissance role. They put packets together to brief the rest of the squadron. Alpha Troop's interpreter was from Zaganiyah and he was able to give an update as to what had been taking place since they had left.

The missions began with a recon of several routes in and out of the area. No one had been there in a long time so there was a whole set of intelligence requirements that needed to be determined. Where were the likely points of enemy contact? Where were the various police and army units? Which ones were willing to operate in the area? What was the general disposition of locals?

As the situational awareness picture was sharpened, the fire support plan began to take shape. Staring intently at the high-resolution imagery spread before him, Captain Andy Hercik, the squadron's fire support officer, mentally reminded himself that the goal of lethal fires was to "shape the battle for maneuver, set them up for success and in turn facilitate the killing and or capturing the enemy in the objective area." Hercik was adamant about using lethal fires to deny the enemy their terrain by fire. Even though the contemporary operating environment of counterinsurgency in Iraq depended on precision fires using coordinate bombing and GPS-guided artillery rounds, Hercik noted that "attacking a trail so the enemy couldn't use it was definitely outside the fire support norm for the Iraq theater of operations."[3]

Andy knew that tubed artillery couldn't always reach Headhunter in the Diyala River Valley. He could only depend on what was organic to the squadron, the 81mm and 120mm mortars that were part of Alpha and Bravo Troops along with Charlie Troop's 60mm mortars. There was limited attack aviation and air support because they were in what was termed a "benign area," miles away from anybody.

Asking for close air support or Apache air weapons teams each night routinely received the "request denied" stamp from higher authority. Part of the game would be how the request was sold. Hercik was from the old acetate-overlay-and-marker generation. During the train-up for Iraq, Hercik first learned that it was all about digital files prepared from PowerPoint. Brett Sylvia began to school Andy in the art of the PowerPoint brief. According to Hercik, Sylvia "broke my chops" in order to give him the finer points of how to sell his plan.[4] It was a skill that was most useful as Hercik's fire plans became such a critical piece of the Diyala fight.

CHAPTER 15

Marathon

The background that Alpha Troop had provided was the first step in the intelligence preparation of the battlespace. In Brett Sylvia's effort to keep the Ancient Greek heritage to the operational forefront, the first operation would be named Marathon. A series of zone and area reconnaissance missions were to be conducted. In order to develop a campaign plan for the Diyala River Valley detailed information concerning all routes, obstacles, terrain, and enemy forces had to be found. Al Qaeda, Sunni and Shia extremists had all had free rein in Diyala since Alpha Troop had left back in November. Operation Marathon was the first operation conducted by Task Force 300 to further degrade Al Qaeda.

Alpha Troop worked the western and northern portion of the battlespace. They stayed on the west side of the river and worked to the east. Several IEDs were discovered. Charlie Troop had the eastern and southern portion of it. They linked up with an Iraqi army outfit at a small base in a town called Al Abarrah. The Diyala River snaked its way through the center. Charlie Troop started to recon south from that Iraqi base. They began making heavy enemy contact as they moved to the south towards a place called As Sadah. It was telling of what was to come.

One of these 24-hour missions was being run by a four-truck platoon-size reconnaissance element moving down the canal road between Zaganiyah and As Sadah. The patrol's assignment was to watch a dangerous stretch of road in the hope of catching insurgents placing IEDs. The paratroopers had been out all night and had captured several insurgents. On the way back to the patrol base, the patrol took a detour to observe a nearby town that was supposedly controlled by Al Qaeda.

On the outskirts of town, the lead truck got stuck in a mud hole and began to sink. Doctor Larry Robinson, "Doc Rob", the squadron surgeon, was riding in the right rear seat. Doc Rob observed angry villagers approaching the column armed with Kalashnikov assault rifles and a few rocket-propelled grenades. The .50-caliber machine gun turret on the lead truck had malfunctioned and wouldn't swivel. The gun truck was pulled clear and the decision was made to report and disengage rather than confront this group of unknown belligerents.

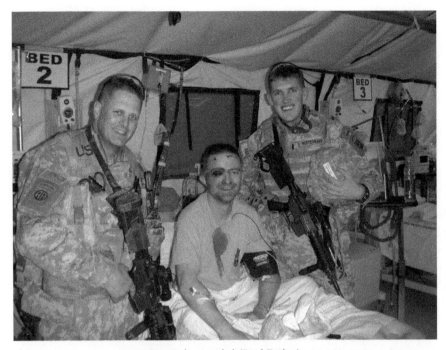

Doc Rob wounded (Brad Rather)

Doc Rob's helmet (Brad Rather)

At this point, the column was on a hard-packed road with a canal approximately 30 feet wide by 10 feet deep paralleling the road and an eight-foot chain link fence on the opposite side. The patrol was boxed in.

The situation suddenly and drastically changed.

A command-detonated explosive built into the berm of the canal detonated, sending shrapnel sideways into the lead gun truck. Doc Rob's position received the brunt of the force. Shrapnel struck his helmet and immediately rendered him unconscious. The truck had been torn open by the explosion, and there were several large holes in the truck skin. The entire right side of the truck was blackened, the rear tire was flat, and the cargo compartment appeared to be on fire. Larry was quickly removed and laid in front of the gun truck. The right side of his face was covered in blood. He was now conscious but had an altered mental state.

Andrew Harriman, the medic assigned to the patrol, rushed forward and began to perform a patient assessment. He wasn't aware that Doc Rob was on the patrol and thought that Doc Rob should be notified of the casualty and his condition. He looked at his patient's body armor and saw captain bars. It wasn't until he checked his nametape that he realized that it was Larry Robinson. The head injury dictated immediate casualty evacuation. However, due to the restricted terrain and imminent threat of a follow-on attack by the enemy, the only choice was to turn the column around and retrace their path. Unable to fit him on a backboard, which would have been the optimum way to transport him, Larry was moved to one of the other trucks for the trip back to the base.

As Larry was carried into the treatment area, his facial expression told part of the story: he was in excruciating pain. The other telltale sign of intracranial pressure or brain bleed was the condition of his helmet. The right side had been torn open, exposing and dislodging the Kevlar fibers that make up the dense protective layers. The helmet had literally saved his life. He was quickly flown to Camp Anaconda, Balad, for treatment.

The shrapnel had caused several comminuted fractures of Larry's skull along with facial bone fractures and epidural, subarachnoid and subdural hemorrhages. The increasing intracranial pressure from the bleeding inside his skull caused extreme nausea and unrelenting vomiting. The pain and confusion made Doc Rob's condition increasingly unbearable for him.

Lieutenant Colonel Poppas and the squadron physician assistant Major Rather along with a few other friends from the squadron arrived to check on him. When they explained what had taken place and how severely he'd been injured, Doc Rob couldn't believe it.

"Let me see that CT scan," he demanded.[1]

The Purple Heart was pinned to his hospital shirt and Doc Rob joked that it wasn't the medal he had envisioned receiving for his service in Iraq. Rather and Doc Rob had often referred to the Purple Heart as the "Iraqi Marksmanship Badge."

Evacuation and surgery in Landstuhl, Germany soon followed. A craniotomy with evacuation of the epidural hematoma along with cranioplasty to stabilize the fractures was performed.

As Emily Robinson, Larry's wife, hurried through her morning routine to get to work, the ringing of the phone startled her. The voice on the other end was distant, official sounding, and unknown. The rear detachment commander at Fort Bragg was delivering the dreadful news that Larry had been wounded. Stunned and horrified, she passed the phone to her dad. As he got the details the look on his face gave definition to the gravity of the situation. Hearing skull fracture had brought Emily to tears at the thought of Larry being so grievously injured.

Praying with family members, Emily sat painfully spellbound by the message, "Larry had sustained a skull fracture and they'd call us when they had more information." An eternity later, the phone rang, and Larry was on the other end. With slurred speech, he reassured Emily that he was going to be OK and that he loved her.

Four days following the surgery, Doc Rob was transferred to the National Naval Medical Center in Bethesda, Maryland, to continue his recovery. When Emily finally got to see him 67 surgical staples were holding Larry's scalp together. Both eyes were blackened as a result of the fractures to his face as well as the head injury and one eye was blood red. Despite his frightening appearance, Emily was thrilled beyond words to see him alive. The recovery process was to be a long one and included bouts of horrible nightmares where Larry perceived that the nurses were trying to kill him. He recovered from his injuries, returned to civilian life and is currently practicing medicine.

Enemy weapons cache during Turki Bowl I (Marc Adams)

Conducting house-to-house searches during Turki Bowl II (Sergeant Armando Monroig)

Larry "Doc Rob" Robinson sustained serious injuries following an IED detonation (Brad Rather)

Delta Troop crossing the Diyala River (Doug Yates)

Evacuating wounded soldiers during Operation Minotaur (Staff Sergeant JoAnn Makinano)

Sniper and spotter working (Matt Guza)

Air assault (John Ferrante)

An explosive ordnance disposal technician preparing to make an entry (Craig Honbarger)

Charlie Troop members performing building searches during Operation Minotaur (Staff Sergeant JoAnn Makinano)

Staff Sergeant Geriah McAvin searches a spider hole during Operation Minotaur at Qubbah, Iraq, March 24, 2007 (Staff Sergeant JoAnn Makinano)

Members of 5-73 working feverishly to rescue their fellow paratroopers after the double vehicle-borne IED detonation at the As Sadah patrol base on April 23, 2007 (Zach Carpino)

Memorial service for the nine 5-73 paratroopers who were killed in As Sadah (Zach Carpino)

Sergeant Christopher Harmon, Bravo Troop, 5-73 CAV, executes a shotgun breach of a door lock during house-by-house clearance, Operation Pericles (Sergeant Angela Widener)

Bravo Troop react to contact during Operation Ithaca, August 12, 2007 (Senior Airman Chalanda Roberts)

Restraining and searching a detainee following a brief engagement (Senior Airman Chalanda Roberts)

Bravo Troop documents injuries to an Iraqi civilian who had been held and tortured by insurgents, August 12, 2007 (Senior Airman Chalanda Roberts)

CHAPTER 16

Troy

Charlie Troop was getting ready to make As Sadah their new home. After only two days back on the Iraq–Iran border in Khanaqin with the continuing mission to train the border guards and assist with curtailing the smuggling from Iran, word had come down to return to Warhorse. Captain Carson was handing over command and returning to Fort Bragg as the rear detachment commander. The new boss would be Captain Jesse Stewart. Stewart had done his platoon time with the 82nd in Afghanistan and had been serving as Headhunter's assistant S3 Operations. This was also about the same time that General David Petraeus assumed command of operations in Iraq bringing with him the counterinsurgency strategy. This was nothing new to 5-73 CAV. Headhunter had been pressing ahead with this approach since Alpha Troop had been in Zaganiyah back in October 2006.

The second operation conducted by Task Force 300 would be Operation Troy. Al Qaeda had been identified as having a stronghold in the town of As Sadah, allowing enemy IED cells to proliferate along Route Blue Babe. Nearly every day this extremely well organized Al Qaeda cell attacked combat logistics patrols travelling this route.

The task for this mission was to seize As Sadah, in order to destroy enemy safe havens and cache locations, reestablish a legitimate authority, and provide a secure and stable environment for the townspeople. By separating the insurgents from the populace of As Sadah, friendly forces would be afforded freedom to maneuver in the town.

Known as "the gateway to the Diyala River Valley," As Sadah would be key to ridding Diyala Province of Al Qaeda. Initially, Charlie Troop's plan was to locate the mukhtar, and begin an area reconnaissance of the village. There was a small Iraqi army outpost right on the southern edge of the Diyala that would be used as a temporary patrol base. Stewart and Charlie Troop conducted a link-up with them. Accompanied by the Iraqi army commander, a mounted patrol set out to recon the immediate area. Before they could get back

Operation Troy (Richie Donely)

to the patrol base three improvised explosive devices had been emplaced along the route after they had passed.

Several days before the plan was put in motion, Stewart got some additional intelligence. A buddy with special operations provided a reality check.

"You are crazy if you think that'll work. You'll get blasted by IEDs, and every military-age male will move into the palm groves and open fire on you," Stewart's friend warned.[1]

A Special Forces team had run into a firefight with 40 to 50 enemy fighters while on an earlier mission in As Sadah. They'd engaged in a running gun battle that showed that the enemy was tough, organized, and well established. Following the firefight, a drone flew over the area that night and observed insurgents dressed in hoods and black pajama-style clothing moving in a tactical formation patrolling the area. When the enemy detected the drone, they broke off into squads. This was going to be a tough fight.

The original 5-73 plan was scrapped. Reconnaissance and surveillance teams would establish observation posts at various points in an effort to find and fix the enemy. The teams were also expected to counter attempts by the enemy to maneuver or escape. It was anticipated that the insurgents would use the palm groves since these provided good cover and concealment. The teams comprised a team leader (section sergeant), three soldiers, and a medic who under the cover of darkness would enter the palm groves and set up hide sites to pinpoint the enemy fighters who were using the palm groves for training and placing weapons caches. Undetected teams could be out for 36 or more hours before being relieved. They carried food, water and ammunition for the duration.

A mission brief or fragmentation order was issued and included what the team was doing, what to look for, intelligence requirements of the commander, the rules of engagement if compromised, and maneuvering to a secondary location so eyes on the original objective could be maintained. If compromised, the team would call in air support or a drone to determine if the enemy was maneuvering on them. Primary and secondary routes of escape had to be identified if the team made contact and needed to leave the site quickly. Recon teams were inserted on foot from an Iraqi patrol base. Occasionally, they would dismount from gun trucks, check for buried explosives, enter the palm grove and then a portion of the dismounts would return to the gun trucks leaving the recon team in place.

Visibility with night vision goggles was extremely limited due to the heavy foliage canopy in the palm groves. These groves were shaped like a maze with walls and vegetation so dense that it was difficult to obtain a GPS signal until reaching a clearing. There were trails throughout that were bordered by walls 10 to 15 feet high and a foot thick. Doors were placed to allow farmers to enter the orchards and tend their crops. There was also a canal that provided irrigation water. The canopy was so thick that there were instances when Apache gunship crews could not see the signal smoke due to the overhead vegetation trapping it.

One of the first teams inserted reached their position just before daylight. It was imperative to conceal the hide site before first light. Gunfire from an unknown direction and distance added to the tension. Then a farmer and his wife stumbled on the recon team. Dropping her fruit basket, the woman ran off screaming with her husband following close behind. The team had to move quickly. As they maneuvered towards their secondary site, the team came upon and quickly detained three insurgents armed with Kalashnikov rifles who were removing rocket-propelled grenades from a weapons cache.

Having linked up with the rest of the platoon, the recon team maneuvered towards the gun trucks that were going to transport the detainees. A two-story house, with the windows covered with blankets, came into view. It gave everyone an uneasy feeling. One of the detainees suddenly stopped, fear etched on his face. As the paratroopers moved around the front, an insurgent suddenly appeared clad in a black hood and tactical vest, chambering a round in his Kalashnikov rifle as he ran out the door.

Accurate rifle fire instantly killed the enemy fighter. The entry team threw grenades into the building before entering to kill any remaining insurgents. Ultimately, two more enemy fighters were captured. Antiaircraft rockets and triggers that led to IEDs were found in the house as well as on the roof. One of the enemy fighters was a sniper who had been active in the area and was on the wanted list.

After turning the prisoners over, the recon team moved back into the palm groves and established a circular patrol base. As several members were allowed to grab a few minutes' rest, the other members took up defensive positions to protect against enemy attack. Instantaneously, the chatter of machine-gun fire broke the morning calm. Enemy fighters had been observed moving towards them.

"They're flanking us," shouted the team leader.

Indirect fire support from the troop mortars was called for and suppressive fire from the team continued.

"We've got to get the hell out of here," the team leader ordered.[2]

As mortar fire began to land, the team disengaged and moved towards the Iraqi army compound located on the northern edge of As Sadah.

The decision was made by command for the team to remain in the palm groves. As they paused to reconnoiter the area, eight more enemy fighters were observed. Flares were requested to light up the area. The goal was to startle and disperse the enemy patrol due to the concern that the paratroopers might not have enough firepower to overwhelm and destroy the insurgents.

A bone-chilling rain fell steadily all night long. The paratroopers were resorting to using extra socks to warm their hands. They were running out of rations. Food like summer sausage and protein drinks had already been consumed hours earlier. As the sun rose, the recon team slowly and deliberately moved through the rows of fruit trees and vegetable beds.

During a stop to clean their weapons, the decision was made to send out a small patrol a short distance so early warning of any enemy threats could be given. The patrol had been out only minutes when automatic-weapons fire caught their attention. They quickly circled around and found the rest of the team engaged in a firefight. Insurgents armed with Kalashnikov rifles and grenades had been caught by surprise walking through a palm grove gate. The brief gunfight had killed one of the enemy fighters outright and forced the others to retreat. A substantial blood trail found a short distance out was a sure sign that at least one more of the enemy had been hit.

After being out in a hide site for several days, recon teams needed to be either resupplied or relieved. Lying in a rural surface site meant being covered up with vegetation in a heavy canopy and jungle-like foliage, which created an extremely limited field of vision of no more than three to four feet. This meant that intruders could be virtually on top of the team before they were detected. Team members were unable to stand, had to relieve bladder and bowel with the minimal amount of movement, and were in constant danger of being discovered by the enemy. If they were lucky, a team could use an abandoned building. First, though, these urban sites would have to be cleared to ensure that the building was not occupied by the enemy or booby-trapped. Once inside, the structure provided protection from the elements and allowed for some freedom of movement.

Sergeant Geriah McAvin was leading such a patrol charged with placing ground sensors that could detect enemy movements and relieving a team that had been out for several days. The pace man indicated they were within a couple of hundred meters of reaching the site. He was responsible for keeping the patrol on the correct heading. Suddenly, movement was observed just as the team was reaching the edge of the palm groves. McAvin signaled a halt and contacted the Iraqi police to determine if they had personnel outside the wire, patrolling the area.

"Red 5 Romeo [the patrol] to Red 1 [platoon leader] in contact! Man down!"[3]

The sounds of small-arms fire could be heard in the background. Red 1 (Lieutenant Bajema, platoon leader) acknowledged and Charlie 6 (Captain Stewart) was monitoring as events unfolded. Deadly bursts of small-arms fire shattered the night stillness. The ambush site appeared to be a choke point, a narrow space that limited movement. There was a canal on the right, a wall on the left, and a dirt road on the other side of the canal. It was just shy of where the team had planned to enter the palm groves, north of As Sadah. Turning left and walking a short distance would have put the team in the palm groves.

McAvin immediately signaled the team to shift to the wall, which provided some cover from the enemy fire. The quick reaction force was alerted and began moving towards the firefight. Carrying a squad assault weapon, Private First Class Dary Finck was covering Sergeant Tim Cole who was on point. Finck was immediately struck by enemy fire coming from a building directly to their front. Multiple rounds tore into Finck's buttocks, scrotum, urethra, pelvis and legs. Both of his femoral arteries were severed, causing life-threatening bleeding.

Specialist Harriman, the medic assigned to the team, immediately moved forward to treat Finck. Dragging his 80-pound medical bag and rifle, Harriman crawled about 30 meters to reach the wounded soldier. Due to the ever-increasing intensity of the enemy fire, Harriman was forced to treat Finck while lying on the ground. Harriman's aid bag had absorbed multiple enemy rounds, destroying much of his equipment. A rapid assessment revealed major trauma to both of Finck's legs. Harriman placed three tourniquets on the gravely wounded paratrooper's right leg before the bleeding was controlled.

The hemorrhaging left leg was controlled by using a cloth cravat, feeding through Finck's belt and then looping the makeshift tourniquet through his groin, pulling it up on the backside and cinching it down. After the bleeding was controlled, Harriman inserted an intraosseous device, forcefully placing a needle through Finck's sternum so intravenous fluid could be pushed to deal with the large amount of blood loss. Finck also got some morphine to deal with his extreme pain.

Attempts by other team members to reach Finck were stopped by the enemy along with fire coming from their rear. The team had maneuvered to the south to suppress enemy fire. Gunfire was also coming from the Iraqi police who mistakenly believed that the patrol was the enemy. The police station had been attacked earlier in the day but the team had been unaware of this, so they had unknowingly walked into a deadly trap.

Having reached Finck and Harriman, McAvin began moving Finck to safety while Harriman continued to care for him. All three were flat on the ground and crawling due to the intense enemy small-arms fire snapping perilously close to their bodies. Sergeant Tim Cole moved forward to help bring Finck to the cover that the wall provided. Once under cover, Lieutenant Bajema, who had arrived with reinforcements, transmitted a medevac report detailing Finck's condition and the need for aerial evacuation. The helicopter was dispatched to rendezvous with the team back at the Iraqi outpost.

The reaction force got the Iraqi police to cease firing and simultaneously began laying down suppressive fire on the enemy position with the large-caliber rounds from the gun trucks' machine guns.

Finck had to reach the trauma docs as quickly as possible. Even with the rapid aid administered it was impossible to tell how much blood he had lost and if the bleeding had been completely controlled. Harriman had his doubts that Finck would survive without immediately extracting him. Unable to lay him down in a Humvee, the decision was made to commandeer a Toyota pickup truck to transport him. The wounded paratrooper was placed in the truck bed and the roughly four-mile ride through the enemy-infested area began.

They reached the outpost to find that the inbound medevac helicopter was seven minutes out.

"He's not going to make it, there's no way in seven minutes," Harriman insisted.[4] Fortunately, two minutes later the Black Hawk landed, and Finck was quickly turned over to the flight crew.

Writhing in pain, Finck was losing control of his motor functions due to blood loss and the accompanying shock. Finck recalled that, "I couldn't control my arms. One of the door gunners reached over and was grabbing my arms to hold on to me."[5] As he struggled to breathe, a panic state was setting in, causing the convulsive movements. When the medevac bird landed, Finck felt as if the short flight had taken an eternity. He was quickly wheeled into the emergency room and the trauma team began to rapidly assess, treat and move him to the operating room.

Dary Finck was to survive his ordeal and while recovering at Walter Reed Medical Center he got married. He and his wife started a family and Dary became a small commercial plane pilot.

The main assault on As Sadah began knowing that the enemy was dug in and well armed. A squadron-level cordon search of the village was conducted bringing elements in by both ground and air assault. To trap enemy fighters and stop any attempts to flee further north, fighter aircraft destroyed the road at the north end of As Sadah. Covert teams were placed to the north and east while to the west teams remained to ensure that escape wasn't possible. The air force dropped several 2,000-pound bombs at road intersections. The two main roads that led out of town to the north had to be rendered impassable so the enemy would not attempt to escape by vehicle. The craters that were created by the exploding ordnance were 40 to 50 feet wide, at least 20 or 30 feet deep, and rapidly filled with water.

The assault came from the south, and the town was flooded with tanks followed by gun trucks along with dismounted troops. Each building had to be entered and cleared. For every entry there was the continuous danger of being confronted by an armed insurgent who knew that the entry team had to come through the doorway or that the building had been rigged to explode. If the entry didn't go smoothly, the consequences could be deadly.

An infrared weapon system mounted on one of the gun trucks had eyes on a compound, trying to determine if there was any potential danger. The shadowy figures they observed were guarding the compound, weapons at the ready while others appeared to be digging a hole. The word came down to make the entry. The door of the first building was breached, and instead of the paratroopers moving smoothly through the doorway, everybody got "bogged down in the fatal funnel,"[6] leaving the paratroopers exposed to potentially lethal enemy fire coming from the interior of the building.

"Holy shit, it's not working," shouted the platoon leader, Tye Reedy.[7]

The lieutenant grabbed one of his paratroopers and started clearing rooms. As each room was entered the young platoon leader took the initiative, searching out any potential threats. It wasn't the platoon leader's job, but he made the snap decision to take charge and attempt to unscrew things. His approach had been unorthodox, but it ensured that this kind of cluster fuck wouldn't happen again.

Over 200 houses were cleared, six insurgents were killed and 12 detained. Six weapons caches had been uncovered that included a 60mm mortar tube and a 107mm rocket.

The enemy continued to make every effort to attack the paratroopers by any means possible. Returning to their gun truck following a building clearance, the crew noticed that the ground around the truck seemed to have been disturbed. Further investigation discovered that they had been sitting on an IED. The propane tank packed with three artillery rounds would have created a catastrophic explosion that most certainly would have killed or maimed the entire crew along with anyone close by. It was a sobering moment and a near miss.

After the clearance was completed, a patrol base was established in the center of As Sadah. This allowed Charlie Troop to control all the traffic that came in and out of Diyala and that was the foothold for the squadron as other clearance operations were planned and executed from south to the north up through the Diyala River Valley.

Originally, the patrol base for Charlie Troop had been in the north of As Sadah. The north end of town appeared to be abandoned. Captain Stewart conferred with Poppas and Sylvia on how to proceed. They decided to move closer to the center of town (close to Route Blue Babe) and provide support to most of the inhabitants.

It was all part of winning their hearts and minds. Hold the place and build the relationship. There was a school, an L-shaped structure with a wall surrounding it. There was a mosque to the west of it, a market to the north, a canal on the east side, and on the south side was a vacant lot that was used for a helicopter landing zone. This put Charlie Troop in the center of the village. The goal was to ensure that the villagers were provided with the resources to succeed and to support their leaders. There was a mukhtar in power, a hospital was opened, and weekly meetings between Stewart and the local leaders gave a real sense of hope. The market was beginning to see customers, and people were returning to the mosque.

Patrols went out every few hours and included continued surveillance of the palm groves. The routes were varied to help protect against being ambushed. Route Blue Babe went from nearly daily attacks warranting designation as a Tier 1/highest degree of danger, to having only two IEDs discovered in a subsequent 90-day period. The reduction in the number of hidden explosives didn't eliminate the threat. Receiving information about the location of a particular IED, a patrol was sent out to investigate. Before they realized it, faulty information had put the Joes directly over it. The only reason it didn't detonate was because the radio-controlled detonator battery was dead. The artillery shells were daisy-chained together and would have surely caused heavy losses if they had detonated. Despite efforts to drive the militants out, As Sadah still faced the threat of extremist violence.

CHAPTER 17

Suicide Attack

Each day became increasingly like the one before it. Captain Stewart, Charlie Troop's commanding officer, had the three platoons on a daily rotation of performing dismounted patrols, guard duty and quick reaction force/refit missions. The patrol base force protection consisted of concertina wire strung at the front gate and concrete jersey barriers at the approach. This particular day Lieutenant Nick Bajema was joking with Ben Sebban, the senior medic of the 5-73 CAV medical team attached to Charlie Troop. Their friendly banter centered around the best places to get fish and chips back in the States. Being from Perth Amboy, New Jersey, Ben insisted that his home town had the best while Bajema's loyalty was to Seattle fish and chips.

A close friend of Ben's, Geriah McAvin, was returning from a patrol cycle. One section was back at the Warhorse base for refit so McAvin was pulling double patrol duties. He wanted to make sure that his guys got some chow. It would only take 15 minutes. In the mean time, McAvin went to have a cup of coffee with his buddy, Ben Sebban. Lieutenant Bajema had gone to his gun truck to read. The truck doors were open and Bajema's driver was seated next to him. It was late afternoon, and Joes were milling around, eating chow or going about their duties preparing for the next mission.

"VBIED, VBIED get down!"[1]

The calm was instantly shattered by the shouts of Ben Sebban's warning. A truck laddened with explosives with a suicide driver at the wheel had begun to approach the gate at an increasing rate of speed. Ben's warning had coincided with the roof guards engaging the truck in an attempt to stop it before it did any damage. A gravel pit at the entrance to the base stopped the truck from going any further.

Bajema was no more than 30 meters away from the ensnared attacker when the two of them locked eyes. Bajema remembered that the suicide driver was "lifting his hands and clapping them together" in an effort to detonate the device. Seconds later, a flash of light followed by the deafening sound and shock wave drove Bajema to the floor of the truck. Instantaneously, windshield glass showered the inside of

Staff Sergeant Sebban and his Cheez Doodles (Brad Rather)

Sebban and Rather (Brad Rather)

the truck. The ensuing smoke and debris cloud created a thick wall of black death. It consumed and shrouded the scene momentarily so that only the eerie sounds of those screaming in pain or shouting orders could be heard.

"Are you alright, you alright?" Bajema remembered that his driver had been next to him.

"I'm fine, I'm fine," came the reply.

A follow-on attack was a threat, so as the smoke began to dissipate, Bajema stepped out to take stock of the situation. Who was injured? How much damage had been done by the bomber? Who was still able to make decisions and issue orders? Placing his foot on the ground next to the gun truck, Bajema felt something soft under his foot. He looked down to find a severed arm. The sight of the limb gave him a nauseating pause.

One of our guys is out there with a missing arm or worse, he thought.[2]

Unbeknownst to him it was the bomber's. Bajema's next thoughts were to locate Captain Stewart. He found Stewart along with another platoon leader, Lieutenant Walsh, and the Charlie Troop First Sergeant John Coomer, wounded from flying glass. They were in the building organizing a defense and advising Headhunter of their situation.

McAvin recovered from the initial effects of the blast and ran towards Sebban. Sebban indicated that he was OK and that he had to treat the wounded, the number of which was steadily rising. He worked feverishly to go to the aid of his fellow paratroopers. Suddenly, Ben dropped to the ground. He was rushed to the aid station, where his comrades tried to resuscitate him. It turned out that he had received a penetrating wound to his hip that had lacerated several of his vital organs and he bled out.

Ben Sebban was the consummate medic. Brad Rather recalled that, "He died taking care of other people. Not even caring that, I doubt he even realized he was wounded but even if he had he probably wouldn't have stopped." Ben had just found out that he had made the promotion list for platoon sergeant. Rather continued saying that "he was a great guy, a real straightforward guy and he'd have been a great platoon sergeant."[3] Everybody was very excited for him. Ben had been thinking about leaving the army but when he made the list, he had decided to stay in a bit longer.

Sebban was always a prankster. There was a Hickory Farms sausage that managed to find its way into Doc Rather's sleeping bag, and even into his duffle bag when he went home for mid-tour leave. When discovered, it would be hidden somewhere in Ben's gear (usually in a sleeping bag or under a pillow). The day they left for Diyala, Ben had zip tied the sausage to the bumper of Rather's gun truck. There it stayed. After he was killed, the sausage remained there until it eventually fell off during a mission. To this day Rather can't look at a Hickory Farms Summer Sausage without thinking of Ben Sebban.

The medevac helicopter landed and the wounded were quickly hustled onto the waiting bird. A total of 12 were evacuated by air while seven lightly wounded were transported by ground for further treatment. There had been a wide variety and severity of wounds, from a bone-deep laceration to the calf created by rocketing shrapnel to another who had multiple shrapnel wounds to the knee, liver and head. One paratrooper had the right side of his face horribly damaged. The skin from his right eye down his nose to just above his jaw was peeled back exposing his skull and he was spitting up blood.

This attack had been an obvious attempt by Al Qaeda to stymie efforts by Headhunter to restore As Sadah and eliminate the militant threat.

The next day, Charlie Troop ran a scheduled medical clinic for the people of As Sadah. Many of the civilians had wounds that they had received as a result of the previous day's explosion. Everyone was suffering the effects of the evil that the insurgents were attempting to foment. For Charlie Troop, it was just the beginning of the battle to thwart the enemy's campaign of terror. McAvin reflected on the loss by saying, "You get hit, you continue on." Stoic, resolute, determined. For Ben's sake. In Ben's memory.

Months later, "Doc Rob" Larry Robinson found a video message from his old friend, Ben Sebban. Larry was recovering from his wounds and was still trying to come to grips with the effects of his injury. Ben and Larry had spent time talking about their spiritual paths and had shared hopes of being with the Lord.

"Hey sir, what's goin' on? It sucks that you got hit but I hear you're doing pretty good. I told you you'd be alright. Enjoy your R&R, take some time and get better. I don't know if I'm going to see you again in the 82nd, but we appreciate everything you did. You were a great TC [truck commander], and I appreciate everything along the way."

Ben told Larry to drop him a line and that they would "get together sometime in the future." It was not to be.[4]

CHAPTER 18

Minotaur

The Islamic State of Iraq, known as the political organization of Al Qaeda in Iraq, had taken over the towns of Zaganiyah and Qubbah since the departure of Alpha Troop the previous November. Al Qaeda had built training camps in the palm groves between the towns and the Diyala River, as well as numerous fighting positions overlooking a main route in and out of both towns. Furthermore, a bomb-making cell working along major avenues of approach to Zaganiyah targeted coalition and Iraqi movements into and out of the area. This area would be the focus of Task Force 300's next mission, Operation Minotaur.

The brigade leadership had to be briefed up before the operation could be approved. To maintain operational security, the Headhunter leadership met with the brigade commander in private to avoid the possibility of a leak. The plan was to employ a feint to take Qubbah first in order to shape the fight in Zaganiyah. The goal was to convince the insurgents that coalition forces would use the main road into Zaganiyah. What they weren't counting on was the fact that Alpha Troop knew the terrain. They had developed plenty of intelligence back in the fall of 2006.

The elaborate Al Qaeda infrastructure included training camps along with a planning cell and court complete with a detention center and a torture chamber. The power base for the Islamic State of Iraq needed to be dismantled. Captain Few remembered that as part of the effort to confuse the enemy, word was spread that the coalition forces were "coming back up the main road into Zaganiyah to fuck them up."[1] Headhunter had eyes on Al Qaeda placing IEDs in anticipation of the battle. Great pains were taken to confuse the enemy into thinking that Zaganiyah was the main effort.

Prior to commencing Operation Minotaur, various Headhunter elements were working route reconnaissance using a combination of small kill teams and searches while working out of a patrol base located between As Sadah and Zaganiyah. A series of IED detonations began to give new meaning to the deadly effects of these homemade bombs.

Clearing Zaganiyah (Staff Sergeant JoAnn Makinano)

Harriman treating a wounded soldier (Staff Sergeant JoAnn Makinano)

Searching for hidden enemy fighters and weapons (Staff Sergeant JoAnn Makinano)

The first was detonated while searching cars. About two hours after the first one, Wade Sharbono and Josh Kinser were probing the edge of Zaganiyah to see how the enemy sentries would react. Sharbono was an experienced staff sergeant, a former Marine who had received extensive training as a combat medic prior to being assigned to 5-73. Josh was driving for Wade because his truck had been damaged in the prior blast. Sharbono's driver had been injured and medevaced out along with several other paratroopers. "I needed a ride and Wade needed a driver," Josh recalled.[2]

Proceeding cautiously, they rounded a corner and observed two motorcycles speeding off in a nearby field. Simultaneously, an explosion consumed the road on the driver's side of the gun truck. Josh woke up leaning on the steering wheel with Wade yelling over the ringing in his ears to hit the brakes. The armor had maintained its integrity while the glass had spiderlike cracks. According to Kinser, the huge blast appeared to have been set wrong "and some of the shrapnel was blocked by the road and asphalt."[3] The explosives techs had to detonate a bomb that another crew had spotted. So, while they anxiously waited, Sharbono checked Josh's level of consciousness, looked at his eyes and had him follow his fingers.

Although shaken, Josh appeared to be OK. On the other hand, Wade was beginning to show signs of the adverse effects of detonations. Kinser recalled that "it was like he was drunk or something, his speech had just slowed and slurred."[4] The following evening, they returned to the site of the second explosion to bait the bomb makers with a set of wires and a fake artillery shell. They wanted to send a message to the insurgents that "we were here to stay." The fake bomb had a GPS chip installed in it. The hope was that the enemy fighters would recover the explosive and lead the paratroopers to their cache. The fake device was buried, and the detonation wires were run across the road, effectively blocking any enemy attempts to escape.

No less than six insurgents at various points further up the road watched their movement. The Al Qaeda members were certainly astonished and confused when they saw U.S. Army soldiers emplacing an explosive in the road. A large sign in Arabic taunting the enemy was staked in the road pointed towards Zaganiyah declaring, "Ali Latif—How do you like those apples. We own you. We will crush you and the women who fight with you."[5]

Sharbono and his team left the site, rounded the corner and were rocked again by another explosion, which they were able to drive through. Ultimately, three detonations within 36 hours would be more than Sharbono could handle. He was in such bad shape that Captain Few was going to give Kinser command of his section and have Sharbono sit in the back seat of the gun truck. Kinser protested because although Wade was his friend, at this point he was a liability. Sharbono was passing out in the mess hall during lunch. He was so dizzy he couldn't do anything. He was vomiting, pale and complained of jaw pain. The pain was so bad he couldn't chew his food.

Finally, on the first morning of Operation Minotaur, Kinser insisted that Wade was getting on a chopper to get much-needed medical care. Kinser demanded that "you can either do it this way or we can do it at gunpoint."[6] It was tough for Josh. He and Wade had been through all sorts of tight spots together so being such a hardass about the threat Wade posed made a bad situation feel even worse to him. It was an entirely different Wade Sharbono who got on that medevac than the one Kinser had known just days earlier. Wade was in for a new battle, fighting the insidious effects of traumatic brain injury or TBI.

A combination of 120mm mortars close into the ground assault along with the 155mm howitzer artillery were used in fire plan Samson, which had 155mm and 120mm rounds walking around in the palm groves during the air assault in order to keep the enemy from escaping. The air force dropped 2,000-pound bombs around Zaganiyah to draw the enemy's attention away from the actual landing zones in Qubbah.

After extensive bombardment of the western side of the road leading to Zaganiyah, the air assault flew past and Operation Minotaur began with the clearance of Qubbah. The operational security was so good that the general in overall command was on the radio declaring in a general-sized voice that they were on the wrong landing zone. Captain Dobbins and Bravo Troop along with Captain Stewart and Charlie Troop entered the battlespace by air assault. Within minutes, the fight for northern Qubbah had begun. Firefights ensued for the next four hours or so resulting in numerous enemy dead. Having nowhere to go and being completely taken by surprise and vertically enveloped, as Major Sylvia would say, the enemy had no recourse but to stand and fight.

Captain Stewart observed that "as soon as they realized how much they were getting their butts kicked they either laid down arms or squirted into the palm groves and continued moving up north."[7] Alpha Troop entered the battlespace by ground convoy and cleared southern Qubbah. Among the evidence discovered during the clearance was an American passport of a foreign fighter with stamps showing recent visits to the U.S. Dug-in entrenchments had been established in preparation for the extremists to make a last stand. An enormous number of houses had to be searched and the pace was grueling for the paratroopers.

According to First Sergeant Clemens, Bravo Troop's senior sergeant, the enemy fighters were dressed in "fedayeen-type garb. They were in black pajamas and black robes carrying bandoliers and weapons." As the clearance began, a support by fire position would be set up on a roof to protect the entry team. Clemens recalled that "all of a sudden four guys came out of a building two blocks up all dressed in black, running right at us and shooting. That was the kind of resistance we encountered in that area. They didn't really seem to have a plan or be well trained. They were fanatical fighters."[8]

Shrouded in darkness, assistant team leader Justin Young along with other members of Charlie Troop stepped forward into the fight with the eerie green glow of their night vision goggles illuminating potential threats. As they moved toward the house that was designated as their first objective, tracer fire appeared off to their south. This meant that the enemy was now aware of their presence. An explosive charge quickly solved the problem of a locked courtyard gate, and the entry team found nothing out of the ordinary as they proceeded towards the house. An overwatch position was quickly established on the roof of the house to help protect those clearing the compound.

As Young and his fellow 2nd Platoon paratroopers moved forward two Apache attack helicopters alerted the team of what appeared to be enemy movement in the courtyard. The clearance team had also picked up on the movement and as they approached an inner fence, they carefully scanned the area. As Young and his team crossed the threshold, Young identified a partially concealed enemy fighter. The insurgent was forced to surrender. He was detained along with a pistol, grenade and Kalashnikov rifle. A shack located in the back corner of the yard was their next objective and the Apaches indicated that they had a "heat signature" in it.

"White three Alpha, element clearing the northside of building 22 and will walk in on the shack, over..." was the report transmitted to the troop commander.[9]

The Apache pilot monitored the white-hot images of Young and his team as they cautiously moved forward, knowing that the enemy lurked inside. The long narrow tree-lined section of the courtyard served to block much of the ambient light, which limited their night vision capabilities. Before clearing the adjoining bunker that served as an enemy fighting position, Young made entry into the shack while the others kept watch on the house, which turned out to be a duplex that still needed to be searched along with a bunker. Young switched on the flashlight attached to the stock of his rifle and—

"Fuck, fuck they're shooting friendlies, goddamn it!" The Apache pilot's voice betrayed his momentary horror at viewing what appeared to be the death of a fellow soldier.[10]

Justin Young was no more than five feet from a rifle-wielding enemy dismount. He saw the wide-eyed enemy fighter who immediately began firing his Kalashnikov rifle on full automatic, the red tracers flying within feet of Young's body. Justin quickly returned fire lying on his back, with his weapon between his legs. Justin quickly assessed his injury and found blood on his neck. "I'm hit," Justin declared as two members of his team rapidly moved forward to defend their wounded buddy.[11] They entered the shack to find the enemy fighter who had tried to kill Young near death. He mumbled his final words, "Allah Ahkbar, Allah Ahkbar."

As Young stumbled out of the kill zone, he was helped to a covered position out of the line of fire. Shouts of "medic" gave added seriousness to an already adrenaline-filled fight. Thinking that the round had found the gap just above the wounded paratrooper's body armor, the medic quickly began removing Young's kit to expose the wound. Miraculously, it appeared that a ricocheting round had caught the corner of Young's vest plate producing a minor wound. Another enemy bullet had damaged his rifle, destroying the charging handle, optics, and grenade launcher attached to the rifle rail, all of which made the rifle useless. A minor scratch to his hand was the only other wound that could be found. Justin had escaped death by mere inches.

"These guys are hunkered down in this little shed, continuing to return fire. We can't get a frag in there because there are too many friendlies in the immediate vicinity," the platoon sergeant reported.[12]

The decision was made to clear the area of friendlies and let the Apache take care of the shed with a well-placed Hellfire missile. The attack helicopter pilot walked through the targeting process with his weapons officer, detailing weapon selection, distance to target, and confirmation that the Headhunter paratroopers were safe from the blast. Obtaining the initials of the officer requesting the strike gave a clear understanding that this would be "danger close." The white-hot explosion signifying that the missile had done its job quickly followed the transmitting of "missile away."

"Fuckin' nothing left to that building," the pilot declared.[13]

Young was ready to return to the fight. He looked at the medic and refused evacuation. But what to do about a replacement weapon? Seeing a pile of seized enemy rifles, Justin had an idea.

"What the fuck are you doin'?" demanded the paratrooper guarding the captured weapons.

"I don't have a weapon," Young responded.

"What do you mean you don't have a weapon?"

"I got shot, it destroyed my weapon," Young said.[14]

The paratrooper looked on in amazement as Young picked up a Kalashnikov rifle and several spare ammo magazines so he could continue the fight. Young led his team for the next five days and never sought medical attention for his wounds.

The day ended with Headhunter taking control of several buildings and conducting patrols in preparation for clearing the palm groves. "I got a really bad vibe" in Qubbah, Lieutenant Mike Anderson recalled.[15] He couldn't pinpoint it but his uneasiness with this majority-Sunni village was palpable.

CHAPTER 19

Qubbah

The following day, Headhunter began clearing the palm groves, which were thick, dense and wet with vegetation that limited the field of vision to just a few meters in some cases. Bravo's Captain Dobbins remembered that as the clearance teams walked online, the paratroopers were "constantly hopping fences, going over walls and traversing canals."[1] The locals used the palm groves to grow dates and fruit. Fences that marked off individual groves subdivided the fields. The thick vegetation gave the insurgents the cover and concealment needed to ambush any intruder. Enemy fighters suddenly appeared or began their assault from hidden firing points.

The paratroopers were soon waist deep in water and surrounded by thick marsh grass, which placed them at a major disadvantage. Row after row of dirt roads every 300 meters or so, with roads connecting them approximately every 300 meters, created a grid system network. Each grid was fenced off with chicken wire that was a dangerous obstacle whether troops were initiating contact, attempting to maneuver or breaking contact with the enemy. Wire cutters were an essential piece of equipment needed to deal with these obstacles.

Soon after Bravo Troop entered the palm groves, enemy movement was detected. It appeared that the insurgents were attempting to re-enter the town and flank the paratroopers. The enemy fighters were stopped before they were able to counterattack. First Sergeant Clemens remembered that they "hadn't been in the palm groves for more than a couple hundred meters when one of my sections off to my right was in contact with a machine gun in a building. There were little mud huts that had machine-gun positions set up and rocket-propelled grenades cached in them." At one point, Clemens "turned the corner and there was a guy coming out the gate with an AK47. He saw me and I saw him, but I was just faster."[2] There were dug-in enemy fighting positions with weapons cached in them.

Alpha Troop had established a temporary limit of advance, a stopping point that was designated by Captain Few that was used to consolidate his forces and make sure they weren't over-extended. It was located at a Y intersection with a bus stop in the center. A makeshift patrol base was set up so they could strong point the intersection.

Qubbah clearance (Staff Sergeant JoAnn Makinano)

The headquarters platoon was on the intersection securing the inside perimeter and 2nd Platoon was off on a berm road to the northwest covering the palm grove. 1st Platoon was on the northern portion of the Y intersection and part of 3rd Platoon was to the south watching that part of the intersection. Few and Anderson were in the very middle of it, near the bus stop. A couple of headquarters trucks were floating around here and there watching the northeastern portion of that Y.

To reach out to the villagers, some of the paratroopers were handing out candy to children. Smiling and interacting with these kids was the compassionate side of this complicated fight. Amidst the hatred and unrelenting violence, this simple act offered hope to the young Iraqis.

Lieutenant Anderson noticed that several of the Joes were a bit too relaxed, so he instructed the sergeant to tighten things up and get the paratroopers back in their gun trucks. After the completion of the clearance, the guidance that had been received from squadron was "let people live their day-to-day lives. We're trying to be the kinder, gentler counterinsurgency." So, the villagers were trying to go about their daily business. Anderson had a "fucking really bad feeling about guys being out of their trucks" walking around talking to the locals.

"Don't worry sir, I'll fix it right now," the sergeant responded.[3]

Anderson returned to Captain Few's truck and saw a group of maybe 15 or 20 military-age men, looking at them.

"I feel like shooting them all right now," Anderson said, looking at Few who also had his gut aching over their presence.

Anderson grabbed an interpreter along with one other Joe and walked over to the group.

"I'm going to go find out what the fuck is going on," he told Captain Few.

As they moved towards them, the Iraqi men dispersed. Several of the Iraqis were rounded up to figure out what they were up to.

"What the hell were you guys talking about?" the interpreter inquired.

They just got the same old bullshit answers: "Nothing, we're just hanging out talking, wondering what you guys are doing."[4]

As Anderson walked back to his gun truck, he found the paratroopers milling around. He repeated his order to the sergeant to get those paratroopers back in the trucks. A battle update brief was in progress when Anderson returned to the captain's truck. The briefing would provide the squadron leaders with a complete picture of how the operation was proceeding.

Anderson was momentarily distracted by a "troops in contact" radio report coming from Delta Troop paratroopers. They were in a firefight with insurgents and were requesting assistance from Apache gunships. Anderson turned around and noticed that the Joes were still hanging around the bus stop.

I'm getting fed up with this shit, thought Anderson.[5]

As he was climbing out of his truck to chew the sergeant's ass again, an Iraqi man appeared, walking towards the troop commander's truck with a bicycle. The turret gunner was told to stop him. He was checked out by Captain Few and was allowed to pass. Anderson eyeballed him too and didn't see anything on the guy either. He was wearing very light clothing that the wind pressed up against his body. If there had been anything underneath, he would have noticed it.

Walking towards his gun truck, flanked by the seemingly harmless bicyclist, Anderson felt a sense of dread that could only be eliminated by erasing its existence. He clutched his pistol grip, determined to engage the perceived threat. The urge passed as the haunting figure made his way past Anderson's gun truck. Once again, his attention circled back to the paratroopers who had stopped to take a respite at the bus stop. Made with cinder blocks and a concrete roof, it could easily fit eight or nine people.

Seated in the enclosure or standing close by, Sergeant Jason Swiger, Corporal Jason Nunez, Private Orlando Gonzalez, Private Anthony White and Private Anthony Wurster had no idea of the perilous fate that awaited them. Suddenly, the Iraqi was now running towards the unsuspecting Joes who had congregated at the bus stop. In an instant, blistering shock waves, a sea of desert dust and deadly ball bearings hurtled in all directions. The Iraqi suicide bomber had used a hand-held triggering device to detonate a bomb previously hidden in the bus stop.

Anderson quickly recovered from the blast. He'd been behind his truck, which shielded him from the explosion. Picking himself up off the ground, Anderson began running towards what was now just a pile of concrete rubble. The dust cloud created by the explosion was beginning to dissipate as he reached the devastation. One of the interpreters was already attempting to lift the concrete off Wurster's legs. Wurster had been leaning against the outside wall so the deadly explosive effects of the blast had gone past him. Within moments, Captain Few arrived to take charge of the rescue effort after reporting the attack on the squadron radio.

When Anderson reached the blast site, Captain Few was holding Wurster's hands trying to reassure him. Few would later remember that "so many thoughts went through my head that I hadn't done my job. Not just searching that guy but letting my boys get overconfident." Few believed that the squadron "could go anywhere and do anything and the enemy just couldn't touch us. Your pride has gotten your soldiers killed." Mike Few was kicking himself for allowing his guys to get too confident. "I had this intense anger of wanting to destroy fucking everything and everyone associated with this blast."[6]

Other paratroopers quickly moved forward to assist their injured brothers. The concrete slab trapping Wurster was broken into small pieces using an ax, which allowed Wurster to be freed. Once the roof was removed, the grim task of recovering those crushed by the explosion began. By this time, Lieutenant Colonel Poppas along with Bravo Troop had quickly moved towards the blast site to help secure the area and be of any other assistance.

The first body to be uncovered was that of Sergeant Swiger. "I couldn't even tell who it was," Anderson noted with shock. "His face was completely gone. It was discovered nearby, lying on the road. His body was so badly burned that his body armor had to be opened to reveal the nametape on his uniform," which was used to identify him. One of the mechanics, Anthony White, was the next to be recovered. As the unrecognizable trooper was lifted from the wreckage his arm almost came off. It was just dangling by flesh. Anderson recalled that it was "weird placing them into bags and making sure all of their teeth were there."[7]

After recovering Orlando Gonzalez and Jason Nunez, one of the medics couldn't take the pressure anymore. He was found squatting on the pavement staring at pieces of human flesh. The blast had also wounded one child and killed another. Barely clinging to life, the injured child was placed on a medevac helicopter and died en route to the hospital. Iraqi authorities never told the family of their loss. It would be months before the child's family would know that their son would not be returning.

As he stood over the carnage, Chaplain Honbarger recalled how he had kidded with Swiger earlier in the day, joking around and briefly switching ranks. Now he couldn't remember what Swiger's face looked like before the blast had torn it away. The smell was unforgettable. The mix of cordite from the explosives and the thick odor of iron that came from blood penetrated his nostrils and became imbedded. Later, Honbarger felt as though he should have said to some of the rescuers, "even though you're telling me you can keep going on and you don't want to leave your buddies behind," you need to step back.[8] It's too much to handle.

Lieutenant Anderson walked over to check on Wurster. He knelt to comfort him just as the medevac birds were landing. The remains of their comrades rested next to him all in a row. Suddenly, someone was challenging Anderson. "What the fuck are you doing?" the intruder demanded. Anderson was on the verge of snapping at this point. He told the sergeant not to put his wounded man on the bird with those who had been killed.

"Why, who the fuck are you?" the sergeant retorted.

Anderson bolted upright, turned and faced this offending sergeant.

"I'm fucking Lieutenant Anderson!" Anderson was pointing at the body bags of the deceased paratroopers that were nearby.

The bewildered sergeant quickly apologized for his indiscretion and moved off.

Anderson recalled that "you always wonder how much to blame someone else, or if you should blame anyone at all, or how much you blame yourself. I don't know if there was anything I could have done to change what happened."[9]

That night, Bravo Troop relieved Alpha Troop temporarily. They moved north and found a school that could be used as a patrol base. Mike Few went from truck to truck, explaining how the attack had occurred. He told them how close they were and what this loss meant to him. It was essential that they remain focused. Few had been deployed multiple times and had never lost a soldier. These losses were his first and it would leave an indelible mark on him.

Airlifting the remainder of the paratroopers the following night, Charlie Troop staged as the double-bladed heavy lift Chinook helicopters approached the landing zone. Captain Stewart had communications with the lead bird. The paratroopers were inside a small perimeter as the Chinooks flew closer.

"Hey sir, is that going to land on us," a paratrooper observed as the Chinook approached.

"Oh no, it's gonna move, it's gonna move," Captain Stewart replied.

"Sir, I don't think it's gonna move," the paratrooper repeated.

"Oh no, we need to move," Stewart declared.[10]

Everybody ran to avoid being crushed by the incoming helicopter. Captain Stewart and Doc Harriman happened to be the last two getting on the aircraft. The Chinook loads and unloads from its rear so a ramp was lowered to allow the paratroopers to step onto the helicopter. As Harriman moved onto the deck, he stepped on a piece of wire from the rear gunner's machine gun; it was on top of the butterfly triggers. The gunner had not set the weapon's safety so as Harriman stepped on the triggers, several rounds struck Harriman, tearing into his lower leg. Despite Harriman's massive leg wound, he applied his own tourniquet. The aircrew quickly diverted, became a medevac and transported him directly to the surgical hospital. Harriman, who had saved so many lives, would survive his injury. He returned to his civilian job as an emergency medical services provider and became a flight paramedic assigned to a medevac helicopter.

CHAPTER 20

Hardship of Loss

The "Stairway to Heaven" memorial platform was expanded to accommodate the four fallen comrades: upturned rifles with fixed bayonets, helmets resting on each rifle butt, dog tags draped over each rifle pistol grip and a pair of boots placed to the front of each position as if standing at attention. To the rear, the crossed flags of the 5th Squadron, 73rd Cavalry Regiment and the American flag framed this solemn memorial to the dead.

Everyone had liked Jason Swiger, and everyone messed with Jason Swiger. He seemed to crave the attention and relished the opportunity to push their buttons. Jason seemed to have a perpetual smile on his face and a snappy comeback to whatever was thrown at him. Always in a good mood and exuding a positive attitude, Swiger was always willing to keep someone company when they were having trouble staying awake or Lieutenant Anderson needed a hand.

In his presence, there was never a silence to fill. Despite any hardships the troop faced, they could count on Jason to make them laugh. Swiger's signature vehicle was his junky, spray-painted van, complete with doorway beads on the inside and a rubber chicken on the bumper. Later, his van became a Fort Bragg landmark for weeks after the driveshaft fell out. Directions around the neighborhood included "yeah, take a left at Swiger's van... you know, the one with the chicken."[1]

He always sought advice when he needed it. He gave it, too. He had known the boys in the platoon a lot longer than Anderson had, so when there was an issue, Swiger provided the background. He was the guy on the inside. He kept an eye on the younger soldiers in the barracks. He would go get them if they needed a ride, he'd counsel them when they needed it, and he always gave them a pat on the back when they deserved it. Behind closed doors, he always had positive things to say about the guys.

The day he was killed, Jason Swiger was taking a detainee to Charlie Troop's patrol base. On the return trip to Qubbah, they dismounted to assess some battle damage from an earlier attack. On the way back to the trucks, Jason was doing what he

Swiger clowning around (Sean Ventura)

always did, cracking jokes and taking photos. As he was talking about taking one more "cool guy photo," his batteries died. He said he'd get more from the truck, but Anderson told him not to bother, that they'd have another opportunity soon enough. "The next time I saw him, it was too late. I wish that I would have taken that photo with him," Anderson said.

Orlando Gonzalez was one of the first cavalry scouts that replaced some of the infantry guys. He was a young kid who seemed to have suffered some significant emotional trauma in his life. He started getting into trouble as soon as he arrived, but as he began to share his background it was easy to understand why he was struggling. His dad had disappeared when he was young and showed up at basic training graduation begging for money. After Orlando gave him some cash, his dad left.

Despite all of life's challenges that were thrown at him, Gonzalez would shine at 5-73 CAV. While at the Joint Readiness Training Center at Fort Polk, Louisiana for pre-deployment training, Alpha Troop ran into a simulated ambush and firefight with the opposing force better known as OP4. The Observer-Controllers were declaring paratroopers killed left and right. Gonzalez was the only guy left in his section; the only kid left alive. He was driving around in a Humvee with no one else in it, into the firefight and then he jumped in the turret and started shooting at the opposing force. He ended up getting the Hero of the Battle award at the end of the JRTC rotation. He was the last kid you'd expect to do something like that because he was so quiet.

Jason Nunez's job as a nuclear, biological and chemical specialist was to help protect against exposure to these deadly agents. With that threat just about non-existent in Iraq, Nunez became Captain Few's driver. Jason wanted to be on the front lines. He wanted the opportunity to take the fight to the enemy. He found that opportunity in Alpha Troop. Nunez had planned to reenlist as an airborne cavalry scout knowing that this was his opportunity to pursue his dream.

After all, he had to think about his future with a wife and young baby to care for. His family said he was a good kid who didn't smoke or drink. He knew the risks, having been wounded several months earlier by an IED detonation. He'd suffered a partial hearing loss but was allowed to return to duty. Just before his death, Jason's dad had spoken to him asking if he was frightened. "A little bit, but not too bad," Jason responded.[2] Did he have a sense of what was to come?

Jake St. Laurent, the Delta Troop commander, shared his thoughts about Anthony White. "I will always remember the huge ear-to-ear grin that he always had, even when the going got rough," recalled St. Laurent. According St. Laurent, Anthony was "quick with a joke to lighten a situation or just to get a smile on your face. It was not just me who thought White was always smiling. Every person I spoke to talked about how happy he always was and how he always had a smile on his face." He was "bound and determined to ensure that everyone around him was kept in a good mood, whether by telling a joke or acting like the class clown."[3]

White had been a member of Alpha Troop's maintenance support team, working as a mechanic. "One night when Alpha Troop had just returned from a mission, White and Wurster were elbows deep in grease with an engine hanging precariously above an Alpha Troop truck. When asked why they were working this job late into the night, White replied with a big grime and grease grin that it had to be completed by the next afternoon. St. Laurent declared that "the following day that truck was up and running."[4]

Anthony White had the ability to take the adversity that plagued him prior to the deployment and turn it into the driving force that made him a mechanic and soldier that matched someone with 20 years' experience. His drive and determination would surely have made him a superior leader. No matter whether he was on the basketball court or attacking damaged vehicles that seemed to multiply in the motor pool, Anthony lived by the mantra "work hard, play hard."

St. Laurent ended his remembrance by saying, "Anthony, you have touched every person in this squadron. We are all better people for having had the opportunity to know you and work alongside you. Your infectious spirit will live forever in our hearts and minds. The sound of your voice will continue to echo through the halls and maintenance bays of the motor pool."[5]

A short time later, Anthony's father, a retired army sergeant major who had spent time with the 82nd Airborne Division, sent a request to Senator Jim DeMint's office requesting that DeMint investigate his son's death. The "Congressional" was forwarded through the chain of command and eventually reached Captain Few. Required to respond to the questions, Captain Few delineated the circumstances surrounding the attack. In the course of the reply, he shared his remembrance of Anthony:

> Never one to complain, he always had a smile on his face. When a truck was damaged and brought in for repairs, Anthony would grin, and say, "Sir, don't worry. We'll have this truck back up tomorrow." With Tupac playing on his CD player, he'd get to work. As paratroopers returned from patrols, Anthony would fire up the grill and begin preparing a meal for them. He would greet them with a smile, a new joke, and a burger. "His enthusiasm and spirit allowed the troop to accomplish more in three months than most companies accomplish in a year in Iraq.

The grieving Alpha Troop commander closed, expressing his deep sorrow for the loss:

> I cannot imagine the pain and suffering relating to the death of your son. I cannot hope to quell the grief that you and your family are currently sustaining. I can only provide these facts surrounding the events leading up to that tragic day. I can empathize with the loss of Anthony. I personally pulled his remains from the site. I personally watched as he was placed into the body bag. There are many nights that I privately mourn his loss. In the reprieve of my own room away from my soldiers, I will cry and ask God why. When I walk into the chow hall, I still see his smiling face.
>
> When a vehicle is damaged and returned to our patrol base and the mechanics begin working on it, I sometimes walk over to inquire why Anthony's not listening to Tupac while he works until I remember that he is no longer with us. This is my burden. I will live with this day for the rest of my life. The pain and grief of his loss is felt throughout our troop. We continually look to that day to ask what went wrong. How did we mess up? What did we do wrong? The answer is nothing. Death is a part of combat, but that is hard to accept. Ultimately, it is my responsibility.[6]

CHAPTER 21

Long Shots and Landslide

After the injured and dead had been recovered, the job of figuring out what happened began to take shape. Possible suspects were rounded up, and Kinser along with Alpha Troop's interpreter, Moose, questioned them, asking what the enemy had used to cause such destruction and determine if the culprits could be found. Numerous members of the troop had occupied the bus stop during the past two days. Kinser had even sat down to share a drink with a reporter.

It turned out that there had been two explosive charges placed there. One was under the bench and the second device a bit higher in the wall. Both were covered back over with concrete. With faces covered, the possible informants were instructed that if they wanted to provide information all that was necessary was to raise a hand. Three of them came forward and identified the two ringleaders. When the suspect house was raided, rockets and detonating cord were found in the house. The tip had born fruit. The informants also showed where several improvised explosive devices were buried and how the aiming site, located behind a wall, functioned. A well-placed hole and chair gave the bomber a good view of his intended targets.

Some additional intelligence gave the location of another house that was identified as the location of an Al Qaeda planning cell. Kinser led the raid with 1st Platoon covering the flank. Black masks and some Al Qaeda "don't fall prey to the Christian crusaders and slaves to the cross" style propaganda was all that was found. While searching the building, one of the paratroopers came around the corner with his bloodshot eyes watering, choking and spitting. A yellowish-green chemical powder was spread on the floor and everyone that came near it was showing signs of a severe response to the chemical exposure. They began to vomit as they rapidly exited the building and could barely make it back to the gun trucks. The medics began giving oxygen to all those who'd been affected as they were having a tough time breathing. There weren't any chemical specialists available to assess the product until days later, and by that time the powder had disappeared. Rather than expose anyone else to the hazardous chemical, permission was given to destroy the building.

Guza making the long shot (Matt Guza)

The snipers were also looking for the bad guys. Matt Guza had lost a good friend the previous day in Qubbah. Guza and Swiger had become friends after they were teamed up to complete their "Spur Ride" during their time as members of Charlie 73rd.[1] Guza now found himself in a position that might give him the opportunity to eliminate the enemy fighters who had killed his friend.

The .50-caliber Barrett sniper weapon system that Matt Guza had been issued required constant attention to detail. He'd perfected his skills with "Binky" by constantly "collecting data," firing the Barrett in all sorts of conditions, day, night, all sorts of weather and at different elevations. The results were recorded in a table that Guza could refer to as necessary. This log told the story of how the rifle and sniper performed. The sniper team would set up targets and vector them using a laser range finder to establish an accurate distance to target. Often the team found itself positioned on the roof of a two- or three-story building in an overwatch position. So, to simulate that height a ridge would be chosen and Guza would be shooting down on his target usually at a distance of between 800 and 900 meters. He'd adjust based on windage and the other data collected including temperature, wind speed/ direction, humidity and altitude also known as "slope dope," compensating for the angle to ensure an accurate shot.

The day following the explosion at the bus stop in Qubbah, Guza, along with another sniper and their spotters, was positioned on a building roof "rotating," or scanning for roadside bomb emplacers. It was late afternoon when they spotted someone digging a hole in the road that ran parallel to Route Barley. The sniper teams "started burning in on him a bit more" and examining the area immediately surrounding the site.[2] There to the left of the suspected enemy was a white Toyota parked in the wood line, partially concealed by bushes.

As they pushed over to the left, the full silhouette of an insurgent dressed in black appeared in Guza's sight. He was placing a wire in the road that would be used to detonate an IED. Their observations gave the snipers the positive identification that would be needed to get the order to take the shot. Captain Dobbins, Bravo Troop's commanding officer, gave the green light, and Guza ranged the target with his Barrett at 1,561 meters. He factored in the elevation. With a steady, smooth pull of the trigger and the report of the rifle, the first shot traveled forward at supersonic speed. The round struck its intended target, and the insurgent fell from sight.

The team now switched its attention to the truck. They had momentarily lost sight of the digger, so Guza fired three well-placed rounds into the vehicle thus ensuring that it could not be used to make an escape. Both snipers began working to locate the digger. Suddenly, the insurgent appeared and was looking around with shovel in hand, leery of exposing himself. Guza quickly fired a snapshot, knowing that his opportunity would be based on the enemy popping up only briefly. The first shot hit left. Guza recalled that, "I fired the second shot and that's when we lost visual with him."[3] Pink mist. A pair of Apache gunships confirmed that the snipers had exacted vengeance. Yes, war is personal.

The next objective was to clear Zaganiyah. There were several fighting positions that had been set up on the edge of the town. These proved to be abandoned. Alpha Troop's interpreter had information that a nearby house was occupied by Al Qaeda. The front gate was kicked open, and a car with wires running from an open trunk was discovered. The clearance team immediately sought cover and the explosive ordnance disposal team was called in. It turned out to be a hoax. The clearance continued, and soon another device was discovered. A bomb detection robot was sent in, and once again it was determined to be a hoax. The clearance was completed, and the decision was made by the squadron leadership to use the house as headquarters.

Kinser recalled being "really nervous about this house.[4]" He approached his platoon leader and got permission to double-check the place. Kinser and another paratrooper walked into the first room, looking for anything out of the ordinary, and found it empty. The second room was empty except for carpet covering the floor. Walking across it, nothing seemed to be out of place. Moments later, they reentered the same room from a different angle.

As they both stepped forward, a cracking sound was detected as though the wood was breaking. The carpet had been cut into sections, and upon moving these they discovered thin sheets of plywood covered by notebook paper. A red cord ran underneath the flooring. Cautiously lifting the plywood, they found a large deep freezer with the cords running directly into it. Not wanting to cause a panic as well as signaling the enemy that the device had been detected and possibly causing them to detonate it immediately, they followed a set of spliced wires into an adjoining room beneath the subfloor. Peering around the corner they saw a "huge bomb" with lights attached that were rapidly blinking. The feeling of impending doom crept over them. Sweat poured down their backs, their hearts raced and they felt a sick feeling in the pit of their stomachs. Kinser's instincts were correct. "It's a time bomb. They've hooked up some sort of timer, all I see is numbers." He watched as the timer ticked off the seconds.

2nd Platoon was already on the roof establishing the guard posts. The explosive force that this device carried would surely kill all of them and collapse the building. If the explosion didn't kill them, they would certainly be trapped and crushed by the debris. There was no other choice… "Landslide, Landslide!" The code word warning everyone of an impending explosion carried up the stairs to the paratroopers on the roof. Thinking that Kinser had discovered a hidden enemy fighter, two of the sergeants quickly headed downstairs to see if he needed any help. "There's a fucking bomb, get your guys outta here," Kinser shouted.[5]

They raced back up the stairs to retrieve the unsuspecting paratroopers. While extricating themselves from imminent death, it was difficult not to lose one's composure and balance. Kinser turned around and quickly realized that he was the last one in the building. The explosive ordnance disposal team arrived after dark and conferred with Kinser. A tracked robot with a camera configured to enter, locate, and disarm the explosive was sent in only to run out of power. A second robot entered only to lose signal.

Eventually, a bomb technician used the robot to disconnect both devices. Donning the entry suit made of various protective layers, including a protective shield and a helmet that weighs in at over 75 pounds, the tech retrieved the robots along with some sensitive items that had been inadvertently left on the roof.

The detonator was removed and brought for examination. It was made up of several D cell batteries with a two-way radio attached to it. All that was necessary was to depress the "push to talk" button—that would initiate the explosion. Kinser mentioned that the light was blinking green and that meant that the enemy operator was attempting to complete the circuit.

Confused as to why it hadn't worked, the bomb technicians did some further testing and determined that the blasting cap was faulty. When they checked the probability of this occurring it turned out that only one in 10,000 caps fail. The robot went back in and set an explosive charge in order to destroy the devices in place. When it detonated, the entire house disappeared. Kinser stared at the pile of rubble, shaking his head in disbelief. It had been all too close.

CHAPTER 22

Tragedy for Delta

With Qubbah and Zaganiyah secure, Alpha Troop had established their patrol base in Zaganiyah to keep the pressure on the enemy and support the population. A combat logistics patrol run was scheduled to move supplies from FOB Warhorse to the base, and Captain Jon Grassbaugh was hitching a ride out and back. Whether it was pushing fuel out, moving the self-propelled 155 mm guns to Butler Range, getting HESCO barriers to Bravo Troop's patrol base in Turki or conducting dismount patrols in As Sadah, the paratroopers of Delta Troop were always in the thick of the fight.

The gun truck that Captain Grassbaugh climbed into on April 7 was crewed by Specialist Emolo, Specialist Hoover, Private First Class McCandless and Staff Sergeant Bobby Henline.

As the patrol began their return trip to the Warhorse base after an uneventful transit to Zaganiyah, they proceeded down the same route. Without warning, a thunderous explosion that could be heard for miles and a thick, black column of smoke that rose into the afternoon sky signaled another violent tragedy. The logistics Humvee had struck a command-detonated IED made of three 155mm artillery rounds. The explosion was so powerful that it lifted the truck into the air, flipping it upside down, and consumed it in a fireball.

Staff Sergeant Bobby Henline was new to the squadron, serving as the truck commander, riding in the right front seat. Along with Jon, who was riding behind him, he was ejected from the vehicle. They were both on fire when they hit the ground. The other three paratroopers, Levi Hoover, Rodney McCandless and Ebe Emolo, were instantly killed by the explosion and ensuing fuel- and ammunition-fed fire. Henline was walking around incoherent. Somebody ran up to him and smothered the flames that were consuming his flesh. Jon was found on the ground badly burned and having trouble breathing. A tracheotomy was performed to better manage his breathing. A medevac helicopter arrived, and the two survivors were quickly loaded. Tragically, Jon did not survive the flight to the hospital.

Grassbaugh, Tarazon and Booth, April 7, 2007 (Jenna Grassbaugh)

From dry socks to making a giant 60-box pizza run one night from Balad to nine different landing zones during the Turki Bowl II fight, Jon Grassbaugh had always put his magic on it. He saw to it that all hands were quickly put to work loading pallets of water, MRE rations or whatever else was necessary to sustain the fight. The squadron marched on "Wild Tiger" energy drinks and Jon made certain that they were kept well stocked. He would take the occasional "tremendous ass chewing" that went with the job, knowing that some things were just totally out of their control. But hearing comments from the squadron's paratroopers like "the S-4 rocks" made it all worthwhile.

Jon's switch was always on. "He never had those tired moments," recalled Nick Bajema. "He was the guy who would wake up at 0600," ready to go. "As soon as he woke up it was as if he had 10 cups of coffee, without drinking coffee. He was just so in tune, always hopping and popping." Nick continued, "This was the guy who would be doing deals on his computer while IM-ing his wife while talking to two privates and telling me what to do all at the same time." His ability to multitask was unsurpassed. No one ever had a bad word to say about Jon. "He was just that kind of guy. People wanted to be around him because of his personality. He would just put you into a good mood."[1]

Levi Hoover was an infantryman by trade who wasn't all that interested in working with the "loggies" or support troops. That said, Levi quickly found his comfort zone working alongside the members of the distribution platoon. The consummate rifleman, he spent hours cleaning his weapon or sharpening one of his many knives. He was happiest when given the chance to go outside the wire and work dismount patrols.

Ebe "Eb" Emolo's unique character was always on display. College educated with a master's degree, Ebe had been a French teacher and a hospital security officer prior to enlisting. When describing his desire to serve, Ebe explained that he was "proud to be an American citizen." He exuded military respect when he would "lock up" at rigid attention whenever he was in the presence of an officer. Originally from the Ivory Coast, Emolo had royalty in his blood, the youngest son of King Nanan Boa Kouassi III. He had received his American citizenship just prior to deploying, proclaiming the event to have been one the proudest moments in his life. Extremely strong and athletic, Emolo was always willing and able to offer friendship and support. He was serving as the gunner on this trip.

Rodney McCandless or "Candlestick" often began or ended a story or greeting with, "You freaky freak." His small stature was overshadowed by his enormous heart and willingness to get the job done no matter what the assignment. His superior storytelling abilities were renowned despite his stutter that he accepted "as a badge of honor." That stutter quickly disappeared when the adrenaline level increased and Rodney took control of solving a problem.

Several days later, 5-73's paratroopers came together once again to mourn and remember their fallen comrades.

Major Brett Sylvia spoke first about Jon Grassbaugh. As he closed his remarks, Brett said, "As I sat at the explosion site that night, the sun went down, and the stars came out. I could not help but think that if Jon were one of these stars, his was one that would have shone brightest in the sky. It is always those stars, the ones that shine brightest, that we do not get to experience for long but that we are glad we did... the ones that burn forever in our memories."[2]

Lieutenant Sal Candela also eulogized Jon:

> It was truly the guy to his left and right that made Jon get up every morning. When I first heard that he had died, of course I was filled with anger. That night seeing him at the morgue in Balad, I even told myself that this place is not worth it. Why are we here, losing the best people America has to offer? Then I realized that Jon would not stand for that kind of thinking. He would want us to carry on with business as usual.
>
> He would want us to continue to work for each other and our families, and he would want us to continue our mission of bringing freedom to this part of the world. A piece of our heart is missing right now, but that will grow back with time. Things will get back to normal and the mission will go on. We must make sure that the memory of Jon is never forgotten and that his example is always alive within us. A friend was taken from us, but a legacy was left behind that will enrich us every day of our lives.[3]

Jenna and Jon Grassbaugh's relationship exuded an almost visible glow. Each moment spent together brought with it a desire to never be apart. Their time in college lit this fire, and that continued to burn strong after they were separated. They knew that being apart was a piece of their reality. Both had chosen the life of an army officer, so when Jon graduated several years ahead of Jenna, he was off to Ranger School, then to his branch course followed by an overseas tour in Korea. After a year in Korea, Jon returned to the States to an assignment at Fort Bragg with the 82nd Airborne Division. With the expansion of the cavalry scout function, Jon would be needed in the newly formed cavalry squadrons.

Jenna's turn to begin her army career arrived. Graduating in May of 2006, and marrying Jon in June, it was a whirlwind of happiness. Even the loss of several close friends along with her parents' struggling marriage couldn't dampen her excitement. Their wedding seemed like something out of a storybook with Jenna in a long, flowing strapless white gown and Jon in his army dress blue uniform; they were radiant. As they departed for their honeymoon, hanging over their heads was Jon's deployment to Iraq.

Rumors swirled as to whether Headhunter would even deploy. Everyone went on leave anxious and uncertain. It soon became apparent that the decision had been reached as deployment orders were issued, and the shipping containers were packed. There was a frantic rush to get Jenna settled in at William and Mary to begin her law studies. If the deployment had been delayed until February of 2007, which was the period of time that had originally been discussed, Jon wouldn't have deployed with his unit due to his position on the promotion list. Instead, he would have gone to the career course, then to the civil affairs school at Bragg. Their joyous but brief time together as husband and wife was about to take a turn.

That morning in late July, as final preparations for the Iraq deployment continued, Jon was sharing a tearful goodbye with Jenna. Being part of the advanced echelon team, Jon was departing with a small group of paratroopers that would make sure all was ready to receive the remainder of the squadron upon their arrival in Iraq. Emotions ran high as Jon and Jenna tried to remain positive. Heading off to the middle of a war zone filled everyone with a certain dread that was difficult to contain. Being separated for a year was bad enough, but the possibility of injury or death was never far from one's worst-case reality.

Describing his sense of humor, Jenna characterized Jon as "hilarious," often wondering, "Where is this stuff coming from?" Along with his sense of humor, he was "extremely intelligent, a good officer and tactically strong."[4] Jon was the total package. And then there was the wedding video.

Jenna and Jon had the entire ceremony and reception filmed. In fact, Jenna had been trying to get copies made so that they could hand them out as gifts to family and friends. Jon loved showing the video to anyone who would agree to watch it. "You want to watch my wedding video?" He was so in love with Jenna. They kept in touch through emailing, instant messaging, and satellite phone when it was available. They seldom went any length of time without checking in and sharing.

Then, the losses began to take their toll. Dennison and Schiller in November. Jon returned home for his mid-deployment leave at Christmas to a whirlwind of activity. Spending time with his family in New Hampshire along with Jenna's, their time together went all too quickly. The death knell continued with the loss of Swiger, White, Nunez, and Gonzalez in March, further shaking Jenna's confidence that everything would be all right, that Jon would make it home safely.

Weeks later, under a rain-filled sky, Jenna clutched the American flag that had draped Jon's coffin. Carefully folded, it represented so much but offered so little to her at this moment. She was dressed in her army dress blues, stoically trying to maintain proper military bearing. Arlington National Cemetery had seen all too many funerals these past years, and there would be so many more.

Sole survivor Bobby Henline remembered his four paratrooper brethren this way:

> My four Angels talked to me today during my run this morning. Yes, it takes four to keep Henline in line.
>
> Emolo, my Strength Angel, born in Africa, came to the states to join the army and became a U.S. citizen.
>
> McCandless, my Wild Child Angel, a lot like me when I was young. That's all I'm saying.
>
> Hoover, my Tough Guy Angel, young, strong, fishing, hunting, with a wad of chew in his cheek and charm.
>
> Grassbaugh, the Brain Angel, smart, business-sense, decision-making, leadership.
>
> They all have big hearts. I draw strength and wisdom from them.
>
> Although they have admitted from time to time they let me mess up just to see what happens because it gives them a good laugh.[5]

On April 17, 2007, a letter from Major General David Rodriguez, Commanding General, 82nd Airborne Division was distributed. In it came the announcement that Secretary of Defense Robert Gates was ordering the extension of current combat tours from 12 to 15 months. To the members of 5-73 CAV it meant three additional months of patrolling and all the dangers that seemed to grow ever more menacing in the Diyala River Valley. Their concerns would soon be realized once again. For the families, it would mean that the daily worries that went with having a deployed service member had to be faced no matter how they felt about the war or what the Pentagon had decided was best for Iraq.

CHAPTER 23

"Another Normal Day"

The Turki patrol base that Bravo Troop occupied and Alpha Troop's patrol base in Zaganiyah had significantly different force protection footprints from As Sadah. HESCO barriers, giant concrete T-walls, triple-strand concertina wire and sandbags weren't being used in As Sadah. The standoff appeared to be minimal.

Charlie Troop's commander, Jesse Stewart, wanted to send the message to the villagers that a different approach was being tried. Stewart declared that, "I can go out there and I can kill all the bad guys I want day in and day out for a 12-month rotation, but that's not what's going to win the war."[1] Rebuilding the Iraqi security force and Iraqi political infrastructure would be a strategic success. Stewart believed that supporting the reconstruction piece of the counterinsurgency doctrine or the third side of clear, hold, build would ultimately return stability to this area. The local leaders were told if they helped identify the insurgents living amongst them, in return they would receive the support and funds needed to rebuild.

One of the challenges that confronted Charlie Troop was a lack of a strong local leader. The previous mukhtar had been killed and his son had become the de facto leader. Unfortunately, he had little interest in the position and resigned the following week. It seemed that Al Qaeda's tactics of fear and intimidation were highly effective. One villager who stepped up resigned the next day after he received threats of assassination. Another candidate for mukhtar was found, and he was quickly attacked by a car bomb that injured him. He left the next day. Eventually, by constantly making the rounds looking for support, Stewart found another mukhtar to represent the village. It was important to have this leader so that funds and projects to improve sewerage, water, electricity and transportation would show the villagers that the Iraqi was a strong leader and that he could get their needs met and work with the Americans.

Six towns surrounded As Sadah with a mix of Sunni and Shia citizens. The mukhtars began meeting with Stewart to determine needs. The allocation of food for families needed to be addressed. Each family would be allotted 40 kilos of rice

2nd Platoon Bravo Troop (Willie Lillie)

and flour each month. Food distribution centers would be established to support the effort. Al Qaeda figured out that they could steal the food and then blackmail the locals into supporting their terrorist activities.

To counter that threat, a list of families was developed to make sure they received their rations. Another issue was the restoration of electrical services. Electricians were hired to restore power. Every couple of weeks the mukhtars would convene a leaders' council to receive a progress report from Stewart. Eventually, the province governor and military leaders began attending. As stability returned, sympathizers of Al Qaeda realized that it was in their best interest to switch sides and they began to turn in the insurgents.

Sadly, these Iraqis were accustomed to violence and the threat of death. When Saddam had been in power there wasn't any sectarian violence. Mass punishment was the order of the day. People wouldn't allow somebody bad to move into town because if they did, everyone knew that the entire town could suffer. Not providing information to the authorities and being discovered meant that 10 people would be executed for your crime. Members of the Iraqi army were suspect, since the Iraqi soldiers tortured civilians. The Iraqi army leaders were harsh towards their own troops, unable to lead without using a heavy hand. First Sergeant Coomer observed that you "can't blame a dog that bites when it's beat all the time."[2]

April 23, 2007 was shaping up to be what Willie Lillie described as "another normal day."[3] 2nd Platoon of Bravo Troop, which was commanded by Kevin Gaspers, had moved to As Sadah so Nick Bajema's platoon could go for a refit, taking a brief break from the rigors of patrol base duty. There had been a morning patrol that was uneventful, amounting to a morning meet and greet. Afterwards, one of the medics had made hamburgers for lunch.

Lillie, Clint Moore, the Bravo Section Sergeant in 2nd Platoon, and Adrian Godoy, the Alpha Section Sergeant in 2nd Platoon, were playing rummy. Moore had a previous combat deployment to Iraq during the initial invasion and had been a cavalry scout since joining the army in 1998. Godoy had been born in Santiago, Chile and his family had immigrated to America when he was 13. He'd enlisted in the army in 2002, had a previous deployment to Iraq and had reenlisted. He wanted an assignment with the 82nd and got to 5-73 CAV in March 2006.

The conversation happened to turn to Iraq and dying.

Moore said, "Yeah I'm not trying to die in this bitch."

Lillie agreed with his friend. "I hear that, man. Yeah, they tried to get me when I was wounded, they tried to get me, but they didn't," Lillie said, remembering his experience in Turki Bowl I.

Moore got up to leave the game in preparation for the afternoon patrol that he would be leading. "Play another hand," Godoy urged him.[4] Lieutenant Kevin Gaspers came in to inform Moore of the route he wanted them to follow during the patrol. As the platoon leader, Gaspers not only had command of the platoon, he had the authority to dictate details of what route these patrols would follow. The young officer had graduated from the University of Nebraska and was commissioned through the ROTC program. He'd wanted an army career since he was a young kid in middle school back in his hometown of Hastings. Godoy was within earshot and reminded Gaspers that was going to be the same area his patrol would be covering later that night. Kevin wanted them to check out several abandoned houses. Godoy headed out to his truck to check the battle tracking system and perform a map reconnaissance in preparation for the night mission.

As the Bravo Section leader of 2nd Platoon, Bravo Troop—better known as "Workhorse" Platoon—"White 5" (call sign) Moore would be leading the patrol. Willie Lillie described Clint Moore as "a tough guy with a no-bull type of attitude, a tough taskmaster who didn't play favorites. Everything from mentoring to training was always combat focused."[5] He could always be counted on to tell you exactly what was on his mind whether you liked it or not. He was hoping to spend his entire career in the 82nd. His dad had been there for 15 years and Moore figured that with the four cavalry squadrons in the Division it would be easy for a cavalry scout to find a home at Fort Bragg.

Despite being tough, he wasn't one to miss having a good time. He had recently returned from his mid-deployment leave with plans for a platoon-sized pig roast and concert featuring him on his new keyboard that would take place after their return from Iraq.

As well as the card players, others in the platoon were relaxing in the base. Specialist Michael "Robo Cop" Rodriguez was all army. His old man was an 82nd Airborne alumnus having retired as a first sergeant who'd also served as a Ranger instructor and was jumpmaster qualified. Rodriguez was living his dream. He just wanted to be outside the wire chasing down the bad guys. According to Sergeant Lillie, down time found him "reading army field and training manuals, even looking through the squadron's study guide then quizzing the other paratroopers in the platoon."[6]

Sergeant Lillie remembered that Staff Sergeant Kenneth "Chuck Norris" Locker was always smoking a cigarette as if "the cigarette had done something wrong to him and he was mad at it." There was this story that circulated around about Locker working on a range with a young paratrooper who hadn't received any training on setting a claymore mine. Locker laid a few choice words on him as he snatched the mine from his hands declaring, "If I would have known we were blowing claymores we would've been training for a week."[7]

Brice "Wildman" Pearson was the old man of the platoon. At 29, the army had offered him the life change he was seeking. He could keep up with and run circles around the youngsters and they were drawn to him for advice and counsel. The crazy situations Pearson found himself in, like giving driving classes to British soldiers, had earned him his reputation and nickname. Always willing to stand up for what he believed in, he was the unofficial section advocate. He was the official face of the squadron, having found himself on the Headhunter poster. His goal was to be the oldest command sergeant major in the army.

Specialist Michael Vaughn always seemed to have a story about his crazy weekend adventures. He was, according to Lillie, "always making everybody laugh."[8] He started out driving for Sergeant Lillie. Eventually, he got moved to the .50-caliber machine gun. He was always smiling, and Lillie couldn't figure out if it was because he didn't have to listen to Sergeant's Lillie's yelling or because he just loved being a gunner.

Specialist Jerry R. King had been with Workhorse Platoon since 2005. He could be counted on to take his job seriously and to perform flawlessly. He had this "get after it mentality" which drove him to accomplishing the mission no matter the obstacles. He was able to maintain an upbeat mood with what one of his platoon mates, Adam Benaway, called a "quick wit and sly smile."[9] He'd been used for sniper missions as a spotter and was highly dependable in the toughest of environments.

Private Randell T. "Junior" Marshall was the "FISTer" or fire support specialist on this patrol, responsible for coordinating calls for fire. Marshall was the kind of soldier that every platoon sergeant wanted to have 10 of in the platoon. He never hesitated to help out a buddy or offer a friendly anecdote in any situation. With a warm smile and jovial personality, Marshall was a favorite among his superiors and peers alike. According to Sergeant Lipscomb, a fellow fire support specialist, "even when he was kicked by a 2,000-pound bull and bit by a brown recluse, he kept his spirits up and his focus on his duty." His sole concern was to get in shape "so he could return to jump status and get back on the line," Lipscomb recounted.[10]

Garrett Knoll was the medic assigned to the patrol. Knoll was a new and young paratrooper, a little guy with a big heart and strong drive. Upon arriving in theater several of the medics ran Knoll through all sorts of drills to ensure that he was ready to provide patient care under combat conditions. New medics were given strenuous patient treatment scenarios with all their gear, at all hours of the day and night. They had to start IVs on everyone who would volunteer a vein. They low-crawled to a simulated patient, dragged the wounded to safety and administered treatment. The squadron's physician assistant, Major Rather, gave some additional training on pain management and IV antibiotic treatment to make certain Knoll had the latest techniques available in the field. A senior medic supervised each new medic and Idi Mallari was Garrett's. Mallari ran Knoll through the drills for his own satisfaction. They had some time before the next patrol and it gave Knoll a chance to build his confidence and take the edge off being nervous. It didn't take long for Mallari to acknowledge that Knoll had what it would take to care for a wounded soldier. "Go get some rest," Mallari told him.[11]

A short time later, Mallari stopped in to visit with his friends from Workhorse platoon. They were his first-line platoon and he had been with them through all their training and Katrina, so he had a special affinity for them.[12] Everyone agreed that Knoll was a good medic and they all appeared to have taken to him already. On his way back to the aid station, Mallari ran into Lieutenant Gaspers. Mallari jokingly told the lieutenant that he was going to hijack Knoll back to Charlie Troop to work for him. "No way," Gaspers replied. He was tired of "losing his medics to other troops." Mallari smiled at having gotten a rise out of the lieutenant. Gaspers' response was a good sign; it told him that the lieutenant also approved of Knoll. Mallari recalled that, "I was glad that the Workhorse platoon had a good medic."[13]

The members of the patrol formed up in the courtyard for the pre-combat checks and pre-combat inspections. These were done beforehand to make certain that all the members had the proper equipment and that their weapons were in good order. Gaspers began to brief his soldiers when the distinct chatter of a Kalashnikov rifle alerted them to a potential threat. The enemy small-arms fire appeared to be coming from a building that was just on the other side of the road that paralleled the patrol base. The roof guards began to engage the insurgents. The enemy fire rapidly intensified and was coming from the north, south and east.

Eight members of the patrol returned to the protective cover of the building, entering the rooms that were serving as the platoon's sleeping space. Staff Sergeant

Clint Moore grabbed Privates Tempke and McDonald, guiding them to a room that was in between the stairs and the aid station, ultimately saving their lives. Moore quickly left that room and headed towards the room where the eight other members were located, presumably to alert them of the danger. Private Marshall had taken cover behind a pillar that was adjacent to the stairs. Sergeant Adam Benaway was the sergeant of the guard when the attack began. He was heading down the stairs towards the platoon's room to gather his gear.

Simultaneously, two vehicles were approaching the patrol base. At first, they appeared to be part of normal street traffic. However, their intent became horribly apparent as soon as they made the sharp turn at the intersection and began accelerating towards the compound.

The first dump truck struck the jersey barriers that were situated at the entrance to the market which was parallel to the patrol base. The size of the truck made it easy to drive through and over the barriers and it proceeded to make a sharp right turn heading straight for the room where Lieutenant Gaspers and his paratroopers were located. The truck came to rest next to the outside wall and immediately detonated. A large portion of the building collapsed. The detonation and collapse killed or mortally wounded everyone who was in that room.

A second truck immediately followed the first. Apparently, the suicide bomber driving the second truck became disoriented due to the debris and dust cloud that was created by the first explosion. In the confusion, the bomber detonated his deadly cargo next to the market, demolishing a large portion of the shops that lined the road that separated the school and the market. Calls for help began to fill the air.

Sergeant Benaway had narrowly missed being killed by the first truck bomb. As he regained his senses, Specialist Cain appeared climbing over the rubble pile that had been created by the explosion. Cain had been one of the roof guards who had engaged the enemy when the attack started and was blown off the roof by the explosion.

Marshall was found lying on his back and had taken the full effects of this deadly blast. His right arm was torn off at the shoulder and it had been blown out into the courtyard. Marshall's arm was retrieved, and he was carried to the aid station by Cain and Benaway. One of the other roof guards, Private Gonzalez, was partially trapped by the rubble and was extricated by Specialist Carpino and Sergeant Doherty. With extensive wounds to his left arm and buttocks, Gonzalez was bleeding profusely and couldn't see or walk.

Doc Rather and several medics including Mallari were hard at work sorting and treating the casualties. Marshall had suffered a shrapnel wound that was essentially non-compressible. The bleeding was extremely difficult to control. Even with a tourniquet in place, he was rapidly bleeding out. Doc Mallari was working feverishly to save Marshall.

Sergeant Lillie had rushed out of the tactical operations center as the firing commenced. He was crawling out of the room just in time to be slammed against the wall in the hallway, knocking him out momentarily. He let his training and experience take control, assisting with treating one of the wounded and establishing a security detail to cover the courtyard and protect the incoming medevac helicopters. With his weapon buried in the rubble, one of the paratroopers retrieved a weapon from a wounded Iraqi soldier and the security detail headed towards the courtyard. Lillie entered the aid station and saw Marshall with his detached arm placed between his legs, obviously in deep shock and with multiple wounds. The sight before him was mind numbing.

One of the Bradley Fighting Vehicles was used to punch a hole in the wall adjacent to the landing zone, allowing the wounded to be moved more quickly to the waiting helicopter. They had to cross 150 meters of open terrain with the wounded. Several enemy fighters appeared and began shooting at the litter teams as they moved the wounded. The security detail covering the alley returned fire, killing the insurgents.

Suddenly, Lillie switched gears and ran over to the room his platoon had occupied and began to assess the damage. The injured had been evacuated from the remains of the roof. He could account for himself and four members of the platoon. The outside wall was gone. The interior wall was separated from the ceiling, and it looked as though it had been peppered by a series of shotgun blasts. The fragments had splintered the little bit of furniture that was visible.

Lillie tried to locate his uniform shirt and pull the battle roster out of it. He couldn't find it, so a nearby MRE rations box would have to do. As he made a list from memory, the list of missing quickly grew.

I've got some of my best friends down there, he thought with a sense of dread.[14]

Lieutenant Colonel Poppas arrived, and Lillie gave him a situation report. "Guys made it through 9-11, they found guys in the rubble, I think we'll be alright," Lillie told him with cautious confidence.[15] Lillie hoped that they could survive being buried. The support beams had to be moved. Additional help arrived along with a wrecker, which was used to help pick up some of the bigger pieces of concrete and steel beams. All the digging was done by hand.

Approximately two hours into the ordeal, Sergeant Moore was located. They uncovered him partially and he moved his shoulder. Told to do it again, Moore did so and that got everyone motivated. Although severely wounded, Moore had a strong pulse in his wrist that indicated a workable blood pressure, so his treatment was aggressive. Despite being grievously injured, Moore was able to alert the rescuers to the whereabouts of his trapped friends, once again heroically placing the well-being of his comrades above his own.

Pearson was lying on top of him and had to be removed before Moore could be extricated. Even though Pearson was dead, Doc Rather worked on him out of respect for those around the scene. Pearson had so much debris in his airway that a hole had to be surgically cut into his throat. Pearson had already begun to stiffen.

Lieutenant Gaspers was found next, followed by Vaughn. An interior wall separated the area, so digging on both sides lengthened the amount of time it took to locate the others. They knew Sergeant Locker had gone back in the corner to take a nap. After Locker was found, Knoll and Rodriguez were uncovered at the same time.

The smell of death swirled around the paratroopers. They worked feverishly to rescue their trapped comrades. The dust hadn't settled, and the partial ruins of the school lay before them. It was a stark reminder of the brief but violent firefight that had just ended.

The entire squadron knew of the double vehicle-borne IED attack on As Sadah patrol base. They had heard the explosion miles away and knew it was As Sadah. The notification came soon after with a transmission over the communications net. The battle roster numbers quickly identified each member who had been lost.

Poppas walked towards Nick Bajema with what appeared to be a small notebook. As Poppas moved closer to Bajema he could hear the battle roster numbers of his fallen comrades tolling in his head. Reaching Nick's side, Poppas appeared to tower over everyone around him as he handed Bajema a blood-splattered photo album. It was the one Nick's wife had given to him before he deployed to Iraq. "Hey Nick, I found this in the rubble, I think it's something that your wife would probably want you to have," Poppas said with a sense of profound sadness.[16]

Nick was overwhelmed with emotion. It had come out of the wreckage of the patrol base where just days before his platoon had been sleeping. They had skirted death only because after a brief refit at the Caldwell base, a truck breakdown had kept them at the motor pool just long enough to miss the attack. 2nd Platoon had taken their place. *Why were we six hours late that day?* Nick wondered *Why them and not us?*[17]

The loss of Kevin Gaspers and his fellow paratroopers had been the largest single loss of life for the 82nd Airborne Division since the Vietnam War. The personal tragedy reverberated through the squadron. Many who knew them were also close to them and felt the searing emotional pain of their loss. Nick Bajema remembered Kevin Gaspers "was probably the nicest guy I've ever met." He'd be the guy to step in and defend someone who was being abused. He always had something nice to say. He was an honest and trustworthy friend who was loyal to his peers and cared deeply for the paratroopers in his platoon.

He always put the needs of his troops ahead of his own. "I don't think he ever made a decision without considering how it would affect each of them," Bajema said. He continued to recall that Kevin felt that, "The guys on his crew were good luck because they always seemed to be one truck ahead or one behind when the convoy hit an improvised explosive device."[18] The irony was inescapable. That luck had run its course.

Efforts were made to recover some of the equipment and sensitive items. Finally, around midnight the survivors stopped and attempted to comprehend the tragic events. Sergeant Lillie was told that Moore and Marshall had died from their wounds. Everyone had hopes that both would survive since they had pulses when they were medevaced. Lillie and Moore had been especially close. The loss hit Lillie hard.

Working his men to keep them busy, Lillie continued the process of accounting for equipment and weapons of all the dead paratroopers. Having to share the devastating news of the additional losses was almost too much to bear. Lillie declared that, "This ain't going to let us down, we still got to honor our brothers, their memory. They're going to be watching us. We're going to find these guys that did this."[19]

They began to talk about their fallen comrades, telling stories and sharing memories. It would be a long, sleepless night. When they finally tried to sleep, any small noise would wake them. Closing their eyes meant seeing the horrible images of their friends as they were being pulled out of the rubble.

The only thing keeping me sane is, if I lose it, I'll lose the guys that I have left, Lillie told himself.[20]

Several days later, the remnants of the platoon would form the Patriot Line that would escort and pay tribute to their friends as they began their final trip home.

Now it was time to rebuild the platoon. A new platoon leader was assigned along with enough soldiers to return the platoon back to full strength. The senior commanders had to think about Willie Lillie and decide if he could soldier on. What would it take for someone to return from the tremendous grief that comes with such a horrific loss and be able to set the example for this new collection of paratroopers? After what he'd been through, he deserved the chance. Captain Stewart, Charlie Troop's commander, recalled that, "We could have pulled out, and we could have left very easily. I'm sure that if I had asked the battalion and brigade commander, they probably would have moved another company in. But then what are we saying to all those guys who we just lost, we're saying we're quitting, we're done, and we cannot do that."

Charlie Troop seemed to take hold of that sentiment and Captain Stewart observed that his paratroopers "realized that the only way we're going to be able to personally vindicate each one of these guys is by continuing to fight day in and day out."[21] In some small measure of exacting revenge, the next night a small kill team was able to locate an enemy mortar emplacement and destroy it. Satisfaction tempered by sadness.

Willie Lillie rebuilt his shattered platoon. The platoon had gotten replacements who were fast learners. On their first raid as a new platoon, they were in the blocking position and got into a firefight. Two insurgents who had taken off running to the east ran right into 2nd Platoon's position. One of the enemy fighters came out screaming Jihad with a pistol and the other one had a Kalashnikov assault rifle. They were quickly engaged and wounded. Three other jihadists attacked the platoon and they were also wounded. 2nd Platoon, Bravo Troop had proven that their loss would not deter them from accomplishing the mission.

CHAPTER 24

We Regret to Inform You

Ever since he had entered middle school Kevin Gaspers knew that being in the army was what he wanted to do with his life. His dad had other ideas for him. John ran his own construction business and Kevin had been learning the trade helping him. John thought that would continue. As Kevin got older, John tried to convince him to steer clear of the military. "I didn't want Kevin to join the army," John said. His father's dread continued to grow in intensity. "When he got into high school and I could see the direction he was headed, I began to fear for him."[1]

Trying to convince Kevin to reconsider proved fruitless. John remembered that, "I told him, Kevin, you can do what you want to do. I don't want you to hate us for life. It's your life. But I'll buy you a Hummer. I'll paint my equipment camouflage. If you want to jump in sand, let's go out to western Nebraska and we'll jump in sand."[2] Kevin would not be deterred from his dream.

"We taught our kids we would respect what they did in life as long as it was something honorable," Kevin's mom, Pam, reflected.[3] Kevin began his college education at the University of Nebraska in Lincoln and signed up for Army ROTC. His parents gave their blessings to Kevin and hoped for the best.

Police officers and firefighters have dangerous jobs too, his mom thought.

Four years later, Kevin graduated and received his commission as a Second Lieutenant in the U.S. Army. His dream had come true. Now it was time to be tested. After attending Officers Basic at Fort Knox for his Armor/Scout branch, jump school at Fort Benning to earn his paratrooper wings, and Ranger School, Kevin was assigned to the 82nd Airborne Division. He was going to be a platoon leader in 5-73 CAV. The die had been cast.

When Kevin arrived at Fort Bragg, he became fast friends with guys like Jesse Bolton and John Dennison. As their deployment to Iraq drew closer, they got some leave that allowed four of them to go on what was dubbed as a "Lieutenants Gone Wild" trip to Key West. Their first order of business was to head straight to the beach. The perfect location was found: bleach white sand and crystal-clear water. Kevin dove in first as if he'd been waiting his entire life for the opportunity. The

Kevin Gaspers (Pam Gaspers)

summer waters were the perfect temperature. Kevin appeared a few moments later with a puzzled look on his face. "Why's it so salty?" he asked. No one else thought anything of the taste, Jesse Boulton remembered that everyone suddenly realized "that was the first time Kevin had ever been in the ocean."[4]

When Kevin deployed to Iraq, John told Pam that he felt like he had signed his son's death certificate. At Christmas, he told her that he felt that Kevin wasn't going to make it home. His premonitions continued to haunt him. Kevin's mid-deployment leave was delayed several times due to hardship needs of other troops. He finally got home March 25, 2007, right before Easter, for a well-deserved two-week break from the stress of the deployment.

The following week Kevin went to visit a class of third graders from Pam's hometown school in Alma, Nebraska, about 80 miles away. They had befriended him by way of his grandmother. She was friends with the class teacher and had the class write Kevin, send him cards, and stay in touch with him. He visited with his grandmother and got to spend some time with his sisters, especially his younger sister Audrey.

Pam could detect that he was troubled, recalling that, "You could see it in his eyes, you could see it." When she inquired about it, Kevin said, "I'm on a 24-hour anxiety level, and I can't rest. At home I can rest, I can go do what I want to, and I don't have to worry about a bomb blowing up, I don't have to worry about anything." He wasn't looking forward to returning to Iraq because everyone was always on edge.

Kevin described the confusion of battle to his mom, saying, "I only have a little bit of this huge puzzle and things aren't clear. It's smoky, you have noise going all over the place, you don't know where some things are coming from, and sometimes you don't even know where your own men are let alone everyone else."[5] During one battle, Kevin put in a call for close air support. That must go to an air force joint terminal attack controller who in turn relays the strike information. Kevin knew where his guys were so when he heard the coordinates that were sent by the controller, he knew they were wrong. Not only were they incorrect, the mistake was putting his troops in danger of being hit by friendly fire. "Cancel that strike, it's the wrong grid," Kevin hollered but it was too late. Fortunately, the aircraft missed the target, because if it hadn't, Kevin said, "They would have hit my men."[6]

As the days grew closer to Kevin's departure date, he grew quieter and more withdrawn. On the way to Omaha to catch his plane Kevin told his sister that he was "going to a bad place" and not to tell their parents.[7] They would only worry even more. His parents knew all too well. The news was full of the daily horrors of war. Even without the political slant some of the networks put on it, Iraq was a powder keg full of violence. The sectarian strife placed Kevin and his soldiers squarely in the middle of a fight that made it difficult to distinguish between good and evil, the tormented and the torturers.

Soon after Kevin left, Pam found a green government-issued notebook in her bedroom. Opening it, she found all sorts of phone numbers associated with the military. Thinking that Kevin might need it, she called him. Kevin told her, "Mom, I left it on purpose. I don't need it, but you probably will. Just keep it."[8] Pam put it away and didn't give it any more thought.

As the casualty notification officer and the chaplain approached the front door, Pam saw them from the front window. She began to scream, "He's dead! He's dead!"

We regret to inform you...

"You cannot describe the pain that you feel when you see the chaplain and a soldier walk up to your door and you hear your wife screaming," John Gaspers said. "It's unbearable."[9] The news of the attack and the deaths of the nine paratroopers in As Sadah were going to be released shortly. Pam and John had to make some calls. She remembered the green notebook. When she opened it, there were all the phone numbers that she needed.

The funeral had all the pomp and circumstance that goes along with honoring a soldier who died in combat. Paratroopers from Fort Bragg were there to serve as an escort. The flag that draped Kevin's coffin was carefully folded and presented to the family. Another flag would be given to the parish priest, so it could be flown at the school each day. Mournful notes of taps followed a rifle salute. Pam wanted Kevin buried close by so family and friends could visit and tend to his grave. Hastings is a small town and it seemed as if everyone was there to show their support.

They appeared as if their grief would overtake them. How would they make it through this tragedy? Each member of Kevin's family had to cope with it in his or her own ways. John feels that they will carry the burden of Kevin's death with them as long as they live, as if it is their fault. Pam observed that John, "is angry. I don't know if that will ever go away." She finally told him to, "Just get mad at Kevin for doing this and get it done and out of your system and you'll feel better."

Pam thought, *There's a lot worse things than death.*

Your child coming back brain damaged, limbs lost, unable to function. Pam knew that Kevin "would never want that."[10]

Weeks after the funeral, Pam and John had to decide what Kevin's headstone would look like. There was a picture of Kevin and John working up in the rafters of a house that they had been building. "We'll put that on the tombstone. Leave me out of it, it'll just be him,"[11] John suggested. In the meantime, Kevin's truck arrived from Fort Bragg, and John began to clean it out. As he moved the visor on the driver's side, to his surprise the same photograph fell into his lap.

A few days after Kevin returned to Iraq, Pam and John had attended a fundraiser for the Hastings Catholic schools. After the parish priest asked for those in attendance to pray for Kevin and another area soldier who were both in Iraq, the bidding began on a plaque that had been created by a renowned artist who had donated her work, and the plaque was to be donated back so it could be hung in one of the schools. The title of the piece is the "Armor of God" and is a biblical quote taken from Ephesians 6:10–6:18. Kevin's mom and dad were the highest bidders. As funeral preparations got underway, Kevin's parents thought that this plaque should be displayed next to Kevin. Up until this point neither Pam nor John were aware of the exact verse but quickly realized that the plaque seemed to be made for them.[12]

Weeks later, Kevin's personal effects began to arrive. The case officer assigned to the Gaspers had received the bins after the mortuary services team at Dover Air Force Base had cataloged, cleaned and packed all the items that Kevin had when he was overseas. The only item that hadn't been cleaned was a tan baseball-style cap with the arrowhead symbol and the word "RECON" on it that one of Kevin's friends, Jesse Boulton, had sent. Jesse told Pam that Kevin would put it on after returning from each mission. It still smelled like him.

The bins were opened in front of Kevin's parents. An inventory sheet documented and confirmed the contents. Uniforms (which along with some of Kevin's other clothing Pam used to have three beautiful remembrance quilts made for her and the girls), boots, even 37 pairs of socks were accounted for. There was a beautifully ornate box that contained personal items like Kevin's wallet along with the military pocket bible that Kevin had with him when he died. Pam began to flip through it and came to a dog-eared page. To her surprise, it was Ephesians 6:10–6:18 underlined! Kevin had never known about the plaque's existence.

To establish a lasting memory of Kevin, "the Armor of God" memorial plaque along with a plaque bearing an image of Kevin in his dress uniform and red paratrooper beret were placed in St. Cecilia's, Kevin's high school alma mater. A yearly scholarship in Kevin's name was established using all the contributions that people had sent.

To the Gaspers, these were clearly signs "from God that he is taking care of Kevin and his men!"[13]

There were other messages that appeared over the next year.

Pam and John were in the basement, and Pam was vacuuming. In one corner there was a shadow box with Kevin's medals in it. She shut the vacuum off, and suddenly they heard consecration bells ring twice in that corner. There aren't any bells in the room.

"Did you hear that?" Pam asked John.[14]

Stunned by the religious bell ring John acknowledged that he too had heard the bells toll.

A friend of the Gaspers had lost his son, and he recounted getting a curious phone call that didn't show up on his caller ID in the early morning hours. John's call came about a year later at 5:00 a.m. on Veterans Day while Pam was away at a speaking engagement. Pam was speaking to the third-grade class that Kevin had corresponded with in nearby Alma, and John was speaking at Adams Central High School in Hastings. John let the phone ring two or three times: there was no caller ID, and when John picked it up there was no one on the other end.

Pam began reciting a novena to Saint Theresa soon after Kevin left, asking for an orange rose to indicate that her son was OK. It seemed that at least once a week an orange rose would appear in her travels. It happened often enough that Pam was convinced it wasn't just a mere coincidence. While Kevin was home on leave no orange roses crossed her path. Then, the first flowers to arrive at their doorstep after Kevin's death was announced were orange roses.

Audrey is the youngest of the Gaspers children. Her sister had gotten married and moved to Tampa, and with Kevin gone she felt especially alone. Her emotions were even affecting her high-school volleyball game. Finally, one night she just came unglued: "Kevin's gone; he'll never see me play."[15] One Friday evening Pam got a call from an acquaintance by the name of Cathy. She was hesitant to begin the conversation with Pam because it had to do with a dream or maybe it was a vision that she had the previous night.

She continued, "I woke up last night to popping noises in my bedroom. I remember sitting up, hearing the noises, I looked over at the chair by my bed and there's Kevin sitting there, popping balloons." Cathy stopped for a moment to convince herself that she wasn't losing her mind. Pam urged her to continue. "Kevin smiled at me and said I have a message for you to give to my baby sister. You are to tell her I am there for her, I'm watching her, I am in the gym. She can't see me, but I am there, and I want her to know that. The entire time he's talking Kevin is popping balloons, 17 in all and then he leaves."

"Why the balloons?" Cathy wondered.

Pam said Audrey's birthday was coming and she was turning 17. That was the number of balloons that Kevin had popped.

She continued to quiz Pam, "Well, how come me?"

Pam speculated that if it had come from someone she knew real well that she might not have believed the story. The conversation ended with Cathy's admission that she had not attended church in a very long time having lost spiritual faith.

"Go back to church," Pam urged her.[16]

There were even humorous moments that helped relieve some of the pain. The third-grade class that Kevin had corresponded with had written notes to the Gaspers offering their condolences. Pam, John and several close friends went through them. Lots of tears were shed until they arrived at one particular card. "Dear Mr. and Mrs. Gaspers, I'm so sorry about Kevin. He was a wonderful person. I just don't know why this happened. Well, I've gotten on with my life now." Everyone just started laughing. Out of the mouths of babes.

While Kevin was home, he'd shown Pam some photos including one of a destroyed gun truck, which upset her. Kevin told her that a healthy way of dealing with it was to "learn to laugh."

Pam thought for a moment then said, "I'll take it where I can get it."[17]

Joking one day about moving flowers from one cemetery headstone with an abundance of flowers to one with too few, Kevin's older sister Katie said that was exactly what Kevin would say. He'd go and pick someone else's observing that they'd never miss them. Their new normal would take getting used to. "We closed one book and now we have to open the other one up and start writing in it," Pam reflected.

Pam committed to getting others through their grief. Pam's mom was struggling with the loss of Kevin. At one point she said to Pam, "I don't know why you pray anymore; your prayers weren't answered."

Pam looked at her in amazement. "You know what mom, my prayers weren't answered."[18]

But somebody else's prayers were granted that day. Pam went on to remind her that someone who couldn't handle the painful loss as well as she was able to was blessed to not have had their child taken from them. Don't ever say prayers weren't answered, Pam insisted.

Pam and John waited almost 11 months to receive the autopsy report along with the after-action report describing the attack. Apparently, they should have had it within six weeks. Pam finally had to reach out to Senator Chuck Hagel's office to get action. Twelve days later a package containing the reports arrived. The Gaspers approached their family doctor with a request to review the documents first. He agreed to do so, then called them in.

According to the autopsy, "Kevin died instantly," the physician declared. The cause of death was from "blast and ballistic fragment injuries." Nowhere in the report was asphyxiation mentioned. The manner of death was "homicide." What a twist of irony; would a suspect be brought to trial?

"My son is gone, but at least he hadn't suffered and that was a blessing," Pam said.[19]

Pam wrote letters to all the families who had suffered the loss at As Sadah. She shared with them how proud Kevin was to be their platoon leader and how much his soldiers meant to him. Pam hoped they had no hard feelings or felt it was Kevin's fault for what had happened. "You never know where people are going to put blame," she said.

No one blamed Kevin for what happened. His dad respected the fact that his son had chosen to be an officer in the army. John acknowledged that "now we have to carry that cross for the rest of our lives. That's what I'll hate the most."[20]

CHAPTER 25

Rest in Peace

The enemy continued to probe Charlie Troop in As Sadah, looking for opportunities to inflict harm. A nearby cemetery, no more than 200 to 300 meters away from the old patrol base, was a favorite spot for the insurgents to bury weapons and set up ambushes. They liked to put their improvised explosive devices near the cemetery. The dismounted patrol that stepped off from the As Sadah patrol base on June 6, 2007, was no different than so many other patrols. In fact, an identical patrol had moved through the same area on the previous day. They'd swept the cemetery checking for wires to eliminate any danger from enemy explosives.

This patrol's mission was to observe any enemy movement and engage as necessary. The thought was that a resupply convoy that was scheduled to arrive would spur the enemy to react. Leading the patrol was Staff Sergeant Tim Cole. The 27-year-old former Marine had decided to join the army in 2005, becoming a cavalry scout and shipping out to Iraq with 5-73. The platoon sergeant, Robert Cobb, had originally planned to accompany the patrol. Cobb was working with a detail reinforcing the patrol base perimeter with claymores when Cole approached him. The additional force protection work needed to be finished so Cobb told Cole that he didn't want to hold the patrol up and to go ahead without him.

As Cole and the patrol walked through a field, they came to a mud fence, maybe three or four feet tall, with an opening in it to walk through. A previous patrol had opened it up. It was the only point that the patrol could pass through. There weren't any gates or other gaps that could be used. According to the patrol's medic, Kevin Geis, "They'd used it a couple of times. We varied our route but when we'd go in that direction, we would always go through that hole." One can only speculate but as fate has it, Geis recalled that, "I guess they were watching."[1] It was a pressure wire, designed to explode in one direction—the way they were coming from. The first person would step on it and the shrapnel would strike everyone else. The enemy had cut one-inch pieces of rebar, metal rods used to reinforce concrete, and put it in front of the explosive. However, the explosive device didn't detonate as the enemy had planned. Seven members of the patrol passed over it before it went off.

Tim Cole (Nick Bajema)

The explosion propelled shrapnel and rebar at supersonic speed towards Cole and the remaining members of the patrol.

Geis had made it through the opening in the wall and was about 25 meters away from the explosion. He recounted that he "was the last one or the second to the last one to make it over before it went off."[2] Shrapnel struck Geis and threw him to the ground. The medic quickly recovered and returned to the wall to find mayhem spread before him.

Geis found Cole's lifeless body on top of the mound of dirt that had concealed the deadly bomb. He was peppered with shrapnel and suffering from a massive head trauma. There wasn't much that could be done to save him. Observing that Cole was struggling to breathe, Geis gave him the benefit of the doubt and inserted an airway. Another paratrooper managed his breathing with a bag mask. Next, Doc Geis moved to an injured paratrooper whose left arm was almost completely amputated. He also had a leg trauma and was unconscious. In addition to the Americans, three Iraqi soldiers had been grievously wounded along with their Iraqi interpreter.

At the patrol base, Cobb and the work detail had just finished their assignment. Cobb heard the explosion and immediately began running towards the tactical operations center.

"My guys just got hit," Cobb declared.[3]

Reaching the entrance to the center, Cobb's fears were confirmed as frantic radio reports of the attack were transmitted by the patrol. A quick reaction force raced to the scene accompanied by Cobb and Lieutenant Nick Bajema, the platoon leader. They secured the scene and went to the aid of the injured so they could be medevaced. Lieutenant Bajema tried to comfort two of the critically injured paratroopers knowing that their conditions were grim. These were his guys.

Cole and Bajema shared the same hooch. Cole had the rack next to Bajema's. They spent their down time playing ping pong and Cole was constantly bragging about how good he was, even though Bajema always seemed to beat him. One night they broke open a chem light and poured the florescent liquid all over the ping-pong balls. Tim Cole was quite a character and always wanted to be in the middle of the fight. When Bajema had taken over the platoon after John Dennison was killed, Cobb told him that when the shit was on, Cole would be the tip of the spear. Cole wanted to be in contact with the enemy, to be on point. Cobb emphasized that Cole was "an absolute warrior. He never had to lead through words, he led through action. The guys looked up to him, they wanted to be like him." Cobb declared that he had lost his "little brother."[4] He'd always put a smile on his face no matter what the situation, good or bad.

As he prepared to return to Iraq, Tim Cole told his mom "that he would never live to see 30." Mid-deployment leave had given Cole a chance to reconnect with his wife and kids. Although excited about the birth of a son and already having three girls, he had a sense that seeing them grow up wasn't in the cards. A tattoo with R.I.P. on his stomach was an ominous body art addition.

The Rest in Peace sentiment didn't escape his mother, Connie Cole's scrutiny. "Timothy, why would you say something like that?"

Tim's response was eerily fatalistic: "Because I know."

The scene at the airport was filled with emotion: hugging him as though it would be for the last time. His mom didn't want to let go. Knowing that when she did, it would be all over.

"Stop crying, Mama, I'll be alright," Tim pleaded.

It was so painful for Tim's mom to say goodbye facing the fact that Tim believed his death was imminent. As they walked away, she turned to see her son one last time. *How could this be happening to us? What will we do? How will we cope with this heartbreaking loss?*[5]

His mom bought a black dress in anticipation of Tim's funeral. She needed to be prepared because she felt that Tim wouldn't return. Connie remembered that, "I've never worn the dress again, but I find it very hard to throw away."[6] Tim's gravesite was turned into a monument to the bravery of a fallen warrior. A large headstone bears an image of Tim in his Class A dress uniform. Joes refer to it as the funeral photo because that's what appears in the death announcement. On the back of the marker is a silhouetted photo that was taken when Tim's squad was on the Iraq–Iran border. You can recognize Tim because a halo has been placed above his head. Below the image is the narrative that appears on the Bronze Star with Valor that he received for helping save Dary Finck's life months earlier. Adjacent to the grave is a flagpole flying the American flag. Next to it is a statue of the up-turned rifle, helmet, boots and dog tags that symbolize a fallen soldier, and on the other side of a granite bench there is another statute of a soldier in full combat gear and rifle in hand. It is both a unique and fitting tribute to this proud paratrooper.

Yet another soul had been taken by the demons of As Sadah.

CHAPTER 26

Olympus, Hoplite and Pericles

The squadron continued to conduct operations throughout its extended area of operations. The purpose was to support the defeat of Al Qaeda in Baqubah through the disruption of the enemy and to prevent them from reinforcing from outside of the city. As the operation to clear Baqubah continued, 5-73 CAV systematically cleared the support zone for insurgents north of Baqubah.

Each operation fell in line with the original campaign plan for the Diyala River Valley. In turn, each operation would build on the intelligence of the last operation while deliberately increasing the squadron's hold and decreasing the hold of Al Qaeda in the area. The region was the center of the initial footprint for the Al Qaeda sub-branch or what is now the Islamic State of Iraq. It was where all their key leadership was and where they were trying to begin to emplace their shadow government.

The Al Qaeda fighters continued to rear their ugly, violent heads. Raids conducted by Headhunter were uncovering intel that indicated a need to increase pressure on these enemy cells. An enemy command post complete with a map of the Warhorse base and a Russian-made Dishka tripod-mounted heavy machine gun capable of striking incoming helicopters was discovered during one of the raids. This continued fight for intelligence reinforced the need to continue the drive to eliminate Al Qaeda in Iraq.

Headhunter's plan was to work the opposite side of the Diyala River moving from south to north, conducting troop- and squadron-sized air assaults. Bravo Troop would become an aerial strike force. Their sole function for the duration of the deployment was to perform what could be described as surgical-level, precise air assaults. Bravo Troop got to the Warhorse forward operating base, set up a tent, surrounded it with concertina wire and made it a compound within a compound. The sign read "Strike Force 300, restricted area. You'll be beat down with a bat if you enter."

While plans were finalized for the upcoming operations, enemy contact continued, and Headhunter responded with ferocity. Whether it was enemy rifle or machine-gun fire from a rooftop, sweeping up enemy weapons caches or disarming improvised

Operation Hoplite (Sergeant Angela Widener)

Conducting a rehearsal of concept drill in preparation for Operation Ithaca (Senior Airman Steve Czyz)

explosives, they wanted enemy fighters to regret engaging 5-73. A raid to capture a high-value target, a suspected member of the enemy leadership, began with approaching the target house and initiating a shotgun breach of the front gate. The gate flew open and the suspect attacked one of the paratroopers who quickly responded and killed the enemy fighter with a shotgun blast.

Sometimes though, the enemy was successful. There was a bridge that linked the Warhorse forward operating base with the Zaganiyah patrol base. The bridge was guarded by Georgian troops. On July 11 the enemy successfully detonated a car packed with explosives and destroyed the bridge. The loss of the bridge slowed the logistics resupply to the patrol base until an alternative crossing was established.

Enemy attacks using IEDs continued to plague Headhunter and injure paratroopers. The intelligence continued to be refined resulting in the further isolation and disruption of the enemy. In one instance, information was received from an informant that the insurgents were using boats to ferry explosives to the Zaganiyah side of the river. Several boats were discovered. They were well camouflaged and appeared to contain bags of rice. A closer examination revealed that they were concealing bomb-making materials and weapons.

The enemy threat took different forms. On one occasion a section was conducting one of the numerous daily patrols that took place in and around Zaganiyah. As the gun trucks proceeded down a lateral route on the outskirts of Zaganiyah, they rounded a corner to find an enemy 122mm mortar team emplacing the weapon in preparation to attack the patrol base. This mortar system delivers a projectile that can travel over four miles and has a blast radius of 60 meters. One of the .50-caliber machine guns immediately began engaging the retreating enemy as they fired their Kalashnikov rifles. A second gun truck quickly joined the fight, engaging the enemy fighters. The small pickup truck that had been used to transport the mortar tried to escape with two enemy fighters. As they attempted to outrun the Headhunter patrol, machine-gun fire ripped into it, and the truck rolled over into an adjacent canal.

Sergeant Lewandowski, the patrol leader, ordered two of his paratroopers to clear the vehicle. As the paratroopers reached the burning truck, one of the enemy fighters was trying to pull the pin on an incendiary grenade to avoid capture and take his potential captors with him. The paratroopers killed the insurgent with accurate rifle fire. The other insurgent was trapped underneath the vehicle. The truck was on fire after the fuel ignited. Fearing that the truck would explode, the paratroopers quickly returned to the safety of the gun trucks. The enemy truck exploded in a ball of flames and was totally consumed.

Bravo Troop's first mission as Strike Force 300 was to an area where it was uncertain if Al Qaeda had seized the village. So, they did a soft knock. The area was isolated, the first house was chosen, and a tactical call-out performed. This meant that the occupants were asked to step outside to meet with the paratroopers. It was determined that the area was still friendly. At that point, the mayor linked them up with a schoolteacher who could speak English. Dobbins and his paratroopers were able to determine from the local population that Al Qaeda insurgents were trapped in Diyala. There were Shia strongholds to the north, which is northeast of Diyala, so there really wasn't an area they could move north unless they moved into a different province. The enemy had spent time and treasure ensuring that the foreign fighters were part of their plan to control Diyala. It was a top priority for the senior Al Qaeda leaders to hold it.

The battlespace was under the operational control of a unit with tanks and Bradley Fighting Vehicles. Their sheer size severely restricted their movement into some of the small villages along the river valley. There was no way to get a tank up through the palm groves. One of Charlie Troop's platoon leaders observed that "it's no different than a barrio in one of the bad areas in the states, you know where the gangs say we better go where there's one place in, one place out and where they're going to get the best safe haven."[1] That's what the Diyala River Valley afforded the enemy.

Bravo Troop initiated the first of these efforts to eliminate the Al Qaeda presence. Operation Ithaca was a troop-level mission executed as one of the shaping operations that would lead up to Operation Pericles, which would bring all of 5-73 CAV to bear on the enemy. Ithaca caught the insurgents completely by surprise. The paratroopers encircled the enemy and they had no way to escape. While some of the insurgents attempted to escape, an enemy stay-behind force attacked the paratroopers. Headhunter responded with full force arrayed to destroy the enemy. Besides the accurate small-arms fire from the paratroopers, artillery fire, Apache gunships and the cannon fire from air force fighter jets attacked the dug-in positions, killing the insurgents. The enemy was rooted out, forced into the planned kill zone, killed or captured.

Through the night and into the early morning the enemy was engaged and Headhunter along with Iraqi army troops dominated the fight. The Bravo Troop paratroopers searched and cleared continuously for eight hours, all while taking fire from a disciplined and determined enemy force. Several large weapons caches that contained rocket-propelled grenades, heavy machine guns, Al Qaeda propaganda, Iraqi army/police radios, military uniforms and over 17 IEDs were uncovered.

As the building clearance continued, the brutality of Al Qaeda was once again reinforced. The insurgents had reached a new low. In the village of Abu Tauma eight captives were found by Bravo Troop. They had been marked for execution that very day. One shirtless middle-aged Iraqi man's back was one massive bruise. From his shoulders down to his waist the deep purple marks confirmed his story of having been beaten and tortured by his captors. As they were being questioned, it became apparent that Al Qaeda had trained children to beat the captives and threaten them at gunpoint. One of the captives began to cry uncontrollably when a youngster who appeared to be as young as 12 years old entered the room. The boy's mere presence sent the man into hysterics. Once again, it was apparent that this brutal enemy would stop at nothing to dominate these people.

Through the oppressive summer heat other operations followed with names like Olympus and Hoplite. They all followed the path towards Pericles, the engagement area that was created by the shaping operations that had been conducted over the past five months surrounding the towns of Qubbah and Mukisa in the northern portion of the Diyala River Valley. To ensure everyone knew all the mission details, huge rehearsal-of-concept drills would be run. Laid out on large pieces of black plastic, road networks, buildings, topography and phase lines were all set up in miniature three-dimensional detail. The attack plan would be walked through, and the paratroopers were expected to commit it to memory. The extensive fire support plan made sure that coalition forces didn't become casualties due to friendly fire. Artillery fire would shift as friendly assault forces approached each phase line, a map coordinate that kept troops organized.

Operation Pericles, which was executed from August 12–22, would be the largest of these operations. With the three cavalry troops of 5-73, a Stryker armored vehicle company and an additional airborne rifle company, 5-73 CAV would execute the clearance of Objective H-Minus, the designated engagement area around Qubbah and Mukisa. The concept of Operation Pericles was the isolation of the west, south, and east sides of Objective H-Minus by one troop air assaulting, with another mounted troop seizing key road intersections and routes. To the north, an attached cavalry squadron conducted operations to force the enemy into the objective and then prevented them from escaping. Once the isolation was set, the remainder of the squadron would air assault into the town of Mukisa and systematically clear each structure and the surrounding palm groves.

The goal was to destroy the enemy using artillery and aviation just prior to troops being brought in by helicopter. With the final clearance operations ready to begin in the hottest months of 2007, Headhunter planners had lethal fires down to an art. Captain Hercik guaranteed that his fires plans "whether it was a troop air assault or a squadron mission, we could integrate the full meal deal on every mission."

The enemy's haven and ultimately their route of exfiltration included the palm groves. Rich in cover and concealment, they afforded the insurgents the opportunity to escape and the option to fight from prepared positions. Hercik noted that as the insurgents "hauled ass, we started dropping mortar and artillery rounds in the palm groves and other exfiltration routes. So, the only way the enemy fighters could run, was to where the helicopters were landing, or they could just stay and fight. Lo and behold, they had to stay and fight and we were able to destroy them."

If Hercik wanted a round in a certain place, it didn't have to be shot at that exact point on the map. It's about getting the destructive effect to reach the vicinity. That effect was designed to deny the enemy the ability to move through that area.

With a hint of sarcasm, Hercik pointed out that you didn't want to have to get White House approval for a target because it might hit a house so "now it's 200 yards away, nobody's house is getting hit, the brigade commander can approve it, in case you've never been 200 meters away from a 155mm shell exploding in the air above palm trees, that's a lot closer than you want to be."[2] Headhunter was about to apply these techniques along with others to maximize the destructive force that this kinetic energy provided.

There would be nine separate kinetic strike packages for Pericles. This meant that the operations order included a fire support plan that combined all the different methods that had been used in every other squadron mission up to this point. Hercik described it as "the most robust fires plan to be used in theater" to date. As Hercik stood up to give the fire support brief of the operations order, he could sense some in the audience questioning his level of sanity.

"Is this guy fucking serious? No fucking way. This guy's crazy, he's out of his mind!"[3]

The plan had been sold up through the chain of command with difficulty: Hercik had struggled to explain how his plan would benefit the operation. Many of the decision makers in the higher headquarters had never been in combat. All they were thinking about was collateral damage and winning the hearts and minds.[4]

A division fire support officer called Hercik wondering why it would be necessary to shoot a fire mission at two in the morning at the palm groves. Hercik explained that the target was not who was in the palm groves, since hostile intent had not been established and positive ID would have to be determined per the rules of engagement before firing on suspected terrorists moving through the palm groves. The objective was to "shoot the trails and enemy escape routes through the palm groves" to deny enemy movement. "No shit," Hercik recounted that the clueless officer said, "Well what if one of their children is lost and the man's running through the woods trying to find his child."[5] The dirt bags Headhunter was after didn't give a shit about their kids. No Al Qaeda father was going to be running through the palm groves in the middle of the night. The only motivation the insurgents had was violent extremism.

As the rehearsal-of-concept drills for Operation Pericles were executed there seemed to be a sense of dread amongst the paratroopers. One of those paratroopers, Sean Ventura, recalled that "the plan that we'd received was dangerous and casualties were very much expected." Originally, the deployment had been slated to have ended by now and the squadron would have already been headed home. Ventura continued, saying that they were "extended, tired, and having already lost 22 brothers there wasn't a lot of hope left. People tended to be a lot quieter in that week leading up to Pericles. Groups of friends would cluster around a bunk with weary looks and tired smiles. We would talk about things we had wanted to do as though they would not ever happen. We were resigned to our fate."[6] With the plans approved, the operations order issued, and the paratroopers prepared once again to take the fight to the insurgents, Operation Pericles was launched.

Ten minutes prior to the initial air assault, a B1 bomber made its first pass dropping seven 2,000-pound bombs in the palm groves surrounding Zaganiyah. Headhunter knew from experience that the enemy would use the palm groves to hide their weapons caches. Another goal was to distract the enemy from the actual objective area. The B1 sortie accomplished both.

Five minutes before the Black Hawks and Chinooks carrying the paratroopers landed, artillery from the Normandy forward operating base began firing rocket-assisted projectiles into the palm groves. This suppression of enemy air defense mission would eliminate any anti-aircraft weapons that the insurgents might have waiting for the inbound helicopters. Simultaneously, the multiple rocket system battery at the Normandy base fired 11 guided rockets at suspected cache locations in the palm groves surrounding the main objective area followed by a guided missile at an abandoned school that was known to be rigged with explosives and was less than 200 meters away from one of the landing zones. If the enemy blew that school while the Black Hawks and Chinooks were inbound it would wipe out several of them.

Once the first lift came in, the artillery at the Normandy and Warhorse forward operating bases fired rocket-assisted projectiles that suppressed and neutralized any possible enemy escape routes within the palm groves. Next, a second pass by a B1 bomber dropped an additional four 2,000-pound bombs on road and trail intersections within the palm groves. These strikes were meant to stop any attempt by the enemy to use these in order to maneuver on the coalition forces as they continued the clearance. The jihadists would scurry to the palm groves to retrieve their hidden weapons and return to their fighting positions to await the coalition forces. The goal of Headhunter was to sever those routes of travel so the enemy couldn't bring heavy weapons to the fight.

The Alpha Troop mortars at the Zaganiyah patrol base were also brought to bear to deny terrain to the IED emplacers. In addition, attempts were made to stop the enemy from returning to Qubbah by targeting the palm groves. Snipers were positioned off into the dead space that wasn't being hit with indirect fire or clearing at that time, so there was no way for the enemy to potentially ambush friendly forces.

As the assault forces approached the landing zones, Apache gunships flew overhead protecting the lift aircraft carrying the Headhunter warfighters. When a Black Hawk or Chinook came into the landing zone there was always an Apache watching that landing zone. The Apaches let the inbound aircraft know if it was safe to land.

"Wait, hold on." Kill him and, "Alright, now you guys can land."[7]

So, there were always Apaches in the battlespace and they accounted for many of the enemy kills.

The air assault was initiated at 1:00 a.m., clearing in darkness for four or five hours. Air assaulting onto the objective, landing zones were about 100 meters out from the village so Headhunter was literally running off the ramp of a Chinook or stepping off the Black Hawks into the first building.

LTC Poppas and his command RTO (radio), along with Andy Hercik, lugging the Fires radio and a couple of NCOs for security, made up the "TAC light" or assault command post on every troop level and above air assault. The Tactical Operations Center (TOC) was in the follow-on trucks of the ground assault convoy. Once the ground assault convoy or GAC arrived, the big antennas went up and a static location for the TOC was established.

The S3, Major Sylvia, ran the fight from an ACC2 (airborne command and control) helicopter, which was a specially modified UH60 with a command post inside. It had four seats, each with a computer console and a radio and a blue force tracker. The S3 sat in one seat, the SIGO (Signals) sat in another seat. Another fires guy sat in the back. The aircraft hovered around at about 1,500 feet, outside the range of conventional radios from Warhorse so it had retransmission capability. It was the main C2 (command and control) hub for these air assaults.

Once on the ground, the Joes quickly assaulted the first buildings. An explosive or ballistic breach using a shotgun signaled forced entry into each building. After getting a foothold in that first building, the 240 machine guns and automatic rifles moved onto the rooftops, and provided the base of fire for the assaulters as they pushed in. In the first hour and a half they killed or captured most of the enemy fighters. Many of these villages were so large that the initial focus was on clearing the actual houses and then establishing a temporary patrol base for a few hours. Rehydrating was vital to being able to continue the mission. Medics even resorted to using IVs to get the needed fluids on board quickly.

In the early morning hours, around 4:00 a.m., the paratroopers moved into the palm groves. The goal was to clear them by 8:00 to 9:00 a.m., because the heat became unbearable. "The groves are like nothing that I've ever experienced," declared 2nd Lieutenant Walker Gorham, platoon leader, 1st Platoon, Charlie Troop.[8] In the middle of the summer in the Diyala River Valley it was easily 140 degrees. The paratroopers were wearing 100 pounds of equipment and body armor—it was no small task to work in this kind of heat.

When they hit the swamps, anyone who'd earned their ranger tab had flashbacks of the Florida phase; hot, humid and wet. The imagery showed only that the vegetation was dense. The plan was to get on line and clear, making sure they didn't stray in front of each other. Each plot of land was fenced off. Bolt cutters and Leatherman tools were used to try to cut holes in the fences. Sergeant First Class Pete Johnson was a platoon sergeant in Charlie Troop at the time. Johnson had years of experience in long range surveillance and observed that "progress was so slow, insanely slow." Moving through the swamps with full kit on was hot and miserable. On the map it was only a couple thousand meters. Johnson continued saying, "This'll be done in a half a day, we'll get back, call the helicopters" and exfiltrate. It turned into a daylong pain in the ass and to top it off before the teams could be picked up, they had to "walk back through all that crap."[9]

All the homes were systematically cleared. If no weapons were found, or enemy contact wasn't made in the home, then "identities of the families would be verified and run through a suspect blacklist."[10] ID cards were an important part of the process. Since most of the Al Qaeda terrorists possessed fake IDs, using tactical questioning skills similar to a police investigation to determine who was telling the truth was an important skill set.

Men, women, and children would be separated. An interpreter working with the platoon leader and platoon sergeant coordinated the questioning in order to accurately identify all the civilians. ID cards were taken from the women and the kids. Family and tribal names were cross-matched. It was easy to tell when a family was cooperating and willing to pinpoint on a map where the enemy fighters were living. ID marks were placed on the necks of each person in order to prove that they had been interviewed and cleared.

This ID mark coincided with homes that had already been searched so the villagers wouldn't be able to move from house to house. They were instructed to stay in their homes, or they'd be considered a threat. If the local populace wasn't controlled, the insurgents could force them to serve as a suicide vest bomber and attack coalition forces. The key to success was completely controlling the objective and making sure innocent people clearly understood the need to follow instructions. At this point the insurgents knew that it was a death sentence to fight so they would try to blend into the population. After almost a year and a half, Headhunter had developed what Lieutenant Gorham described as "a keen eye for identifying the telltale signs" of an enemy presence.[11] The lack of women and children in a home, fake ID cards, or large amounts of ammunition were all pieces of the intelligence puzzle to key in on.

Once the clearance was completed, forums for reconciliation between Sunni and Shia leaders were organized. Restoration of essential services became a high priority and both groups would benefit from the effort. The 5-73 paratroopers lived in the towns, helping to ensure the safety of the civilian population and maintain an accurate picture of any potential attempts by Al Qaeda to return.

In addition to the five squadron operations and 18 troop-level operations, countless platoon operations and innumerable patrols were conducted. The paratroopers were able to connect the dots following a mission. They were able to build the intelligence into planning for future missions using techniques like those utilized during criminal investigations. The troop-level leadership was given the leeway to produce missions driven by this robust intelligence. Platoon leaders would write up a Word document, troop commanders would review them and add commanders' comments. The intelligence assessment would be forwarded to the squadron leadership and continuously reinforced the need for 5-73's continued presence in the area.

The platoons were aggressive and encouraged the paratroopers to exploit the intelligence. They were able to develop intelligence to make sure they put the insurgents away for a long time. Often sensitive targets were close to the patrol base. The enemy was attempting to be within striking distance of the patrol base. Once a target building was identified, a patrol quickly moved to the enemy location by foot, isolated it, and grabbed the suspects virtually undetected. These missions were able to beat the insurgents to the punch and destroy the enemy network before it could mature.

Following Pericles, Mukisa became the site of Headhunter's next patrol base. By this time in the deployment Mike Few, Alpha Troop's commander, was headed for a stateside learning assignment at the Naval Post Graduate School. The troop's new boss was Captain Joe James.

One platoon covered Zaganiyah, and one platoon protected Mukisa and Abu Garma from the patrol base. Every three to four days the platoons rotated out, refit and then moved to another patrol base. So now Alpha had two new towns that they needed intelligence on as well as to secure. There was one Iraqi army company inside of Zaganiyah that was split in half, keeping some of them in Zaganiyah and then moving the other half of the Iraqi soldiers up to the Mukisa/Abu Garma patrol base with Captain James.

Initially the Iraqi soldiers didn't want to go up to Mukisa. James was able to calm their nerves and reassure the Iraqis that they were needed to protect the villagers and chase the insurgents out. The Iraqi army troops immediately began to conduct point raids to help develop the intelligence picture. A platoon from Charlie Troop was attached to Alpha Troop. Alpha Troop was stretched thin with two patrol bases and the need to have a quick reaction force for each patrol base in case a patrol was attacked and needed reinforcements.

Several insurgent bomb makers were identified, and raids were conducted on their homes. IED-making materials, blasting caps, and wires were discovered. Homemade explosives were being used. Captain James explained that the bomb makers were "combining fertilizer and whatever else to make some type of explosion."[12]

Despite the successful raids, the attacks continued. Small kill teams were sent out to locate the emplacers. James resorted to using checkpoints to stem the flow of enemy explosives. It was a tough choice because each checkpoint "ate up combat power."[13] Patrols were reduced to one a day. Half the time a patrol would have to depend on a portion of the quick reaction force and fingers would be crossed that things wouldn't go to shit. The next quick reaction force response would mean that anyone that was left in the patrol base would have to go. Any additional enemy action meant calling the platoon from Zaganiyah to respond.

The Iraqi troops had their share of the hardship. An Iraqi company was switching out to take leave. As the column headed north, they struck an IED and the explosion killed two Iraqi soldiers. The detonation was immediately followed by a coordinated small-arms attack that took the lives of two more Iraqi soldiers and left six wounded. Their mangled bodies and grievous injuries were testimony to the hard fight that lay ahead. The villagers of Mukisa denied any involvement, but the intelligence had the enemy fighters using the palm groves as a staging area and women of the village supplying them with food. They were still loyal to Al Qaeda.

Another attack on a joint 5-73/Iraqi patrol was initiated by the insurgents using an IED, followed by small arms and rocket-propelled grenades. The difference was this time it was spotted. The gun truck sped up and drove over the explosive device knowing that if the driver slammed on the brakes the gun truck would have stopped right on top of the device. Speeding past it, the ensuing explosion narrowly missed them. One of the turret gunners saw an enemy fighter preparing to fire a rocket-propelled grenade along with several enemy fighters carrying Kalashnikov rifles and began engaging them with bursts from his machine gun. There wasn't any way to confirm it, but it looked like at least one insurgent had been killed along with several wounded. The quick reaction force reached the ambush site and retrieved the enemy grenade launcher, several rounds and numerous Kalashnikovs. There were blood trails, and the weapons were covered in blood. These Iraqi soldiers were willing to take the fight to the enemy, aggressively getting into firefights to take back the town from the insurgents.

A curfew was established. "Nobody will be out at night. Once the sun goes down, be in your house or you're going to be engaged," James decried. That night, the roof guards at the patrol base picked up movement.

"Hey, they're maneuvering on us, and it's after curfew," observed the Joes.[14]

Too easy! The rapid fire of the paratroopers' heavy weapons cut through the night air.

The next morning a joint U.S./Iraqi patrol left the wire on a routine reconnaissance mission. They started snooping around to figure out what the intruders had been up to. They uncovered a weapons cache that had two surface-to-air missiles, three mortar tubes, mortar rounds, grenade launchers and rockets. The cache was literally on top of the patrol base. It was open to speculation whether the insurgents were moving the weapons, preparing to use them to attack the base or staging it for a future attack. Either way, the alert troops on guard had probably saved quite a few lives.

The dismantling of Al Qaeda was just one part of the complex picture that needed to be addressed. There seemed to be a general mistrust between the mukhtars, sheiks and the local mayors. The provisional government leaders believed that the locals were collaborating with the insurgents. As a result, no services were being provided. There was a lack of employment, so the higher headquarters provided $50,000 towards hiring workers to pick up trash and begin to clean the streets. All three towns were struggling to restore electricity to the area. One of the water treatment plants was disabled, so people were going into the canals to get drinking water. The canal water was heavily contaminated from bathing as well as being full of trash.

Bottled water was trucked in to address that shortage. Even the distribution of food had been stymied. A food bank was started in Mukisa and Abu Garma that allowed foodstuffs to be given out to those in need.

Bravo Troop continued to aggressively pursue the insurgents and engage the population to support the needs of the locals. Captain Patrick Levier was now leading Bravo Troop. Levier had previously served as the squadron's battle captain.

Levier gave his first operations order on September 4, took command from Captain Stephen Dobbins on September 5, and launched an air assault on September 6. As Levier took command, Al Qaeda was moving out of Baqubah and coming back into Balad Ruz. The intelligence was red-flagged and sent up to higher headquarters with an urgent request for combat power.

Everything Headhunter had accomplished in the Turki Bowl operations was, according to Captain Levier, "now in jeopardy of being lost."[15] The insurgents had destroyed all five Iraqi army checkpoints and killed the Iraqi troops manning them. Al Qaeda was extorting food, money and shelter from the locals. If they didn't cooperate villagers would be tortured or killed. The village elders claimed "we're locked into our own houses; we can't move around our own neighborhood. Al Qaeda is burning our houses, killing families and just running everyone out of the palm groves." Al Qaeda preached that "we own you; we own this area; the Americans will never come into the palm groves of Turki."

Suicide vest bombers began to materialize in the Balad Ruz market. Forensic markers indicated that the same individual was fabricating the explosive devices. One by one Bravo Troop hunted the insurgents down. They narrowly missed the local Al Qaeda leader. He evaded capture by being rolled up in a carpet and propped up against a wall.

Levier took a combined force of Bravo Troop paratroopers along with 150 Iraqi soldiers and cleared the length and breadth of the palm groves. They showed the enemy that the Iraqi troops weren't cowardly, Al Qaeda were the cowards. Captain Levier declared that these terrorists "were killing women and children but when the men came to fight them, they hid and ran."[16] Bravo Troop exerted so much pressure on the insurgent leader and his Al Qaeda cell that the terrorist leader sent a letter to the mayor promising to leave the area if Bravo would stop pursuing them.

Not only were Sunni extremists active, violent Shia elements were also posing a threat. The Shia were much savvier. They infiltrated the government and sent their strongest political figure from Baqubah to control the police force. The police force had been heavily infiltrated and Jaysh al-Mahdi death squads were active. The political hack insulted the local police chief in front of his men, telling him he was "inadequate", took over the chief's office, and began taking his men out on patrol.

Levier and his paratroopers went to his house. He was told, "You're not welcome here. You're not a local government official so you don't say who gets hired to be a police officer."[17] His family was politely escorted outside, their house was searched, all the weapons were confiscated, and the politician was escorted out of the city on the brigade commander's orders. He was sent packing back to Baqubah. Upon returning to Baqubah the Shia politician saw to it that an assassination hit was placed on the mayor, the Iraqi police chief and Levier. The contract killers were from neighboring Quinon. Fortunately, Levier and his civil affairs counterparts had spent a great deal of effort in Quinon restoring the local government in the town. The intelligence on the contracted hit quickly came to Levier's attention. Levier had the intelligence forwarded to the province leaders in Baqubah and the Shia hack was fired.

A story surfaced about a local businessman who owned a car wash and fuel point. Jaysh al-Mahdi came to the fuel point demanding money and fuel. He refused to comply. As he was driving home, his car was ambushed. The assassins pulled him out, and he was executed on the spot. The killing was linked to the Jaysh al-Mahdi infiltration of the police. As Bravo Troop began their transfer of authority with the incoming U.S. Army unit, one of their missions was the arrest of the terrorist members who had carried out the killing.

CHAPTER 27

Church, Duran and Home

In the midst of shaping operations designed to force the enemy into an engagement area that was ultimately isolated, seized and cleared during Operation Pericles various humanitarian missions continued to be executed. Trying to win the hearts and minds of the Iraqi people continued to be part of the clear, hold and build counterinsurgency strategy. A report had come in that water from a 20-foot-wide village irrigation canal was not flowing due to an obstruction that had been put in place further north of a small farming village. It was another tactic used by Al Qaeda to control the population.

On August 8 the job fell to Bravo Troop to clear the irrigation canal. A column made up of nine gun trucks along with combat engineers headed out from the Warhorse forward operating base. The engineers would be used to clear the canal with explosives.

Specialist Jeremiah Church recalled the mission brief: "Alright boys we'll be in and out in an hour. We're going to run up north. There's this canal that's blocking people from getting running water in a town that we had been looking after for a while."[1] Simple; piece of cake; too easy.

The column arrived to find local villagers armed with rifles acting as a home guard patrolling the area to protect their homes. Escorted by Iraqi police, the column proceeded north. There was a report from the local cops that one of the villagers had a Russian-made machine gun that would need to be confiscated. It turned out to be "a good 15- to 20-minute drive north," which ended up being out of Headhunter's sector.[2] Word was that the assigned unit didn't want anything to do with that part of their area of operations because they always got into a firefight when they went in there. The Bravo paratroopers didn't have that intelligence. It got tense very quickly.

The two senior scouts' gun trucks held back because they had Rhino mine rollers mounted to the front of the Humvees. These massive devices made it impossible to move any further down the narrow canal road. They secured the choke point in the road, making certain that any threats from the rear could be stopped. The road ran north to south. On the west side was a village, and then on the southeast side there was another village. A spot report team from 3rd Platoon observed someone

Jeremiah Church wounded (Jeremiah Church)

Memorial T-wall (Sean Ventura)

with a heavy machine gun. The remainder of the column was proceeding down the canal road led by an Iraqi police truck along with the mayor and his armed escort.

As the spot report was received—"Troops in contact!"—both ends of the column began to receive enemy fire.

Orders were being shouted to the dismounts to take cover. The high-velocity noise of Kalashnikov rifle rounds sped by them. Sergeant Lillie could see rounds skipping around the paratroopers. Lillie reported that they were "taking fire from the west at this point."[3] The Joes at the choke point quickly returned to the safety of their gun trucks. At the head of the column, the police pickup and the lead gun truck were engaged by intense, accurate fire from a heavy machine gun mounted in a technical vehicle 200 meters north of their position. Rounds struck and destroyed the pickup, killing one Iraqi police officer instantly.

Manning the .50-caliber machine gun located in the lead truck's turret, Specialist Church immediately engaged and killed two insurgents. Simultaneously, large volumes of fire erupted from the trenches that surrounded his platoon's position. Because of the terrain, none of the other vehicles could engage with accurate fire, so Church was now in an intense firefight with over 30 well-entrenched insurgents who controlled the dominant terrain and were heavily armed and well supplied.

Church identified three more insurgents in a nearby canal and killed them with a short burst of fire. A gun truck at the choke point detected an enemy fighter moving along the left side canal. A Mark 19 grenade launcher eliminated the threat. As soon as the round was fired, they began taking enemy fire from three different directions.

The lead trucks in the column were separated from the rear element by about 100 meters. The front of the column was trapped in a complex ambush. The road was so narrow that the gun trucks couldn't reposition. There was a 15-foot-wide canal full of water separating the paratroopers from the enemy and no way to reach the other side without it being suicidal. These enemy fighters knew what they were doing. They were well trained, had sliding positions built on rooftops, had trenches in the canal system, and interlocking sectors of fire.

If this wasn't enough firepower, what showed up next made matters worse. An enemy technical truck with a heavy machine gun appeared. The enemy fire was so intense that it was as though you were standing in a tin building in a hailstorm. The noise was deafening, and it was almost impossible to hear the radio, which was being used to call for fire support. There were three insurgents in the back of the pickup truck firing the machine gun. Church killed all of them, but the truck escaped.

Church continued to engage enemy dismounts to his left and right using the turret-mounted machine gun and the 240 SAW. There were so many targets that as soon as he killed one enemy fighter another would pop up. The volume of enemy fire was unbelievable. Suddenly, Church said, "I hear a deep rumbling again and these sons-of-bitches got a brand-new machine-gun crew, gotten back on this truck and are in front of the road again. So, I took out the truck again."[4] Church grabbed another can of .50-caliber ammo and was reloading the machine gun when an enemy round struck the ammo belt, traveled through it, entered his left wrist, and traveled down the length of his arm. Lead and brass fragments had torn up Church's arm. He grabbed a tourniquet from his battle buddy, applied it to himself, reloaded, and continued to engage the enemy.

Despite efforts by his lieutenant to convince him to exit the turret, Church continued to carry the fight to the enemy, killing several more insurgents. Church recalled that, "I was mad cause I'd gotten shot. I was amped up and I was ready to go. I fought harder than I'd ever fought."[5] The combination of training and muscle memory drove him. As a result of the artery retreating down into his forearm, the tourniquet was not having the desired effect of completely controlling the bleeding. Church finally relented and turned the turret gun over to another paratrooper.

Rummaging through a medical bag, Church found a trauma bandage and applied it to the wound. That seemed to stem the flow a bit. They were stuck in place and couldn't get air support or artillery as they were out of their sector. The only thing to do was to keep firing the turret-mounted machine gun. There was only one problem with that plan—they were running out of ammo in the gun truck cab.

Church knew that there was ammo stored in the trunk, so he grabbed his rifle, pushed the door open and as he laid down covering fire swiftly moved to the rear of the truck to retrieve more ammo. Rather than thinking, *I probably shouldn't get out of the truck, I'm in the middle of a complex ambush I might get shot,* Church was determined to keep feeding the gun. *God damn it, we're out of ammo again, I gotta get more ammo.*[6] Church knew this was making the difference between escaping this wall of enemy fire and their destruction.

Church exited the gun truck twice to retrieve ammunition before they were finally able to extract themselves from the ambush. The rear truck was shot up so badly it was barely running. It had to be pushed out of the kill zone with another truck. With flat tires, shot-up radiators and bullet-riddled doors, the gun trucks slowly escaped the continuing onslaught. The gun trucks were so badly damaged from enemy fire that they couldn't be driven any faster than five to 10 miles an hour.

The firefight had only lasted 10 minutes or so. For now, Church's fight was over. The bullet had destroyed all the ligaments in his left hand except for the pinkie. The median nerve and an artery were severed. Church's left wrist had been destroyed. After being evacuated to Balad, Church continued to demand, "Just give me some chow and let's get the hell out of here, we got shit to do."

The nurses looked at Sergeant Major Edgar and exclaimed, "Are they all like this?"

"Naw, just that kid, he's crazy."[7]

Church wanted to get back in the fight and do it now. He would receive "three ligaments out of a dead guy, a dead guy's nerve and a dead guy's artery in his right hand."[8]

A short time later, Headhunter would take the fight back to the site of the ambush, making the enemy pay in spades, thus denying the insurgents another haven during Operation Pericles.

"Come over and eat with me, dude," came the invitation from Staff Sergeant Joan Duran to Marc Adams, one of the squadron's medics.[9] Adams was feeling down and the invitation was most welcome. Duran was a "funny, nice guy with a boisterous personality. He was well-liked, always had a smile on his face and ready to give anyone a high five."[10] Adams and Duran had served together their entire time at the 82nd. They sat together bullshitting and telling stories like soldiers do. Adams finished chow and headed over to the internet café to check his email and found the café abruptly closed. When Adams asked why, someone told him that Duran had been shot. Adams rushed over to the aid station to find that his friend was dead. Duran was part of a detail handling some Bradley 25mm ammunition. The thought was that possibly a bad round in combination with the heat of the day along with the heat from the gun truck motor had created enough energy for a round to discharge. When it did, Duran was struck in the chest.

During Duran's memorial service, Chaplain Honbarger remembered him for his "ability to see through the brokenness of this world and find objects of value." Duran had the uncanny ability to look at those around him and notice when they were struggling. "He encouraged us, reconstructing us so that we could continue to drive on." He was a great listener and a "friend that stuck closer than a brother." His sense of humor and ability to encourage others were traits he shared. The chaplain concluded by saying, "We dare not say goodbye to such a good friend, for that is far too difficult. Rather we say to our brother and fellow paratrooper we will see you at the final manifest."[11]

The memorial stands in front of the chapel and faces what was the squadron's headquarters. It's a 12-foot tall T-wall also known as a Bremer Barrier, Texas or Alaska wall. Made of reinforced concrete, these walls provide blast protection to various facilities. On the front face of the memorial, starting at the top, the 82nd Airborne Division shoulder sleeve insignia, which is the cloth patch that identifies the division, was drawn: upon a red square, a blue disc with the letters AA in white. The inner elements of the two "A"s are vertical lines and the outer elements arcs of a circle. Attached immediately above the square is a blue tab with the word "AIRBORNE" in white. Immediately below the patch there is a Master Parachutist Badge consisting of an open parachute on and over a pair of stylized wings displayed and curving inward. A star and wreath are added above the parachute canopy to indicate Master Parachutist and signify the high level of jump proficiency. Superimposed on the jump wings is the regimental crest for the 73rd Cavalry Regiment. The shield is divided blue and red with a gold band in the center, representing the three colors of the shoulder sleeve insignia of the armored tank forces. A hand in armor grasping a bolt of lightning is symbolical of the striking power of the organization. Attached below and to the sides of the shield is a gold scroll inscribed "HONOR, FIDELITY, COURAGE" in red.

Below that appear the words "In Remembrance of Our Fallen Comrades" and then the names of the 22 members of 5-73 CAV who died during the deployment. It remains in Iraq silently guarding their memory, standing watch over what these paratroopers endured during those 15 months and hoping that they would not be forgotten. It is a silent testimonial to their bravery and to the ultimate sacrifice that their fallen comrades made.

Headhunter's time in Iraq was growing short. Another unit would soon be taking charge of the Diyala River Valley. The paratroopers of 5-73 had proven that despite the adversities of the months of continuous combat coupled with the loss of their paratrooper comrades they had prevailed, vanquishing the enemy insurgents and returning the Diyala River Valley to its inhabitants. The motto of the regiment, "Courage, Honor, Fidelity" exemplifies the bond that the members of 5-73 would forever have with each other.

Epilogue

For the many who visit there each year, Arlington National Cemetery conveys a deep emotional significance. A little over a year had passed since 5-73 CAV had returned from Iraq when a small group of vets who had pursued the insurgents in the Diyala River Valley were making a reverent visit to this hallowed ground.

March 17, 2008. St. Patrick's Day is normally a day filled with the wearing of the green, parades, and plenty of cold beverages. It's not usually associated with remembering the death of a departed soldier and dear friend. However, it was the anniversary of Ben Sebban's death.

Ben's death hit everyone hard. He was so deeply respected by his peers. All he wanted to do was take care of people and he seemed to treat everyone with the same dignity and respect. His herculean efforts to try to do his job on that fateful day despite his grievous wounds spoke volumes to his character.

The computerized kiosk holds the exact location of each person buried at Arlington. SEBBAN, Benjamin L, SFC Section 60, Site 8613, interment date 29 Mar 07, date of death 17 Mar 2007, date of birth 14 Jul 77.

The ground was soft and freshly turned in numerous rows. The dead were being interred at a steady rate. All the headstones, identical in shape and size, use the same white marble that has been used to identify our military dead for generations. In section 60, many of the fallen warriors who had been laid to rest were combat deaths from either Iraq or Afghanistan.

The group milled around Ben's graveside. To their right a small group approached. As they came into focus an older woman accompanied by a couple of similar age along with two tall young men approached. Ben's mom and his brothers along with a family friend had arrived. There were also two other men who didn't seem to fit in who were several paces back; it turned out that their local newspaper from New Jersey had sent a reporter and photographer to record the event.

Ben's vigil was light-hearted and filled with funny stories about summer sausages and cheese doodles, two of Ben's favorite snacks. A picture floating around of Ben kneeling in front of his gun truck with a sausage strapped to the bumper brought

Ben Sebban's headstone (Arlington National Cemetery)

a roar of laughter from the group. His brothers remembered their childhood with him and what it was like growing up with their younger brother.

A short time later his brothers in arms walked up to Ben's gravestone and silently paid their respects. The sense of loss was palpable.

Fast forward to Memorial Day 2013…

They tended their loved ones' graves as they tended their loved ones in life. Some set up chairs and opened bottles of champagne or placed an unopened bottle of beer on a comrade's grave marker. Others sat as if still in a state of shock. The loss continued to be raw and so painful, despite the years gone by.

A lone bagpiper played "Amazing Grace" and the notes immediately brought many to tears. A friend of Jenna and Jon Grassbaugh spent the day sitting at Jon's graveside as Jenna couldn't, owing to being recently deployed to Afghanistan. The friend told Jenna that she would make sure that Jon was not alone.

Off in the distance the sounds of an artillery salute could be heard as the ceremony at the Tomb of the Unknown Soldier concluded.

People began to surge towards York Avenue as President and Mrs. Obama arrived to pay their respects. They made sure that they spoke with everyone who lined the impromptu receiving line. Visitors continued to come and go. Some were in uniform, their chests covered with the medals and badges that signified their combat service. There were parents, grandparents, wives, children, comrades in arms, maybe some total strangers. They were all here to share the common thread of remembrance. One young man accompanied by his wife and young child walked up to a grave marker. As soon as he saw the name on it he began to cry. Too much to bear, or relief that he had finally been able to make the difficult journey towards recovery?

Warriors have always returned from combat with scars, whether physical or emotional. What they have experienced will never leave them. Terms like shell shock, combat fatigue, and combat exhaustion are all too familiar to previous generations of fighting men and women. Coping mechanisms and the individual's ability to successfully deal with the aftermath are as varied as the person. The effort to effectively understand and treat post-traumatic stress disorder, also known as PTSD, has taken on new meaning during the years that America has been fighting the war on terrorism. With PTSD has also come the clinical realization that there is a correlation between PTSD and traumatic brain injury or TBI.

In the candid and personal insight of one the Headhunter paratroopers who returned from Iraq after their deployment, the suffering is all too real. Out of respect for his anonymity, I'll call him James. James explained that, "Normally I don't talk about this to anybody. I have to talk to a psychologist every week because I have a problem with it sometimes." The therapist thought it would be a good idea to share his story so people could begin to understand what it means to serve, go over there and sacrifice your life.

James continued:

> It started to hit me, because I was relaxed, you know you don't have your life to focus on and other people's lives to focus on, that's a huge responsibility. I tried to stay away from the drinking because I knew it would make it worse, but the mind starts playing tricks on you and the memories start kicking in. Your sleep gets shitty with the nightmares. I don't mean to be rude, but it's personal to me. It's embarrassing because I'd never thought I'd let anything take control of me as much as it does. I get two to three hours of sleep a night. They've got me on sleeping pills to try and help. I hate pills. I hate the fact that the military tries to drown you in the pills.

James concluded by stating that, "The fact that I continue to struggle with it and have to deal with these issues makes my life a living hell."[1]

Geriah McAvin related that "everyone is going to bring a demon back."[2] Chaplain Honbarger observed that he wasn't sure that an accurate gauge could be put on how combat was affecting the Joes. "It's so hard to call. There were probably guys out there that I should have told you've got to get off the line for a little while. Then again, nobody was willing to leave anybody else behind. There were other guys who seemed fine and how do you gauge that, the guy who was fine? Who knows six months from now how it may hit him?"[3]

Alcohol becomes one of the symptoms. Maybe it's self-medicating; Chaplain Honbarger observed that "unfortunately I think it can be hidden very well by saying, hey that's what paratroops do, they go have a beer at night." You can't force them to get better, to face the nightmares, the physical response to what they've experienced in combat.

Honbarger thought that "you can have the greatest psychologist or counselor in the world and if the person's not willing to do any work, then they might as well be talking to a box. I gave everything I had over there. In some sense I think I even gave more than I had." The effects of losing friends and the depression that resulted are part of Chaplain Honbarger's reality. "The adjustment of going through an ordeal like that and coming back to America where people are still buying their Starbucks coffee and going on with their daily business like nothing is happening."[4]

Others, like Wade Sharbono, ended up having to leave the army due to the physiological aftereffects of being exposed to multiple explosions. According to his wife, Diana, when Wade was "medically discharged from the army he was put on the Temporary Disabled Retirement List."[5] This meant that he was supposed to be reevaluated on a yearly basis to see if there had been any improvement in his condition. Based on that, Wade could return to active duty or permanently retire. The evaluation was supposed to take place each year for up to five years.

Four years came and went and still no evaluation took place. Diana maintained contact with the army, attempting to arrange this assessment. She did so twice a year for four years. Finally, they received word that a reevaluation had been scheduled. For two days Wade met with three different doctors, a general practitioner, traumatic brain injury specialist and a neuropsychologist. "Wade was excited to get the results because he knew he had improved significantly," Diana said. The report arrived and the results were, in Diana's words, "devastating."

Diana said that the neuropsych doc "accused Wade of being a malingerer, feigning, exaggerating his symptoms, and playing the victim in order to get benefits through the VA and other veteran programs." How dare they accuse Wade of faking it! Diana and Wade were horrified by the fact that this doctor had spent a mere 30 minutes with Wade before generating what Diana termed the "malicious report."[6]

The fight was on to get Wade the respect he so justly deserved. Diana began combing through Wade's medical files that dated back to 2007 in order to build a medical defense. The army assigned a lawyer to the case and constructed an appeal. Unfortunately, it didn't seem sufficiently solid, so Diana reached out to Wade's current doctors and submitted a second appeal. A lack of response prompted a request for a hearing that required traveling from their home in Colorado to Washington State to appear before the board. Finally, after months of struggling with the army bureaucracy, Diana and Wade arrived to receive an acknowledgment of their claim and an apology for having put them through all the anguish.

In retrospect, Diana advised anyone faced with a similar situation to "Fight! Fight! Fight!" Don't let the process defeat you. It is daunting and you will be told everything and anything. It will be discouraging. Remember, she said, "Your soldier is worth it." With success comes the ability to, according to Diana, "Focus all our energy on healing."[7]

May 5, 2011—3rd Bridge Combat Team, 82nd Airborne Division Area, Fort Bragg, North Carolina. As the formation of red-bereted paratroopers marched towards the reviewing stand, the tops of the unfurled flags appeared first, the national colors and regimental flag. Battle streamers attached at the top flowed in the warm May breeze. As the formation marched forward the squadron emerged from the tree line moving in the direction of the Hall of Heroes and the dignitaries that were gathered to honor 5-73 CAV for being awarded the Presidential Unit Citation. For a moment it was a vision reminiscent of past battles with brave warriors rallying around their regimental standard.

Before the ceremony, members of Headhunter gathered to celebrate what they had earned by their bravery during Turki Bowl I and II. Mike Few, Donnie Workman, John Ferrante, Robert Cobb, and Willie Lillie were still in uniform and at Bragg. Others like Squadron Command Sergeant Major Ray Edgar had retired and returned to celebrate with other members of Task Force 300. Suddenly, a tall figure made his entrance and his comrades in arms swarmed around him.

Colonel Poppas had arrived. Recently promoted, he had traveled from his new assignment as a brigade commander at Fort Campbell to celebrate this high honor. Hugs all around. "You have to give a hug to get a hug"—Poppas' words of wisdom. To these paratroopers it was more like a family reunion than a military ceremony.

Afterwards, all the members of the squadron who had deployed in 2006 who were able to attend the ceremony posed for a picture to commemorate the occasion. They gathered in the squadron area, and Ray Edgar spoke of the tenacity of these warfighters. Despite their different personalities, what they thought of each other and how they were coping, their common thread would always be this shared experience of combat.

Social media became a significant presence in the aftermath of the deployment. The anniversary of each 5-73 paratrooper death was marked by tributes on the Task Force 300 page located on Facebook. Jenna Grassbaugh blogged about her recovery from the loss of her husband Jon. After deployment tragedies were shared, transfers to other units and promotions were congratulated. Those no longer serving talked about their new jobs and their families.

Bobby Henline, the sole survivor from the deadly improvised explosive device that killed Jon Grassbaugh, Ebe Emolo, Levi Hoover and Rodney McCandless, was now breaking into show business. Although badly scarred from burns to his face and having lost his left hand Henline stepped into the limelight as a comedian. He shared his experiences on social media and uses humor to help others cope, as well as using comedy to deal with the tragedy.

Headhunter was a formidable threat to the insurgents. The tenacity of these 300 "Spartan" warriors and their Delta brothers and sisters proved time and again that they kept the phalanx tight, stood their ground and aggressively took the fight to the enemy. According to Sergeant Willie Lillie, "Word had gotten out, just don't bother messing with the guys with the circle and the square" (a reference to the 82nd Airborne Division patch on their shoulder). No unit was more aggressive than 5-73 CAV. Nobody! "You take a shot at us and it didn't matter what it was, we were going to go after you." The enemy knew it. Lillie continued: "By the time summer was over they just didn't want any more of us."[8]

Sal Candela, Alpha Troop's executive officer, felt that the stars aligned with 5-73. They had the right leadership in Poppas and Sylvia and they were given the right mission to rid Diyala of the terrorist threat; it all came together. "All these switches got turned on to enable us to do what we did."[9] It is hard to imagine how anyone could have done it better.

Acknowledgments

First and foremost, I would like to thank my wife Kathy Kahlson for her support. She kept me centered and grounded throughout this long journey. She is my best friend, my confidant and the love of my life.

To my kids, Meredith, Sophie and Nolan: all my love and hope that I have set a good example for what it means to never give up on your dreams.

Thanks to Kevin Maurer for his candid assessments of the drafts that I shared.

An early assessment of my work was done by a colleague of Drew Poppas. Although I do not know the person's name, he provided invaluable early feedback and I returned to it often to gain encouragement as I continued to refine my work.

Joe Craig at the Association of the United States Army Book Program has given me the opportunity to pursue my goal of publishing this book by providing helpful analysis and numerous edit recommendations.

Many thanks to Ruth Sheppard and all the staff at Casemate who supported the publishing process.

The people listed below are those who agreed to be interviewed for this book. Several of them continued to provide me with additional information throughout the process. I could not have completed this book without their vast contributions and willingness to share their stories. I will be forever indebted to them for this opportunity.

Marc Adams	Gates Brown
Mike Anderson	Bill Caldwell
Terry Anderson	Sal Candela
Josh Andrews (USAF JTAC)	Zach Carpino
Mark Atangan	John Carson
Nick Bajema	Jeremiah Church
Jim Barnes	Mike Clemens
Shane Bates	Zach Clements
Adam Benaway	Robert Cobb
Jeff Black	Bryce Cole
Mike Blankenship	Connie Cole
Eric Booth	John Coomer

Debi Curry
Alex Diaz
Stephen Dobbins
Richie Donley
Ray Edgar
Igor Estraykh
Dave Fee (CO 1-82 Attack Aviation
	Battalion)
Danielle Ferrante
John Ferrante
Jenna Ferrell (Jon Grassbaugh's widow)
Mike Few
Dary Finck
Jeremy Fryer (1-82 Attack Aviation)
Jon Gaspers
Pam Gaspers
Kevin Geis
Adrian Godoy
Walker Gorham
Matt Guza
Andrew Harriman
Townley Hedrick
Bobby Henline
Andy Hercik
Craig Honbarger
Joe James
Adam Jeter
Pete Johnson
Adam King
Phil Kiniery
Josh Kinser
Jamie LaValley (1-82 Attack Aviation)
Patrick Levier
Evan Lewandowski
Willie Lillie
Matt Lipscomb
Jeff Loehr
Steve Magner
Idi Mallari
Royce Manis

Geriah McAvin
Justin McLaughlin
Chris Meador
Tim Metheny
Matt Miller
Jake Milligan
Rob Moore
Ben Ordiway
Ford Peterson (2-25th Aviation
	Battalion)
Andrew Poppas
Larry Porter (reporter, *Omaha
	World-Herald*)
Brad Rather
Renee Ray
Tye Reedy
Fisher Reynolds (USN Counter IED)
Dustin Rhoades
Larry Robinson
Lynwood Saville (1-82 Attack Aviation)
Bill Schiller
Hans Schober
Diana Sharbono
Jesse Stewart
Jake St. Laurent
Brett Sylvia
Matt Tarazon
Frank Tate (CO 2-25th Assault Aviation
	Battalion)
Jason Tempke
Shawn Thomas
Haley Dennison Uthlaut (John
	Dennison's widow)
Sean Ventura
John Walsh
Mike Wilburn (USAF)
Donnie Workman
Doug Yates
Daniel York (1-82 Attack Aviation)
Justin Young

Appendix: 5-73 CAV Roster

This is the roster that was attached to the orders dated 21 July 2006. My apologies if there are any names missing. It was the most complete list that I could obtain.

Alpha Troop

ADAIR BENJAMIN	SPC	DELLAROCCO TED NICHOLAS	SSG
ALEXANDER RYAN BLAKE	SPC		
ANDERSON ALEXANDER EDWIN	SPC	DIAZ ALEXIS	PV2
		DICKSON RICHARD PAUL	PFC
ANDERSON MICHAEL DAVID	1LT	DONLEY RICHARD LEE	SGT
		DRURY KENNETH BRENT	SFC
ANDERSON TERRY ROBERT JR	PFC	ELLER AARON THOMAS	PFC
		ESTRAYKH IGOR	2LT
BARNES JAMIESON LINCOLN	SPC	EVANS CARDALE ANTAWN	SSG
		FEW JAMES MICHAEL	CPT
BATES BYRAN SHANE	SFC	FOREMAN NATHANIEL BLAZE	PFC
BAUER BRIAN ALEX	SPC		
BENNETT GLEN EDWARD	SSG	GONZALES MITCHELL JR	SFC
BERNTHAL JOSHUA GRANT	SGT	GONZALEZ ORLANDO ERIC	PV2
BLACK JEFFREY SCOTT	1LT		
BRITTON SCOTT MICHAEL	SGT	GREEN DAVID JOHN	SGT
BROWN GATES MOSLEY	1LT	JACKSON CRAIG ALLEN	SSG
BUTLER DONALD WOODWARD III	PFC	JENKINS NATHANIEL MARVIN	PFC
CANDELA SALVATORE E	CPT	JETER ADAM DAVID	SGT
COLE BRYCE FRANKLIN	SPC	JOHANSEN JASON MATTHEW	SSG
CORDELL RYAN THOMAS	PFC		
CURTIS NATHANIEL RICHARD	SPC	KEELEY HERBERT MCCLINTOCK III	SGT

KIM LAN TAN	PV2	PATTON JONATHAN RAY	SSG
KINSER JOSHUA PAUL	SGT	PAVLIK STEPHEN MICHAEL	SPC
LOPEZROLON LUIS O	PFC		
LYNCH DANIEL THOMAS	PFC	RANDOLPH DENOAH LEE	SPC
MAHLE JASON SCOTT	SGT	REIDY JEREMIAH JOSEPH III	PFC
MCMANN ANTHONY RAY	PFC		
MCMILLAN CHARLES HARRISON J	SGT	ROBLES ADAM AURELIO	PFC
		ROSARIVERA RUFO M	SSG
MENDOZA MARIO LOPEZ	SPC	SANTOPOALO ISAIAH	SGT
		SEBASTIAO CLAUDIO RODRIGUES	SPC
METHENY TIMOTHY LEE	SFC		
MOORE DAMIEN ALLEN	PFC	SHARBONO WADE EVERETT	SSG
MOORE WAKII ABDUL	PFC		
MOREIRATAVARES CARLOS ALBER	PFC	SLACK DUSTIN KEITH	SPC
		SWIGER JASON WILLIAM	SGT
MORRIS JOSH ROBERT	PFC	THOMAS SHAWN LANE JR	SPC
NUNEZ JASON	PFC	VARGAS JAKE CHON	SGT
PARKER CHRISTOPHER WESLEY	PFC	WILLIAMS PATRICK JASON	PV2
PATTERSON JUSTIN DEAN	SGT	YANG BEI CHENG	PFC

Bravo Troop

ADAMO SALVATORE LUIGI	SPC	CLEMENS MICHAEL STEPHEN	1SG
BARBERA MICHAEL	SSG		
BENAWAY ADAM FREDRICK	SGT	COBB ROBERT HENRY	SFC
		COLE TIMOTHY BRUCE JR	SGT
BROWN ALLAN MICHEAL	SSG	COOPER RICHARD WILLIAM III	SPC
BYERLY RYAN MARK	PFC		
CAIN ROBERT RICHARD JR	SPC	DENNISON JOHN RYAN	1LT
CASILLI JASON HEITH	SPC	DIXON DANIEL RAY	SGT
CASTILLO REUBEN ALEC	PFC	DOBBINS STEPHEN GREGORY	CPT
CHURCH JEREMIAH ALEXANDER	PFC		
		DOYLE ALEXANDER GEORGE	SPC
CIBELLI ANTHONY JOHN	PFC		

FESSLER ROBERT THOMAS	SGT		MILLER MATTHEW THOMAS	1LT
FINCK DARY SETH	PFC			
FLEMING WILLIAM DAVID	SGT		MOORE WILLIAM CLINT	SSG
GASPERS KEVIN J	2LT		NEAL SCOTT MICHAEL	PFC
GONZALEZ ADAM	SGT		ODOM DAVID DEAN	SSG
GONZALEZ JOSE LUIS	PFC		ORDIWAY BENJAMIN FORREST	SPC
GRIMSLEY RICHARD JENNINGS I	SGT		PATTERSON STEPHEN TOLMAN	PFC
GUZA MATTHEW ANTHONY	SPC		PEARSON BRICE ALLAN	SPC
HARMON CHRISTOPHER DAVID	SGT		PEMBERTON JASON THOMAS	SGT
HERRON BRANDON REID	SGT		PHAM RYUDO TRUONG	PFC
HITCHRICK TERRY A	SFC		PORTER PHILLIP PAUL II	SGT
HOLSINGER ELI SAMUEL	SGT		RODRIGUEZ MICHAEL JOEL	PFC
KATTER KENNETH	SPC		ROLLINS EARL NEAL III	PV1
KELLY PATRICK JAMES	SGT		ROTH KYLE WESLY	SPC
KING JERRY RYEN	PFC		SANTOSCOLON GABRIEL	PFC
LEWANDOWSKI EVAN	SSG		SHEETZ JACOB RYAN	SPC
LEWIS HARRY ALLEN	PFC		SIGMON TRAVIS DANIEL	PFC
LILLIE WILLIAM ALBERT	SSG		SNOW JASON ISRAEL	SGT
LOCKER KENNETH EDWARD JR	SGT		THOMPSON JOHN EDWARD	SPC
LOPEZ KEVIN LUKE	PFC		URBANEK CHRISTOPHER JOHN	SFC
LOSOYA DANIEL MARK	PFC			
LY THANH XUAN	SPC		VAUGHAN MICHAEL LOUIS	PFC
LYNN STEVE ROBERT	SSG			
MACDONALD JAMES JOSEPH	PFC		WALDBAUER ANDREW THOMAS	SPC
MAREK MICHAEL ROBERT	PFC		WARREN MAURICE ANTOINE	SPC
MCAVIN GERIAH	SSG		WOLTERSTORFF CAMERON TRISTA	PFC
MCELROY DONALD HARVEY JR	SSG		YATES NATHAN DOUGLAS	SPC

Charlie Troop

AMUNDSON BEAU ALLEN	SPC	HODGES WESLEY ALAN	SGT
ARGUELLESCARRENO USIEL	PFC	HONRATH AUSTIN THOMAS	SPC
BELL KYLE FRANCIS	SPC	HUNT ROBERT RYAN	PV2
BLANKENSHIP MICHAEL AARON	SGT	JOHNSON PETER D	SFC
BLOOD JOHN PAUL	SPC	JUSTICE BRANDON EDISON	SGT
BREMER THOMAS RUDY	SGT	KAMARA GIBRIL IBRAHIM	SPC
BURKE CODY PATRICK	SSG	KELLER JOHN MICHAEL	PFC
CANTU RAUL	SSG	KELLER STEVEN RANDALL II	SPC
CARPINO ZACHARY WILLIAM	SPC	KELLY RICHARD GREGORY	SFC
CARSON JOHN P IV	CPT	KOTZIAN JORDAN REICHERT	SPC
CONTRERAS DAVID BRAULIO	SPC	LAWRENCE BRETT JAMES JR	PV2
COOK ALEXANDER SCOTT	SPC	LEEWORTHY JASON FREDERICK	MSG
CULVER JACOB PARRISH	SGT	LESH JOEL ANTHONY	PFC
DAOREUANG KHAMPANE	SPC	LETELLIER LAWRENCE YUN	PFC
DIFFENDERFER DAVID N	1LT	LOEHR JEFFREY AMBROSE	SSG
DOHERTY ROBERT CHARLES	SGT	MAPLES COREY MICHAEL	SPC
DURAN JOAN JOSE	SGT	MCCOY NATHAN TIMOTHY	SGT
EMBRY JASON DEAN	SGT	MCLAUGHLIN JUSTIN RAY	PFC
FERRANTE JOHN JAMES JR	SSG	MEREDITH JOSHUA STEWART	SPC
FIRBY MAX ALLEN	SPC	MIERA JASON BRIAN	SPC
FRAME ROBERT WILLIAM	SSG	MIRAMONTES GABRIEL	SGT
FRY JOSEPH CULP III	SGT	MITCHELL ROY	SPC
GALLAGHER ERIC LAWRENCE	SPC	MOORE ALAN JOSEPH	PFC
GARCIA JUDE	PFC	MORGAN TREVOR DANE	SGT
GEERS SCOTT THOMAS	SGT		

NIELSEN RONALD DANIEL	PFC	SCHILLER RHETT W	CPT
NORFLET RICHARD	PFC	SINCLAIR DANIEL ARTHUR	PFC
ORREN ROY LEE III	SGT	SPEAR STEPHEN KELLY JR	SPC
PALMOORE STEPHEN RAY	SPC	STEWARD SHAWN MICHAEL	SPC
PAREDES JORGE J	SSG		
PIMENTELMELENDEZ EDWIN LUCI	PFC	TODD JESSE JAMES	PFC
		TYNER PHILIP DEAN	PFC
RHODES DUSTIN CHARLES	SSG	VANG HER	SPC
		VIAMONTE ALEXIS	SSG
RIEPE MASON SHAWN	SSG	VOIGT GREGORY MICHAEL	SPC
RIZZO DILLON JOSEPH	PFC		
RODRIGUEZ ERNESTO	SPC	WALSH JOHN B	1LT
SAI HSAING KHWAN	SPC	WENDT ISAAC ROBERT	PFC
SALAZAR RANDY	PFC	WILKS PETER MICHAEL	PFC
SANK JARED ALAN	SGT	WILLIAMS TAYLOR LEE	SPC
SATTERFIELD JOSHUA JAMES	PV2	WUEBKER CHAD THOMAS	PFC
SCANTLIN ROBERT LEE	PFC	YOUNG JUSTIN LEE	SGT

Headquarters Troop

ADAMS MARC GARDNER	SPC	CANALES BENITO SERVANDO	SPC
ATANGAN MARK ANTHONY VILLAFL	PFC	CANNY BRIAN PATRICK	1LT
BAKER BRIAN SCOTT	SGT	CANSINO JESUS	PFC
BARRAZA RODOLFO	SPC	CARDENAS DANIEL ALBERTO	SGT
BIERKORTTE JASON ROBERT	CPT	CARROLL NORMAN JAMES	PV2
BISHOP PHILLIP JOHN	SSG	CAVANAUGH RYAN THOMAS	PFC
BOBKA MATTHEW FRANCIS	SPC	CHARLES JEAN M	SSG
BOOTH ERIC MICHAEL	1LT	CHARVAT ROBERT ANTHONY	SGT
BOULTON JESSE H	2LT	CLOPTON JOSHUA D	2LT
BUSHOVER BRIAN M	2LT		

COLEMAN ISIAH DANELLE	SPC	HONBARGER CRAIG PHILLIP	CPT
COOMER JOHN ROBERT	SFC	HOWARD ANGELO RAPHEAL	SGT
COPELAND TYE JOSEPH WAYN	PFC		
DAVILA MICHAEL ANTHONY	SGT	HUBBARD JERRY ALLEN JR	SPC
		HUDGINS DAYNE CHRISTOPHER	SPC
DUPUIS CHRISTOPHER GLEN	SPC	HUGHES EDWARD CHARLES	SGT
EDGAR RAY	CSM		
ELLIS DEREK FARMER	SPC	INGLE MATTHIAS JAMES	SSG
FEES ROBERT BRUCE	SGT	JAMES JOSEPH CARLETON	CPT
FELICIANO RODNEY	SFC	JENNINGS MARKHAM CARNE	SPC
FILER MATTHEW LEE	SGT		
GEIS KEVIN DOUGLAS	SPC	JOHNSTON MICHAEL ANDREW	PFC
GILBERT JON WILLIAM	SPC		
GORHAM WALKER DEVORE	2LT	KEES WILLIAM MICHAEL	SPC
		KING ADAM GEORGE	PV2
GRASSBAUGH JONATHAN D	CPT	KINIERY PHILLIP JAMES III	CPT
GRAY KENNETH SCOTT	SPC	KRAUS RUSSELL EDWARD JR	SSG
GUNKELMAN BRIAN JOSEPH	SPC	LINNEMEIER JASON MATHEW	SSG
HARRIMAN ANDREW SCOTT	SPC		
		LOTEMPIO JAMES JOSEPH	PFC
HARRIS MARKUS RANDALL JR	SGT	MAGRAS RAUL ANTONIO	CPL
HAYES STEPHEN DOUGLAS	SGT	MALLARI NOCHEBUENA IDI AMINR	SPC
HEDRICK TOWNLEY REDFEARN	MAJ	MANIS ROYCE BOYCE	1SG
		MARSHALL RANDELL TONY	PFC
HERCIK ANDREW M	CPT		
HERNANDEZ RAYMOND SEPULVEDA	SFC	MARTINEZ VELAZQUEZ MIGUEL A	SSG
HESTERMANN BRADEN J	1LT	MAYER JAMES DEAN	SGT
HOCH CHRISTOPHER JAMES	PFC	MCINTURF TYLER DWAYNE	PV2

MCNAMARA ROBERT ALLEN	SSG	SEBBAN BENJAMIN LUCIEN	SSG
MECHAM JONATHAN L	1LT	SHACKLE RYAN DOUGLAS	SGT
MEISMER JOSHUA OINE	SPC	SIEGRIST CHAD MICHAEL	PFC
METOYER RODNEY MAURICE	SPC	SIMMONDS WINSTON FITZGERALD	SSG
MILLIGAN JACOB S	CPT	SLOAN DANNY RAY JR	SSG
MITCHELL MAURICE DARYL	SPC	SMITH KENNETH EDWIN	PV2
MOCK KEVIN DWAYNE	SFC	STEAGALL BENJAMIN FITZGERALD	SPC
MOLINA JIMMY	SPC	STEARNS JAY ALLEN	PFC
MOORE WILLIS CARL III	SGT	STEWART JESSE R	CPT
NAUKANA JOHN DAVID KALANI	SSG	SUMMERS DANIEL SHANE	2LT
NAVARRETE GILBERTO	SSG	SYLVIA BRETT GARETH	MAJ
OBAKRAIRUR MELVIN JOSHWICK	SPC	TARAZON MATTHEW M	2LT
OBRIEN JOHN STEVEN	SPC	TAYLOR CHRISTOPHER ARNOLD	PFC
PARDUN JASON SCOTT	PFC	THIBOU DAVID VICTOR JR	SPC
PARKER SORAN FELICE	SGT	TOLLIVER TIMOTHY ANDREW	SGT
PASTRANA JEFFREY	SSG	TROUT ANTHONY LAUREN	SGT
PETTIBONE ANDREW MICHAEL	SPC	UHLIG DWAYNE CHRISTOPHER	SFC
POPPAS ANDREW PETER	LTC	VERELL BENJAMIN LEE	SPC
RATHER ROBERT BRADLEY	MAJ	WHELAN KEVIN PATRICK	SGT
RAY BRIAN W	CPT	WINDER FULTON JAMES III	PFC
REUTTER RYAN PATRICK	PFC	WOLF JOHN KELLY	SPC
ROBINSON CARLOS AURELIO JR	SSG	WOLFE HAROLD LAVERNE III	SGT
ROCA ROBERT JOSEPH JR	SSG	WOODRUFF JONAS	SFC
ROOT NICHOLAS ANDREW	SPC	YAP ROLAND JASON	PFC
RUDY JOSEPH DANIEL	SPC		
SCHOBER HANS F	2LT		

Delta Troop

ACEVEDO OCTAVIO	SGT	FOWLE BRYANT JAMES WILLIAM	SSG
AGUILAR JORGE JR	PFC		
AGUON VINCENT ISEZAKI JR	PV2	GANTZER STEVEN EDWARD	PFC
ANZURES NATHAN PAUL	SPC	GIBB CHRISTOPHER ALAN	SGT
BAIR MATTHEW BRIAN	PFC	GRAHAM RONALD ROMAN	SGT
BARNES MARK ANTHONY JR	SPC		
		GULEZIAN MARK GERALD	SSG
BILLINGSLEY MYRON BERNARD	SSG	HENRY JASON ALLAN	PFC
		HERNANDEZ CHACON FAUSTINO	SFC
BOATMANALLEN JUSTIN QUINN	PFC		
		HOLEMAN MICHAEL LOUIS	SGT
BRIAN JUSTIN DWAYNE	PFC		
BROWN CHRISTOPHER LAMAR	PV2	HOOVER LEVI KENNITH	PFC
		HUFF MATTHEW	SGT
BURRIS ROBERT GENE	SPC	HUGHES CHRISTOPHER STUART	PV2
BUSH TIMOTHY MICHAEL	SSG		
BYRD JEFFERY DURANE	SFC	HUGHES JESSE RAY	SGT
CHERRY MICHAEL JOHN	PFC	JOHNSON JEREMIAH LEON	PV2
CLASON ROBERT PAUL	PFC		
CONTRERAS MOISES ADAN	PV2	JOHNSON KATANA NORRIS	SPC
COWLES LAUREN ASHLEY	SPC	JOINER DENNIS WALTER JR	PFC
DAMON BRUCE LEONARD	PFC	JONES TRAVIS WAYMEN III	PFC
DAVIDSON RICHARD LEE	SPC	JONES ZACHARY SCOTT	SPC
DEDONATO MICHAEL VICTOR	PV2	KANE JACK ALEXANDER	SPC
		KENNEDY GARY DONNELL	SGT
DOUGHERTY JAMES ROBERT	SGT		
		KLENDA MARIE THEREZE	PV2
EMOLO EBE FIRMIN	PFC	LADSON MICHELE COLLETTE	SSG
EUBANKS JOSEPH JEROME	SGT		
FARNHAM JOSHUA ALLEN	PFC	LAYTON SETH S	2LT
FEBRE GUILLERMO BACANTO	PV1	LYNCH CHRISTOPHER SETH	SPC

LYNCH HAROLD ANDREW JR	PFC	SMITH TYRONE JERMAINE	SGT
MARQUEZ OSCAR JR	PFC	STLAURENT JEREMY LUKE	CPT
MCCANDLESS RODNEY LYNN	PV2	TASSIN MELVIN CHARLES	SFC
MEADOR CHRISTIAN JEREMIE	SPC	THOMPSON ADAM R	2LT
NEAL MILLARD WILLIAM	SGT	THOMPSON ERIC ALAN	SGT
OCONNELL PATRICK W	2LT	VANHAM GEORGE JOSEPH	SSG
ORTIZ ADAM JOSUE	PFC	VANRAALTE BRANDON WILLIAM	SPC
PADILLABUSTAMANTE OSCAR ARN	PFC	VENEGAS MANUEL JR	PFC
PANUSKI ROBERT JOSEPH	PFC	VILLARREAL DAVID LARA JR	PFC
PIMENTEL DIOSEL	PFC	VINCENT JUSTIN MICHAEL	SPC
RAMOS LUIS R	SGT	WARD RICHARD JAMES	SGT
RAMSDELL CHRISTOPHER KELLEY	SGT	WARREN CHRISTOPHER ANDREW	SGT
RANDLE ERIC LAMONT	CW2	WEBER CARL JOHN	PFC
REYES ERIK	PFC	WHITE ANTHONY JAMES	PV1
RICHARDSON COREY	SGT	WIMBERLY JACOUNTRESS KENYEL	SGT
RODGERS AMY ELIZABETH	PFC	WURSTER ANTHONY CARLO	SPC
SHILLING RYAN ALLAN	SGT	YATES DOUGLAS EUGENE	MSG
SMITH CODY LEE	SGT	YOUNG BRANDON ANDREW	SPC

Last Additions

AHLER JOHN	SGT	CAREY KEVIN	SPC
ALVAREZ JOSE	PV2	CHEN JOHN	2LT
ATKINSON TONY	PFC	CLEMENTS ZACHARY L.	PVT
AUTIO ERIC	PFC	CRAFT PATRICK V.	PV2
BAJEMA NICHOLAS	2LT	DAMRON ZACHARY	PV2
BEAUDRY JOSEPH	PFC	DEGARMO JAMES	PVT
BRAMHALL TIMOTHY	PVT	DIGUGIELM JOSHUA	PVT
BRANDT JUSTIN	PVT	DUMYAHN JUSTIN	PV2

EKDAHL GERAD	PFC	MILLIGAN MICAH	SGT
ELLIS ROBERT	PVT	NINH XUANDAT	SSG
FLEMING RYAN	PV2	REFFO MICAH	SPC
FOLEY BERTEL	SFC	ROBERTS MATTHEW	PV2
GATTI PHILIP	PFC	ROBINSON LARRY	CPT
GONZALES MICHAEL	SPC	RODRIGUEZ FLORENTINO	PFC
GONZALEZ JOHNNY J.	PV2		
GROSSINGE SHAWN	PV2	ROMINE KINDRICK	SPC
HARRIS THOMAS	PFC	SALAS MICHAELANGELO	PVT
HAWTHORNE CEDRICK	SGT	SITES BENJAMIN	SPC
HOULE ROBERT	SGT	STAINES GARY	PFC
JOHNSON JASON	SGT	THOMPSON CHAD	2LT
JONES PHILIP	PV2	VALLIERE TIMOTHY	PVT
KEYSER LESLIE	PFC	VELA NORMA	PFC
KIRBY AUSTIN	PVT	WEBER BRIAN	PV2
LIPSCOMB MATTHEW M.	SFC	WHEELER FRANK	SFC
LUCERO PAUL	SPC	WORKMAN DONALD R. JR	SSG
MCCLAIN MICHAEL	PVT		
MERRILL CHRISTOPHER	PVT	YOUNG PATRICK LEE	SFC

Also serving were:

U.S. Air Force Joint Terminal Attack Controller (JTAC) Staff Sergeant Josh Andrews

U.S. Air Force ROMAD (Recon Observe Mark and Destroy) Senior Airman Dustin Hanna

U.S. Navy Squadron Electronic Warfare Officer Lieutenant Fisher Reynolds, Joint Composite Counter-Radio Controlled Improvised Explosives Devices Squadron One

Endnotes

Introduction

This chapter is based on interviews conducted with:
Edgar, Ray
Metheny, Tim

1   Edgar, Ray. December 28, 2009, phone interview.
    Recently, the armor tradition continued with the activation of Alpha Company, 4th Battalion, 68th Armor Regiment with air-transportable/parachute-capable Light Armored Vehicle-25A2 that was acquired from the Marine Corps.
2   A ceremony that is performed when a U.S. Army unit is deactivated or retired from service. The unit's flag is ceremonially rolled and inserted into a protective cover. The colors are then sent to the U.S. Army Center for Military History.
3   In the case of the 82nd, each brigade had been accustomed to having the various "slices" of combat support (CS) and combat service support (CSS) assigned to it. However, in order to create a fourth brigade combat team along with activating a cavalry squadron for each of the four brigade combat teams, the 3rd Battalion of two of the existing three brigades would be deactivated. The troops would then be divided up to help build the new units. Since the 505th Parachute Infantry Regiment (PIR), also known as the 3rd BCT, was in the rotation to arrive home from Iraq and begin its reset time at Fort Bragg, it was decided that Colonel Owens, 3rd BCT commander, and his staff would have the distinction of creating the Transformation pattern for the rest of the Division. Casing the colors of the 3rd Battalion of the 505th Parachute Infantry Regiment, also known as 3-505 or 3 Panther, wasn't going to go over well. One of the original parachute infantry regiments, 3 Panther traced their lineage to the World War II airborne operations in Sicily, Normandy and Holland along with the heroic stand made by American forces in the Ardennes during the Battle of the Bulge.
    A fourth brigade would be added to the Division. The 508th Airborne Infantry Regiment, which had a history with the 82nd from its World War II days, would have its colors uncased and join the 325th Airborne Infantry Regiment (formerly glider regiment during World War II), 504th and 505th Parachute Infantry Regiments. They are regiments in name only. In reality, each is an airborne infantry brigade with support elements attached that were critical to mission success. Artillery was assigned to each brigade along with air defense artillery, intelligence, signals, forward support (including engineers and military police), main support and soldier support (finance and personnel).
    Aviation assets—both attack-flying Apaches and lift assets using the twin-rotor Chinooks along with Black Hawks and air cavalry flying OH-58 Kiowa armed reconnaissance helicopters—were at its direct disposal and organic to the 82nd. The colors of the 3rd battalion of the 325th Airborne

Infantry Regiment and the 3rd battalion of the 504th Parachute Infantry Regiment would be cased and their personnel used to form the 1st and 2nd battalions of the 508th.

According to Command Sergeant Major Ray Edgar, "another unique facet of being part of this complex picture was the 82nd mafia mystic. If you ain't airborne, you ain't shit mentality." A paratrooper rendering a salute to a superior officer often carries with it the declaration "Airborne," followed by the receiver countering with a rousing "All the way."

4   Mass tactical jump description reviewed/revised by Pete Johnson (long-time 82nd member and qualified jumpmaster), and by David Calkins (former paratrooper with the 173rd Airborne Brigade).

5   https://www.youtube.com/watch?v=6ZpYu8sulxs This material originated during World War II. There is speculation that then Colonel James Gavin, regimental commander of the 505th Parachute Infantry Regiment gave these instructions prior to 82nd's jump into Sicily. It could possibly have been part of 82nd commanding general Mathew Ridgway's orders to his paratroopers prior to the invasion of Normandy. Its origin cannot be definitively confirmed.

Chapter 1

This chapter is based on interviews conducted with:
Anderson, Mike
Benaway, Adam
Caldwell, Bill
Dobbins, Stephen
Edgar, Ray
Few, Mike
Gorham, Walker
Honbarger, Craig
Loehr, Jeff
Poppas, Andrew
Rather, Brad
Stewart, Jesse
Sylvia, Brett
Workman, Donnie

1   Honbarger, Craig. November 19, 2008, phone interview.
2   Poppas, Andrew. February 13, 2008, phone interview.
3   Poppas, Andrew. February 13, 2008, phone interview.
4   Edgar, Ray. December 28, 2009, phone interview.
5   Workman, Donnie. November 22, 2008, phone interview.
6   Sylvia, Brett. March 15, 2008, phone interview.
7   Dobbins, Stephen. February 27, 2008, phone interview.
8   Sylvia, Brett. March 15, 2008, phone interview.
9   Rather, Brad. October 25, 2008, phone interview.
10 Rather, Brad. October 25, 2008, phone interview.
11 Ground evacuation of wounded was out of the question due to the long line of evacuation to a combat support hospital so evacuation by medevac helicopter was the only option. If bad weather kept aircraft grounded, performing an auto transfusion using a "walking blood bank", another soldier's blood to sustain the wounded soldier, could stabilize a casualty. Rather, Brad.
12 Rather, Brad. October 25, 2008, phone interview.

13 Few, Mike. December 28, 2009, phone interview.
14 "A variety of rounds are available including high explosive, white phosphorus and illumination. Maximum range is from 3,500–7,200 meters. Dismounted forces can carry medium and light mortars over all terrain, and light vehicles and helicopters can move heavy mortars easily. Mortars can be fired from almost any ground upon which a soldier can stand." (Stewart, Jesse. February 20, 2008, phone interview.)
15 Few, Mike. December 28, 2009, phone interview.
16 Anderson, Mike. December 28, 2009, phone interview.
17 The heavy infantry or hoplites were recruited from the upper class of a town because only they could afford the *doru* or spear, *xiphos* or short sword along with *panoply* or protective equipment consisting of a helmet, breastplate, tunic, greaves or leg guards. Every hoplite carried a large round shield known as a *hoplon*. Their formation was referred to as a phalanx. Both sides, armed with spears, attempted to push over their opposition, and once a phalanx had successfully breached the enemy formation, the soldiers would continue slashing with the *xiphos* or spearing their opponents with the *doru*. The Spartans perfected these fighting skills and tactics by continuously drilling. When not drilling, exercise would be used in order to develop a high degree of stamina knowing that when the phalanxes collided in combat that all their strength would be needed to overwhelm their enemies. http://www.ancientmilitary.com/spartan-military.htm
18 Poppas, Andrew. February 13, 2008, phone interview.

Chapter 2

This chapter is based on interviews conducted with:
Anderson, Mike
Barnes, Jim
Black, Jeff
Caldwell, Mike
Few, Mike
Kinser, Josh
Metheny, Tim
Poppas, Drew
Ventura, Sean

1   Few, Mike. December 28, 2009, phone interview.
2   Counterinsurgency in Iraq (2003–2006). RAND Corporation, pp. 21–34. Bruce R. Pirnie, Edward O'Connell; Santa Monica, CA/2008
3   http://www.understandingwar.org/jaysh-al-mahdi
4   http://www.understandingwar.org/al-qaeda-iraq
5   Caldwell, Bill. November 19, 2008, in-person interview.
6   Few, Mike. December 28, 2009, phone interview.
7   http://www.captainsjournal.com/2006/12/13/the-ncos-speak-on-rules-of-engagement/
8   Ventura, Sean. December 23, 2009, phone interview.
9   Kinser, Josh. May 16, 2008, phone interview.
10 A/5-73 Recon Operational Summary, August 2006.
11 Kinser, Josh. May 16, 2009, phone interview.
12 Kinser, Josh. May 16, 2009, phone interview.
13 Few, Mike. December 28, 2009, phone interview.
14 Black, Jeff. July 11 and 19, 2008, phone interview.

15 Looking through the sight on an Apache is like looking through a plastic tube. If you take a plastic tube and look at a wall two feet away, you can barely read a couple words on a book. But if you take that plastic tube to 2,000 feet and look through it from there, it's super high powered and you can see everything. The backseat pilot is looking at a 1½ inch combiner lens that's mounted to the flight helmet and slides over his eye. It's as though the pilot is watching a 1½-inch TV screen. It's so close to the eye it doesn't feel like it's 1½ inches, it appears as actual vision. Over time the dominant eye becomes acclimated to fly using this TV screen and the other eye essentially shuts down. When the pilot needs to look inside the cockpit the opposite eye is used; switching them back and forth becomes normal. So the front seater is looking through the TADS (short for Target Acquisition and Designation System) searching for the enemy while the back seater is looking through what's called the PINVIS, pilot's night vision sight.

Additional information about the Apache's abilities supplied by LTC Dave Fee, 1/82 Attack Reconnaissance Battalion nicknamed Wolfpack, commanding.

16 Few, Mike. December 28, 2009, phone interview.
17 Few, Mike. December 28, 2009, phone interview.
18 Few, Mike. December 28, 2009, phone interview.

Chapter 3

This chapter is based on interviews conducted with:
Caldwell, Bill
Carson, John
Cobb, Robert
Dobbins, Stephen
Few, Mike
Lillie, Willie
Loehr, Jeff
Poppas, Andrew
Sylvia, Brett
Workman, Donnie

1 Sylvia, Brett. March 15, 2008, phone interview.
2 Caldwell, Bill. November 19, 2008, in-person interview.
3 Presidential Unit Citation narrative, p. 6.
4 Dobbins, Stephen. February 27, 2008, phone interview.
5 Poppas, Andrew. February 13, 2008, phone interview.
6 Dobbins, Stephen. February 27, 2008, phone interview.
7 Loehr, Jeff. October 30, 2008, phone interview.
8 Workman, Donnie. November 22, 2008, phone interview.
9 Workman, Donnie. November 22, 2008, phone interview.
10 Presidential Unit Citation narrative, p. 6 (Turki Shaping Ops).

Chapter 4

This chapter is based on interviews conducted with:
Carson, John
Dobbins, Stephen

Few, Mike
Lillie, Willie
Sylvia, Brett

1   The Turki Bowl operation got its name based on the army tradition of units holding an annual pre-Thanksgiving football game dubbed "Turkey Bowl." It seemed all too appropriate to tag it Turki Bowl based on the time of year and the village that was at the center of the battlespace. Sylvia, Brett. March 15, 2008, phone interview.
2   Carson, John. December 28, 2009, phone interview.
3   Sylvia, Brett. March 15, 2008, phone interview.
4   Few, Mike. December 28, 2009, phone interview.
5   Sylvia, Brett. March 15, 2008, phone interview.
6   Metheny, Tim, *Five Days in Turki Village*, United States Army Sergeants Major Academy, Class 61, December 3, 2010, and Few, Mike. Operational Summary (OPSUM), Operation Turki Bowl I.
7   Lillie, Willie. April 3, 2008, phone interview.

Chapter 5

This chapter is based on interviews with:
Carson, John
Coomer, John
Doherty, Robert
Lillie, Willie
McAvin, Geriah
Metheny, Tim
Ventura, Sean

1   Carson, John. December 28, 2009, phone interview.
2   Carson, John. December 28, 2009, phone interview.
    Recalling a ritual that they'd developed during their short time in Iraq, Dennison's West Point classmate and close friend Matt Miller, who was serving as Bravo's executive officer, remembered that as they would prepare for a mission, they'd give a "man hug, say God Bless and I'll see you on the other side." The day that Turki Bowl I began, in all the confusion, they'd neglected to continue the tradition. In the intensity of the moment, the misstep had gone unnoticed.
3   McAvin, Geriah. June 16, 2013, phone interview.
4   Lillie, Willie. April 3, 2008, phone interview.
5   Lillie, Willie. April 3, 2008, phone interview.
6   Combat Studies Institute, *Operational Leadership Experiences*. (Fort Leavenworth, KS: Combat Studies Institute, June 16, 2008). Interview with CSM Michael Clemens, pp. 13–14.

Chapter 6

This chapter is based on interviews with:
Bates, Shane
Carson, John
Coomer, John
Few, Mike

Poppas, Andrew
Sylvia, Brett

1   Poppas, Andrew. February 13, 2008, phone interview.
2   Carson, John. December 28, 2009, phone interview.
3   Bates, Shane. May 9, 2017, phone interview.
4   Bates, Shane. May 9, 2017, phone interview.
5   Carson, John. December 28, 2009, phone interview.
6   Fryer Distinguished Flying Cross citation, video feed 11-16-06. LaValley, York, Fryer, Saville in-person interviews by author. Flying the AH-64D Longbow Apache attack helicopter were Chief Warrant Officer 4 Fryer and Chief Warrant Officer 3 Saville along with their co-pilot/gunners.
7   Coomer, John. January 31, 2008, phone interview.
8   Carson, John. December 28, 2009, phone interview.
9   Poppas, Andrew. February 13, 2008, phone interview.
10   Few, Mike. December 28, 2009, phone interview.

Chapter 7

This chapter is based on interviews with:
Carson, John
Dennison Uthlaut, Haley
Dobbins, Stephen
Honbarger, Craig
Miller, Matt
Schiller, Bill

1   To make sure that the chaplain was taken care of, a chaplain's assistant was assigned. Sergeant Miguel Martinez took care of all sorts of needs from packing religious materials for deployment to building a small chapel in theater to serving as Chaplain Honbarger's security detail. Craig was "old army" and was willing to go to the field and get dirty with the paratroopers so ensuring his safety and well-being was an important part of the assistant's job. Martinez was Craig's "right-hand man." Always soliciting advice and input from Martinez, Chaplain Honbarger found him indispensable.
2   Honbarger, Craig. November 19, 2008, phone interview.
3   Honbarger, Craig. November 19, 2008, phone interview.
4   Honbarger, Craig. November 19, 2008, phone interview.
5   Honbarger, Craig. November 19, 2008, phone interview.
6   Miller, Matt. January 6, 2009, phone interview.
7   Dobbins, Stephen. February 27, 2008, phone interview.
8   Robert Cobb, digital eulogy for John Ryan Dennison.
9   Dennison Uthlaut, Haley. December 23, 2009, phone interview.
10   Carson, John. December 28, 2009, phone interview.
11   Carson, John. December 28, 2009, phone interview.
12   Carson, John. December 28, 2009, phone interview.
13   Carson, John. December 28, 2009, phone interview.
14   Schiller, Bill. September 27, 2009, phone interview.
15   Facebook Messenger post, Renee Ray to author, September 4, 2010.
16   Schiller, Bill. September 27, 2009, phone interview.

Chapter 8

This chapter is based on interviews with:
Hercik, Andy
Workman, Donnie

1   Hercik, Andy. October 24, 2008, phone interview.
2   Hercik, Andy. October 24, 2008, phone interview.
3   Workman, Donnie. November 22, 2008, phone interview.
4   Workman, Donnie. November 22, 2008, phone interview.
5   Workman, Donnie. November 22, 2008, phone interview.
6   Workman, Donnie. November 22, 2008, phone interview.
7   Workman, Donnie. November 22, 2008, phone interview.

Chapter 9

This chapter is based on interviews with:
Candela, Sal
Fee, Dave
Ferrante, Danielle
Ferrante, John
Guza, Matt
Lewandowski, Evan
Peterson, Ford
Sylvia, Brett
Tate, Frank

1   A key component to these missions would be the extensive use of helicopters. The movement of large numbers of troops by helicopter into combat began in 1963. The 11th Airborne Division, which had seen service in the Pacific Theater during World War II, was reactivated and reflagged as the 11th Air Assault Division. Secretary of Defense Robert S. McNamara instructed the army leadership to "examine aviation in a new light and to be more audacious in using it." Airmobility provided "the capability to sustain a force on the battlefield, to maintain integrity, and to quickly concentrate combat power so that one's resources can be applied with such intensity in time and space as to create a superior force at the point of application."

Airmobile capabilities would be rushed to the jungles of Vietnam. Entire divisions like the famed 101st Airborne and 1st Cavalry Divisions would be reflagged Airmobile and eventually re-designated Air Assault, solidifying the use of helicopters. Eventually every division in the army would have aviation assets organic to it. The Bell UH-1 Huey and later Black Hawks along with the twin-blade Chinooks would provide the lift capability. Huey gunship/rocket platforms, Cobras, then Apaches and Kiowa Scouts would provide the aerial weapons teams (AWTs) that would give ground troops another weapons system that they could call on to destroy the enemy.

Graves, Major Thomas C., *Transforming the Force: The 11th Air Assault Division (Test) from 1963–1965*. United States Army School of Advanced Military Studies, United States Army Command and General Staff College, Fort Leavenworth, Kansas, Second Term, AY 99–00, p. 1. June 1, 2017.

2 Sylvia, Brett. March 15, 2008, phone interview.
3 The five stages of the air assault are ground tactical, landing, air movement, loading and staging. Each stage of the plan is exercised and at the end of the 72 hours troops are being inserted. The process implements a lot of safety factors especially if you're dealing with an untrained or only partially trained force, both on the aviation side and on the infantry side of the house.
4 Candela, Sal. January 2, 2011, phone interview.
5 Ferrante, John. December 22, 2008, in-person interview.
6 Ferrante, John. December 22, 2008, in-person interview.
7 Ferrante, Danielle. December 22, 2008, in-person interview.
8 Details on combat loads for these missions included: 600 rounds for the M249 SAW; 1,200 rounds for the M240 MG, evenly distributed; 210 rounds for each M4 rifle plus the Grenadier was carrying 203 rounds. Rations were Meals Ready to Eat (MRE) (reduced MREs two per day for three days).
9 Guza, Matt. November 9, 2008, phone interview.

Chapter 10

This chapter is based on interviews with:
Adams, Marc
Few, Mike
Lewandowski, Evan
Magner, Steve
St. Laurent, Jake
Sylvia, Brett
Yates, Doug

1 St. Laurent, Jake. November 28, 2008, phone interview.
2 Yates, Doug. July 11, 2008, phone interview.
3 Magner, Steve. November 25, 2008, phone interview.

Chapter 11

This chapter is based on interviews with:
Adams, Marc
Andrews, Josh
Few, Mike
Jeter, Adam
Kinser, Josh
Sylvia, Brett
Wilburn, Mike

1 Kinser, Josh. May 16, 2008, phone interview.
2 Kinser, Josh. May 16, 2008, phone interview.
3 Kinser, Josh. May 16, 2008, phone interview.
4 Kinser, Josh. May 16, 2008, phone interview.
5 Wilburn, Mike. February 27, 2010, written summary of attack.
6 Wilburn, Mike. February 27, 2010, written summary of attack.

Chapter 12

This chapter is based on interviews with:
Adams, Marc
Dobbins, Stephen
Harriman, Andrew
Hercik, Andy
Rather, Brad
Workman, Donnie

1   Harriman, Andrew. November 7, 2008, phone interview.

Chapter 13

This chapter is based on interviews with:
Anderson, Mike
Clemens, Mike
Kinser, Josh
Lewandowski, Evan
Lillie, Willie
Poppas, Andrew
Rather, Brad
Sylvia, Brett

1   Kinser, Josh. May 16, 2008, phone interview.
2   Kinser, Josh. May 16, 2008, phone interview.
3   Kinser, Josh. May 16, 2008, phone interview.
4   https://history.army.mil/html/books/078/78-1/cmhPub_078-1.pdf
5   Clemens, Mike. March 15, 2008, phone interview.
6   Clemens, Mike. March 15, 2008, phone interview.
7   Rather, Brad. October 25, 2008, phone interview.
8   Lillie, Willie. April 3, 2008, phone interview.
9   Sylvia, Brett. March 15, 2008, phone interview.

Chapter 14

This chapter is based on interviews with:
Clemens, Mike
Few, Mike
Hercik, Andy
Poppas, Andrew
Sylvia, Brett

1   https://history.state.gov/milestones/1830-1860/gadsden-purchase
     The Gadsden Purchase was an 1854 agreement between the United States and Mexico, in which the United States paid Mexico $10 million for a 29,670 square mile portion of Mexico that later became part of Arizona and New Mexico.
2   Presidential Unit Citation narrative TF300.

3   Hercik, Andy. October 28, 2008, phone interview.
4   Hercik, Andy. October 28, 2008, phone interview.

Chapter 15

This chapter is based on interviews with:
Harriman, Andrew

1   Robinson, Larry. *The Long Road Back: A family physician recounts his experiences in Iraq.* Journal of the Medical School of Ohio University Heritage College of Osteopathic Medicine—draft of article.

Chapter 16

This chapter is based on interviews with:
Bajema, Nick
Carpino, Zach
Finck, Dary
Harriman, Andrew
McAvin, Geriah
Reedy, Tye
Stewart, Jesse

1   Stewart, Jesse. February 20, 2008, phone interview.
2   Carpino, Zach. June 14, 2009, phone interview.
3   McAvin, Geriah. June 16, 2013, phone interview.
4   Harriman, Andrew. November 7, 2008, phone interview.
5   Finck, Dary. June 25, 2007, phone interview.
6   Reedy, Tye. October 15, 2008, phone interview.
7   Reedy, Tye. October 15, 2008, phone interview.

Chapter 17

This chapter is based on interviews with:
Bajema, Nick
Carpino, Zach
McAvin, Geriah
Rather, Brad

1   Bajema, Nick. October 16, 2008, phone interview. VBIED stands for vehicle-borne improvised explosive device.
2   Bajema, Nick. October 16, 2008, phone interview.
3   Rather, Brad. October 25, 2008, phone interview.
4   Video from Ben Sebban to Larry Robinson.

Chapter 18

This chapter is based on interviews with:
Anderson, Mike
Bajema, Nick
Benaway, Adam
Carpino, Zach
Clemens, Mike
Dobbins, Stephen
Few, Mike
Kinser, Josh
Stewart, Jesse
Sylvia, Brett
Young, Justin

1   Few, Mike. December 28, 2008, phone interview.
2   Kinser, Josh. May 16, 2008, phone interview.
3   Kinser, Josh. May 16, 2008, phone interview.
4   Kinser, Josh. May 16, 2008, phone interview.
5   Kinser, Josh. May 16, 2008, phone interview.
6   Kinser, Josh. May 16, 2008, phone interview.
7   Stewart, Jesse. February 20, 2008, phone interview.
8   Clemens, Mike. March 15, 2008, phone interview.
9   Radio traffic from Apache AWT monitoring ground forces.
10   Radio traffic from Apache AWT monitoring ground forces.
11   Young, Justin. January 13, 2008, phone interview.
12   Young, Justin. January 13, 2008, phone interview.
13   Radio traffic from Apache AWT monitoring ground forces.
14   Young, Justin. January 13, 2008, phone interview.
15   Anderson, Mike. December 28, 2009, phone interview.

Chapter 19

This chapter is based on interviews with:
Anderson, Mike
Bajema, Nick
Clemens, Mike
Dobbins, Stephen
Few, Mike
Honbarger, Craig
Stewart, Jesse

1   Dobbins, Stephen. February 27, 2008, phone interview.
2   Clemens, Mike. March 15, 2008, phone interview.
3   Anderson, Mike. December 28, 2008, phone interview.

4   Anderson, Mike. December 28, 2008, phone interview.
5   Anderson, Mike. December 28, 2008, phone interview.
6   Few, Mike. December 28, 2009, phone interview.
7   Anderson, Mike. December 28, 2009, phone interview.
8   Honbarger, Craig. November 19, 2008, phone interview.
9   Anderson, Mike. December 28, 2009, phone interview.
10   Stewart, Jesse. February 20, 2008, phone interview.

Chapter 20

This chapter is based on interviews with:
Anderson, Mike
Few, Mike
St. Laurent, Jake

1   Anderson, Mike. December 28, 2009, phone interview.
2   Jason Nunez eulogy, http://thefallen.militarytimes.com/army-cpl-jason-nunez/2655429
3   St. Laurent, Jake. November 28, 2008, phone interview.
4   St. Laurent, Jake. November 28, 2008, phone interview.
5   St. Laurent, Jake. November 28, 2008, phone interview.
6   Few, Mike. December 28, 2009, phone interview.

Chapter 21

This chapter is based on interviews with:
Guza, Matt
Kinser, Josh

1   Troopers serving in cavalry units are inducted into the Order of the Spur after successfully completing a series of evaluations set by the command, culminating in the final test; the "Spur Ride", or for having served during combat as a member of or with a cavalry unit.
2   Guza, Matt. November 9, 2008, phone interview.
3   Guza, Matt. November 9, 2008, phone interview.
4   Kinser, Josh. May 16, 2008, phone interview.
5   Kinser, Josh. May 16, 2008, phone interview.

Chapter 22

This chapter is based on interviews with:
Bajema, Nick
Candela, Sal
Ferrell, Jenna
Sylvia, Brett

1   Bajema, Nick. October 16, 2008, phone interview.
2   Sylvia, Brett. March 15, 2008, phone interview.
3   Candela, Sal. January 2, 2011, phone interview.
4   Ferrell, Jenna. December 4, 2009, phone interview.

5   Henline, Bobby. Facebook remembrance. April 7, 2020 and previous posts remembering his angels on what Bobby refers to as his Alive Day.

Chapter 23

This chapter is based on interviews with:
Bajema, Nick
Benaway, Adam
Coomer, John
Godoy, Adrian
Lillie, Willie
Mallari, Idi
Poppas, Andrew
Rather, Brad
Stewart, Jesse
Tempke, Jason

1   Stewart, Jesse. February 20, 2008, phone interview.
2   Coomer, John. January 31, 2008, phone interview.
3   Lillie, Willie. April 3, 2008, phone interview.
4   Godoy, Adrian. November 11, 2008, phone interview.
5   Lillie, Willie. Memorial eulogy for Clint Moore.
6   Lillie, Willie. Memorial eulogy for Michael Rodriguez.
7   Lillie, Willie. Memorial eulogy for Kenneth Locker.
8   Lillie, Willie. Memorial eulogy for Michael Vaughn.
9   Benaway, Adam. Memorial eulogy for Ryen King.
10 Lipscomb, Matthew. Memorial eulogy for Randell Marshall.
11 Mallari, Idi. June 17, 2009, phone interview.
12 The 82nd's 3rd Brigade Combat Team had been part of the federal response to New Orleans immediately following Hurricane Katrina.
13 Mallari, Idi. June 17, 2009, phone interview.
14 Lillie, Willie. April 3, 2008, phone interview.
15 Lillie, Willie. April 3, 2008, phone interview.
16 Poppas, Andrew. February 15, 2008, phone interview.
17 Bajema, Nick. October 16, 2008, phone interview.
18 Bajema, Nick. October 16, 2008, phone interview.
19 Lillie, Willie. April 3, 2008, phone interview.
20 Lillie, Willie. April 3, 2008, phone interview.
21 Stewart, Jesse. February 20, 2008, phone interview.

Chapter 24

This chapter is based on interviews with:
Gaspers, John
Gaspers, Pam

1   Gaspers, John. December 13, 2008, phone interview.
2   Gaspers, John. December 13, 2008, phone interview.

3   Gaspers, Pam. December 13, 2008, phone interview.
4   Kevin Gaspers eulogy delivered by Jesse Boulton.
5   Gaspers, Pam. December 13, 2008, phone interview.
6   Gaspers, Pam. December 13, 2008, phone interview.
7   Gaspers, Pam. December 13, 2008, phone interview.
8   Gaspers, Pam. December 13, 2008, phone interview.
9   Gaspers, John. December 13, 2008, phone interview.
10 Gaspers, Pam. December 13, 2008, phone interview.
11 Gaspers, John. December 13, 2008, phone interview.
12 Ephesians 6: 10: Finally, be strong in the Lord and in his mighty power. 11: Put on the full armor of God, so that you can take your stand against the devil's schemes. 12: For our struggle is not against flesh and blood, but against the rulers, against the authorities, against the powers of this dark world and against the spiritual forces of evil in the heavenly realms. 13: Therefore put on the full armor of God, so that when the day of evil comes, you may be able to stand your ground, and after you have done everything, to stand. 14: Stand firm then, with the belt of truth buckled around your waist, with the breastplate of righteousness in place, 15: and with your feet fitted with the readiness that comes from the gospel of peace. 16: In addition to all this, take up the shield of faith, with which you can extinguish all the flaming arrows of the evil one. 17: Take the helmet of salvation and the sword of the Spirit, which is the word of God. 18: And pray in the Spirit on all occasions with all kinds of prayers and requests. With this in mind, be alert and always keep on praying for all the Lord's people.
13 Gaspers, Pam. December 13, 2008, phone interview.
14 Gaspers, Pam. December 13, 2008, phone interview.
15 Gaspers, Pam. December 13, 2008, phone interview.
16 Gaspers, Pam. December 13, 2008, phone interview.
17 Gaspers, Pam. December 13, 2008, phone interview.
18 Gaspers, Pam. December 13, 2008, phone interview.
19 Gaspers, Pam. December 13, 2008, phone interview.
20 Gaspers, John. December 13, 2008, phone interview.

Chapter 25

This chapter is based on interviews with:
Bajema, Nick
Cobb, Robert
Geis, Kevin

1   Geis, Kevin. March 18, 2012, phone interview.
2   Geis, Kevin. March 18, 2012, phone interview.
3   Cobb, Robert. May 29, 2008, phone interview.
4   Cobb, Robert. May 29, 2008, phone interview.
5   Cole, Connie. July 10, 2012, email.
6   Cole, Connie. July 10, 2012, email.

Chapter 26

This chapter is based on interviews with:
Benaway, Adam

Candela, Sal
Dobbins, Stephen
Gorham, Walker
Hercik, Andy
James, Joe
Johnson, Pete
Levier, Patrick
Lewandowski, Evan
Metheny, Tim
Ventura, Sean

1   Gorham, Walker. October 26, 2008, phone interview.
2   Hercik, Andy. October 24, 2008, phone interview.
3   Hercik, Andy. October 24, 2008, phone interview.
4   Hercik claimed that it should have been as simple as submitting the target list work sheet and the fire support execution matrix. In turn, the response should have simply been, "You need it, you are going to get it." No such luck. Every bone in their body was saying deny the request and you've got to try to figure out, "How to get a guy that hasn't had ground experience but has grown up in the traditional artillery methodology of doing things with an identifiable target and trigger. Now we're shooting targets that seem random if you don't know what you're looking at on what amounts to a time line."
5   Hercik, Andy. October 24, 2008, phone interview.
6   Ventura, Sean. December 23, 2009, phone interview.
7   Apache AWT pilot radio traffic.
8   Gorham, Walker. October 26, 2008, phone interview.
9   Johnson, Pete. December 28, 2009, phone interview.
10 Gorham, Walker. December 2, 2008, phone interview.
11 Gorham, Walker. October 26, 2008, phone interview.
12 James, Joe. April 6, 2008, phone interview.
13 James, Joe. April 6, 2008, phone interview.
14 James, Joe. April 6, 2008, phone interview.
15 Levier, Patrick. May 26, 2008, phone interview.
16 Levier, Patrick. May 26, 2008, phone interview.
17 Levier, Patrick. May 26, 2008, phone interview.

Chapter 27

This chapter is based on interviews with:
Adams, Marc
Benaway, Adam
Church, Jeremiah
Edgar, Ray
Honbarger, Craig
Lillie, Willie

1   Church, Jeremiah. January 13, 2008, phone interview.
2   Lillie, Willie. April 3, 2008, phone interview.
3   Lillie, Willie. April 3, 2008, phone interview.
4   Church, Jeremiah. January 13, 2008, phone interview.

5   Church, Jeremiah. January 13, 2008, phone interview.
6   Church, Jeremiah. January 13, 2008, phone interview.
7   Edgar, Ray. December 28, 2009, phone interview.
8   Church, Jeremiah. January 13, 2008, phone interview.
9   Adams, Marc. September 3, 2009, and July 5, 2020, phone interviews.
10 Adams, Marc. July 5, 2020, phone interview.
11 Honbarger, Craig. November 19, 2008, phone interview.

Epilogue

This chapter is based on interviews with:
Caldwell, Bill
Candela, Sal
Honbarger, Craig
Lillie, Willie
McAvin, Geriah

1   Anonymous.
2   McAvin, Geriah. June 16, 2013, phone interview.
3   Honbarger, Craig. November 19, 2008, phone interview.
4   Honbarger, Craig. November 19, 2008, phone interview.
5   Sharbono, Diana. Facebook post, August 6, 2014.
6   Sharbono, Diana. Facebook post, August 6, 2014.
7   Sharbono, Diana. Facebook post, August 6, 2014.
8   Lillie, Willie. April 3, 2008, phone interview.
9   Candela, Sal. January 2, 2011, phone interview.

Index